The Public Work of Christmas

ADVANCING STUDIES IN RELIGION

Series editor: Christine Mitchell

Advancing Studies in Religion catalyzes and provokes original research in the study of religion with a critical edge. The series advances the study of religion in method and theory, textual interpretation, theological studies, and the understanding of lived religious experience. Rooted in the long and diverse traditions of the study of religion in Canada, the series demonstrates awareness of the complex genealogy of religion as a category and as a discipline. ASR welcomes submissions from authors researching religion in varied contexts and with diverse methodologies.

The series is sponsored by the Canadian Corporation for Studies in Religion whose constituent societies include the Canadian Society of Biblical Studies, Canadian Society for the Study of Religion, Canadian Society of Patristic Studies, Canadian Theological Society, Société canadienne de théologie, and Société québécoise pour l'étude de la religion.

The Public Work of Christmas

Difference & Belonging in Multicultural Societies

Edited by
Pamela E. Klassen and Monique Scheer

McGill-Queen's University Press
Montreal & Kingston · London · Chicago

ISBN 978-0-7735-5678-2 (cloth)
ISBN 978-0-7735-5679-9 (paper)
ISBN 978-0-7735-5795-6 (ePDF)
ISBN 978-0-7735-5796-3 (ePUB)

Legal deposit second quarter 2019
Bibliothèque nationale du Québec

Printed in Canada on acid-free paper that is 100% ancient forest free (100% post-consumer recycled), processed chlorine free

Publication of this book has been supported by the Anneliese Maier Research Award from the Alexander von Humboldt Foundation.

Funded by the Government of Canada   Financé par le gouvernement du Canada

Canada Council for the Arts   Conseil des arts du Canada

We acknowledge the support of the Canada Council for the Arts, which last year invested $153 million to bring the arts to Canadians throughout the country.

Nous remercions le Conseil des arts du Canada de son soutien. L'an dernier, le Conseil a investi 153 millions de dollars pour mettre de l'art dans la vie des Canadiennes et des Canadiens de tout le pays.

Library and Archives Canada Cataloguing in Publication

Title: The public work of Christmas : difference and belonging in multicultural societies / edited by Pamela E. Klassen and Monique Scheer.

Names: Klassen, Pamela E. (Pamela Edith), 1967- editor. | Scheer, Monique, editor.

Series: Advancing studies in religion ; 7.

Description: Series statement: Advancing studies in religion ; 7 | Includes bibliographical references and index.

Identifiers: Canadiana (print) 201900616oX | Canadiana (ebook) 20190061634 | ISBN 9780773556799 (softcover) | ISBN 9780773556782 (hardcover) | ISBN 9780773557956 (ePDF) | ISBN 9780773557963 (ePUB)

Subjects: LCSH: Christmas—Social aspects. | LCSH: Christmas—Political aspects. | LCSH: Christmas—Economic aspects. | LCSH: Multiculturalism. | LCSH: Belonging (Social psychology)

Classification: LCC GT4985 .P83 2019 | DDC 394.2663—dc23

This book was designed and typeset by Peggy & Co. Design Inc. in 11/14 Adobe Garamond.

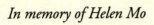

In memory of Helen Mo

Contents

Figures and Table

Figures

Table

Acknowledgments

In a sense, this book is the result of a Christmastime gift. The Alexander von Humboldt Foundation informed us in December 2014 that Pamela Klassen was being awarded the Anneliese Maier Research Prize, which gave us the funding to host an authors' workshop for this volume in Tübingen the following December. We are grateful to the Humboldt Foundation for their invaluable support, which goes beyond the merely financial. We also thank the University of Tübingen and our colleagues at the Ludwig Uhland Institute for Historical and Cultural Anthropology for their generous contributions to realizing this first step in a five-year research collaboration called *Religion and Public Memory in Multicultural Societies*. Special thanks go to Reinhard Johler and Gabriele Alex at the University of Tübingen for chairing sessions and to Helen Ahner for her organizational and poster-design savvy.

All the authors in this volume travelled to Tübingen to present early versions of their papers during our workshop, which fell on the same weekend as the city's Christmas market, giving us a close-up experience of the local seasonal habitus. We thank these colleagues for their intellectual collaboration and generosity of spirit. Other participants, including Andreas Bandak, Marisa Franz, and Amy Fisher, offered valuable comments during our workshop conversations. We are very grateful to Suzanne van Geuns, a doctoral student in the Department for the Study of Religion at the University of Toronto, who expertly and painstakingly prepared the book manuscript for submission to the press, edited the revised chapters in preparation for publication, and offered particularly helpful editorial suggestions. Thank you also to Kyle Byron and Roxanne Korpan for their assistance with the index. It has been a pleasure to work with our editor Kyla Madden at McGill-Queen's University Press, as well as our copy editor, Grace Seybold. We are grateful for the comments of the anonymous reviewers, and for the subventions for this book from the Anneliese Maier Research Award and the Advancing Studies in Religion series.

All the threads of organization for our Christmas workshop ran together into the capable hands of Helen Mo, a PhD candidate in the Department for the Study of Religion at the University of Toronto, and one of the authors who generously shared her work with us. Helen passed away unexpectedly in April 2017. A scholar with a profound gift for drawing people together across disciplines and places, who brought intelligence and cheer to any conversation, Helen made an indelible imprint on the entire project, and on all those who knew her. We dedicate this volume to her memory.

The Public Work of Christmas

The Difference That Christmas Makes: Thoughts on Christian Affordances in Multicultural Societies

Pamela E. Klassen and *Monique Scheer*

Introduction

The modern Christmas is a festival of ample – even aggressive – inclusivity. At once Christian and consumptive, hospitable and hostile, Christmas has become a ritual of gift-giving and feasting that invites, and even sometimes demands, participation regardless of whether one celebrates the birth of the Christ Child. In many parts of North America and Europe, Christmas is a total holiday that commandeers calendars and coffee shops every year, inciting a seasonal habitus of belonging – whether through participation or avoidance – in everyone. This Yuletide inclusivity, however, cannot entirely contain the difference that it encompasses. With a plethora of symbols, stories, movies, songs, and shopping rituals testifying to its seasonal ubiquity, Christmas is a rich site of public memory that can be deployed, revived, adapted, and resisted by all who come within its merry compass.

As is often the case for seasonal public festivals in which hierarchies and schedules are temporarily suspended, the merry-making of Christmas rides on undercurrents of threat or danger, such as overindulgence, over-spending, or family tension. In recent years, the recurring claim that there is a "war" on Christmas has been turned into a discourse of threat that one might call the "weaponization" of the holiday against "foreign" infringe-ments. Exemplified by fears about the suppression of "Merry Christmas" as a holiday greeting exchanged between coworkers or its erasure from coffee cups, narratives of the "War on Christmas" bring metaphors of violence into the workplace, the marketplace, and the public square.[1]

This weaponization of Christmas, however, has its counterpoint in responses that idealize Christmas and the Christian narrative as vehicles for "peace on earth" that embrace the "foreigner." For example, following the large influx of Syrian refugees in 2015, especially in Germany and Canada, many Christmas sermons and speeches, and even public billboards, drew on the imagery of the Flight into Egypt from the Gospel of Matthew to emphasize that "Mary and Joseph were also refugees."[2] Turning to the story of the Nativity to encourage acceptance of the German government's policy of welcoming those fleeing tyranny and war zones, Christmas was used to beat swords into ploughshares. This malleability of Christmas in the service of claims to multiple versions of public memory in multicultural sites is the focus of our volume. Sites of public memory – museums, memorials, print and digital mediations, and even *Weihnachtsmärkte* – are places in which these claims and fears circulate anew with each generation.

Religion and Public Memory

Our wider project, *Religion and Public Memory in Multicultural Societies*, focuses on what we call *modes of apprehension* of religion. Working from the starting point that religion is an historically shaped category that does not have universal meanings, we find "apprehension" to be a useful term because of its overlapping significance as understanding through the intellect, sensations, and emotions, as grasping and seizing someone or something, and as fear or dread. While religion can connote tradition, culture, and heritage, it can also be a code word for fears about the competing loyalties held by people who are at once citizens (or new immigrants) and devout adherents. When people collectively authorize religion – give it power over their social relations – through reference to the past, this authority is apprehended and mediated through public memory. By public memory, we mean narratives, depictions, performances, and materializations of the past addressed to an audience, variously assembled, framed, unified, or diverse, but always collective. Religion may be apprehended or mediated via ancient (or just old) texts, ancestors, relics, stories, vestments, or lineages, for example, and all of these modes of apprehension are soaked in memory, both personal and public.

Apprehension requires memory in cognitive, bodily, emotional, and materialized forms. In the case of Christmas, "getting" the holiday does not require that one is Christian, as its visual and sonic clues (a crèche, a Jesus-focused Christmas carol) are so broadly distributed across markets, workplaces, streetscapes, and schools. The calendrical and material clues of Christmas – which are different in Canada, Germany, and England – inflect what Pamela Klassen has called a "seasonal habitus," or a sense of a feel for the game of Christmas, whether or not one is a willing participant (see her chapter in this volume).[3] In the multicultural societies of Europe and North America, religious difference increasingly makes the Christianity of this seasonal habitus more apparent, as most everyone has a day off work on Christmas and Easter whether or not they celebrate these holidays.

Those not included in the Christian seasonal habitus, whether they belong to another religious tradition or none at all, have long been aware of the ways that North American and European states have recognized and remembered Christianity in particular. Jews, Muslims, Wiccans, and Secular Humanists have all asked states and employers for recognition of their holidays and their times of prayer, with more and less success. These requests for "religious accommodation" now play an important role in shaping the methods by which "religion" comes to be known and recognized. Whether small-scale community negotiations in classrooms, shopping malls, and streetscapes or legal decisions in a Supreme Court, religion is spelled out through deliberation and interaction among people. This deliberation always takes place within particular traditions of public memory; in the cases of Germany and Canada, these traditions are profoundly shaped by a Christian seasonal habitus structured not only by religious difference, but also by racialized, gendered, and class-based attributions of difference. An unavoidably Christian seasonal celebration, Christmas has taken on broader duties within what Pamela Klassen has called "civic secularism," and thus offers a particularly clarifying lens for considering the historical and ongoing intersections of multiculturalism and Christianity in European and North American contexts.[4]

Apprehending Christmas

The Public Work of Christmas joins a long tradition of Christmas critique, but does so with a few twists. First, all of the chapters in the book focus on questions of how invocations and practices of Christmas elicit or create cultural difference, sometimes to overcome it and other times to exacerbate it. The "multicultural" in our title is on the one hand a fairly basic descriptor of the cultural difference and multiplicity that shapes Christmas practices, while on the other hand we use the term well aware of both its local meanings and even its legal weight in particular nation-states. For example, in Canada, a commitment to encouraging people to practise their cultural diversity (up to a point) is actually legislated within the Multiculturalism Act, while in Germany multiculturalism is a term both derided and defended, including by lawmakers, but without the force of law on its side.

Second, and in keeping with the above comparison, the collected essays in this book each focus on specific sites of Christmas, paying attention to how both scholarly and popular narratives of the significance of Christmas are shaped by their framing within national, regional, and diasporic publics. Coming out of a conversation that involved scholars from Germany, Canada, England, Denmark, the Netherlands, and the United States, each chapter evidences the centrality of place for making sense of varieties of Christmases past and present. At the same time, in the sense of Pierre Nora's *lieux de mémoire*, Christmas itself is a place, a site of memory as much as of celebration. Wary of chiming in with the chorus of those who would proclaim Christmas a memorial site in the sense that it must be preserved as cultural heritage, however, this volume seeks to emphasize with its collection of localized studies how the offerings of Christmas lend themselves to performances of power and place shaped by adaptability, inclusivity, and exclusion. The malleability of Christmas is why some people with commitments to Christianity, however attenuated, have so much anxiety around its possible loss as a symbol of broad religio-national public consensus, and, in turn, why they embark on such frequent attempts to firmly lock into place its "true" meaning.

Our approach adds a final twist on the familiar genre of Christmas critique: the question of public memory circulates in these chapters in two related ways. First, shared memories about Christmas, preserved by families and communities, can be viewed as a repository of public knowledge about the holiday, its rituals, and its purposes, which varies according to locality and time period. Second, such local public understandings of Christmas are themselves shaped and developed by scholars producing historical, anthropological, or sociological accounts of the holiday and its meanings. German scholarship long emphasized the susceptibility of Christmas to being drawn into political ideologies – a critique developed in response to nationalist politics and which in turn stoked a broader public conversation about the potentially dangerous nostalgia of Christmas in that country.[5] Studies from the UK and North America, however, often focus on themes of consumerism and materialism. In their own way, these critiques then contribute, perhaps unwittingly, to a long tradition of Christian-based criticisms of holiday buying that assert that consumerism overshadows the "real reason for the season," criticisms which have not abated since the nineteenth century.[6]

In opening the conversation at our workshop in Tübingen in December 2015, Monique Scheer laid out what she called the "coordinates of Christmas." Imagining a field stretching out on one axis between the binaries of materiality and spirituality and on the other axis between the binaries of ideology and authenticity, she argued that the discourse on Christmas pushes back and forth along these axes, all the while making claims about what the holiday is and/or what it should be. Scheer argued (and also does so in her chapter in this volume) that another axis has become relevant in this system of coordinates, one that interacts in complex ways with the previous two: the binary of religion and culture, and the back-and-forth of essentializing and de-essentializing that these concepts incite. Religion and culture are both powerful concepts through which individuals and groups demand recognition and are summoned by the state; "religion" and "culture" are also key terms deployed in debates about Christmas.

Just as Christmas is about much more than just the holiday itself, religion is about far more than a set of moral precepts or narratives pertaining to the supernatural or the afterlife. In contemporary North America and Europe, religion is increasingly an identificatory practice that can bind one closer to one's community or provide a way out of it; it can be so tightly linked to an ethnicity or culture that they seem to be one and the same, or it can form an identity group of its own. In some contexts, religion is a concept that is far more powerful than culture. For example, in courts within both North America and Europe, the frame of religious freedom is increasingly turned to as a legal right that can bind collectives by differentiating them from secular accounts of a public sphere.[7] The law protects freedom of conscience and, to a certain extent, freedom of religious expression and practice, so that the concept of "religion" can sometimes be a useful tool for defending certain practices, such as wearing the hijab or performing infant circumcisions.

In other Euro-American contexts, it is precisely when a specific religion, usually Christianity, transforms into culture or heritage that it is at its most powerful: the collection of Christian symbols that undergird much ceremonial and political power in legislatures across both continents are often deemed "not religious" at all. As many scholars have argued, the "religious" and the "secular" are deeply entangled, forming complementary Christian-inflected grammars.[8] The re-encoding of religious symbols as markers of cultural identity – such as the recent and highly controversial decision by the Bavarian governor Markus Söder to hang Catholic cruci-fixes in the lobbies of all government buildings as a sign of Bavarian-ness – may arguably be viewed as a form of secularization. And it must be noted that the use of religion by right-wing populists as a cultural marker, both of themselves and of the minority groups they vilify, paradoxically (or ironically) correlates with broader processes of declining religious practice. Right-wing populists do not necessarily invoke religion to give their politics a spiritual basis. Religion is often, for them, nothing more – but indeed nothing less – than cultural.

Considering Christmas as a specifically multicultural site of public memory, this book helps to reveal how the concepts of religion and culture work in tandem to frame and reframe questions of belonging and difference. Whether or not a particular holiday with a religious backstory and attend-ant rituals of observance is considered a "public holiday" depends on how cultural it is. Legislated into calendars, commodified into marketplaces, and seasonally habituated into the lives of people belonging to a wide range of communities, including non-Christian ones, Christmas arguably *has* become much more cultural than religious. Furthermore, the economic surplus that retail trade stands to gain each year in December certainly promotes the notion that Christmas can be open to anyone, Christian or not. Religious symbols get recast as "cultural" not only for political reasons, but also through the forces of a neoliberal global economy ever seeking to generate new products and their consumers. Multicultural cosmopolitan-ism can then play into the same logic as globalized, neoliberal capitalism.[9]

But in the increasingly multi-religious and "non-religious" regions of Europe and North America, Christians, non-Christians, and non-religious people are coming to notice how the very cultural ubiquity of Christmas depends on an infrastructure of Christian public memory. This memory infrastructure is materialized through Christian affordances such as historic church buildings on street corners, but also in legal statutes about the seasonal rhythms of workplaces, markets, and schools. Both inclusive and assimilatory, the predominance of Christmas depends on the ways that its cultural forms both mark and mask the ongoing power of Christianity within a deep chain of public memory that orients nation-states in North America and Europe.

By Christian affordances, we mean the ways that public invocations of Christmas – whether in shopping malls, schools, or city squares – depend on this often-obscured memory infrastructure of Christian calendars, narratives, rituals, and symbols for their rhetorical appeal. Even the most baldly consumerist calls to Christmas shoppers are tethered to a calendar organized around the postulated birth and death of Jesus Christ. Whether beginning after Halloween, or after Thanksgiving, or even, most moderately, with the beginning of the season of Advent, Christmas marketing cannot happen in July. (Except, of course, when it does, as in the case of the all-year-round Christmas shops that market themselves within "Christmas" towns, such as the Käthe Wohlfahrt franchise originating in Rothenburg ob der Tauber, Germany, and Bronner's Christmas Wonderland in Frankenmuth, Michigan, which calls itself the "World's Largest Christmas Store.") Narratives of (Christian) charity in the "season of giving" underwrite appeals for tax-exempt charitable donations, and are enabled by the seasonal force of the year-end tax deadline. Rituals of gift-giving and carol-singing at Christmas office parties, in family groups, and among friends carry Christian messages. Symbols of candles, wreaths, and Christmas trees work as codes for genial "season's greetings" as well as particularly Christian rituals to mark the time of Advent and Christmas. Together, these calendars, narratives, rituals, and symbols produce a seasonal habitus born of the coordinates of Christmas.

The coordinates of Christmas, then, are axes that produce tensions at multiple scales and spaces of human engagement and community, including homes, schools, marketplaces, cities, nation-states, and the borders and overlaps amongst all these spaces. Christmas festivities become plot devices in narratives that hope that cultural differences can be overcome through shared food, song, and gift-giving. At the same time, Christmas celebrations necessarily evoke multicultural awkwardness – or even aggression – due to the ways that the liturgical root of Christmas unavoidably reminds some people, whether Christians or non-Christians, of the potentially all-inclusive theology of redemption in which God forgives every human being's sins through the birth (incarnation) of Jesus. In an explicitly secularist context, it becomes problematic that this Christian holiday is enacted as *public* memory. Nevertheless, Christmas continues to be deployed as a materialization of public memory meant to facilitate larger claims about nations and conflicts between them, and to shape the meaning of the past and the future.

The metaphor of triple axes – on their way to becoming a web – along which hopes and fears about Christmas are variously stretched and relaxed is an apt one for thinking through the "public work" done by debates about and practices of Christmas. Here, we borrow and significantly adapt from political theorist Harry Boyte, who defined public work as "a normative, democratizing ideal of citizenship generalized from communal labors of making and tending the commons, with roots in diverse cultures."[10] Not being political theorists, our use of public work is less normative. Instead, we focus on how discourses of Christmas work on issues of public contestation – such as immigration, refugee settlement, and consumerism – to both challenge and define borders of belonging and difference. With Christmas as our focus, these chapters collectively ask about the tactics – in the sense of Michel de Certeau – by which people embrace, resist, and live with Christmas in multicultural spaces shaped by peculiarly Christian affordances.

Chapters

The tensions provoked by the public work of Christmas can be experienced as exciting or entrapping, depending on one's perspective. Expectations of a merry Christmas are regularly disappointed, and it is this sober recognition that has seemed to guide scholarly investigations into the holiday over the last several decades. Together, the chapters in this book examine a multiplicity of perspectives on Christmas in multicultural spaces through a combination of historical, ethnographic, and historiographic methods. We begin with Monique Scheer's overview of both English and German anthropological and historical writing about Christmas, noting that it follows a heuristic of "tension": in trying to understand why there is so much conflict and controversy around the holiday, scholars have construed it as deeply paradoxical. Christmas will always be "tense," they argue, because social tensions come more strongly to the fore during the season in which peace and harmony are demanded, but also because it is given the impossible task of straddling supposedly polar opposites, such as commerce and spirituality. Scheer observes that in the past decade or two, not only have new social tensions manifested themselves during the holidays, but they make it necessary to reconsider the binaries which have structured research on Christmas. Spirituality and commerce have become far less problematic and paradoxical, whereas the boundary between the religious and secular has become more virulent, especially in urban public spaces. As a result, Christmas gets either "religionized" or "culturalized," leading to new controversies.

Isaac Weiner's chapter offers a trenchant – and compassionate – rereading of a Christmas classic, Dr Seuss's *How the Grinch Stole Christmas*, as a tale of resistance to coercive assimilation within a Christian-dominated culture. He posits that we consider the Grinch not as an anomic figure with a heart two-sizes-too-small, but as a member of a minority religious community speaking back to the seasonal habitus of Christmas. Tying his analysis to broader questions of how debates about sound have shaped contests over religious difference in both legal and multicultural urban contexts, Weiner re-narrates the Grinch as a creature who just wanted to be left alone, but who could not avoid the sonic intrusions of Christmas no matter what he did. Reflecting on how Christmas cannot escape its Christian religiosity no matter how cultural it becomes, Weiner raises important questions about the lines between inclusion and assimilation in multicultural and multi-religious societies.

Christmas music is certainly one of the acoustically more aggressive forms of inclusivity, and for those familiar with the melodies, one of the most salient elements of the seasonal habitus. Picking up on what has become the paradigmatic notion that modern Christmas is an invention of the bourgeoisie and its particular configuration of the nuclear family in the second half of the nineteenth century, Juliane Brauer examines this one particular piece of the assemblage of customs that make up Christmas: communal singing. Focusing on a song especially popular in twentieth-century Germany, "Silent Night, Holy Night," Brauer argues that collective singing is a particularly potent emotional practice, tapping directly into childhood memories and deeply felt nostalgia that becomes particularly acute when singers are at war, on the front lines or in captivity. Renditions of the song were implemented on the battlefield and in concentration camps ostensibly to spread Christmas cheer, but rather than bringing together the different communities represented there, the music drew the lines of division between them all the more starkly.

The scholarly theme of the abuse of Christmas for political purposes in Germany has gone more or less in tandem with the intense scrutiny of the history of the academic discipline engaged with studying its customs, traditions, and material culture: German folklore studies or *Volkskunde*, the anthropology of the homeland. Its nationalist and ultimately racist trajectories in the nineteenth and twentieth centuries were reflected in and through its narrations of German Christmas. In his chapter, Christian Marchetti takes a new approach to the Christmas of German *Volkskunde*, construing the mental structures in which these scholars apprehended Christmas as a highly textured terrain in which the holiday was spatially situated. This spatial orientation was then quite literally mapped in the *Atlas of German Folklore* and indeed became implicated in the Nazi regime's aggressive, expansionary vision for the German people. A counter-narrative can be found in the *Volkskunde* of the Habsburg territories, which long after the dissolution of the Empire pursued a different view of culture in its German-speaking scholarship on Christmas. Writing from the margins of germanophone territories in southeastern Europe, these scholars found Christmas to be an object through which stories of transformation and cultural mixing could take precedence over those of preserving "authentic tradition."

Multicultural societies – including imperial ones – are often formed out of people on the move searching for new territory. Pamela Klassen's chapter, " 'The First "White" Xmas': Settler Multiculturalism, Nisga'a Hospitality, and Ceremonial Sovereignty," considers a Christmas celebration on the Pacific Northwest Coast in the early twentieth century. A gathering of new Canadian settlers from a range of national backgrounds and their Nisga'a hosts, the festivities took place on the unceded territory of the Nisga'a and were documented by the resident Anglican missionary on his printing press. A fascinating example of a multicultural Christmas ritual that enacted and celebrated diversity, memory, and whiteness at the same time, "The First 'White' Xmas" also preserved a record of how the Nisga'a, in their hospitality, engaged with the Christian holiday as a means to challenge the supposed naturalness of Canada.

Yaniv Feller's discussion of why a Christmas tree had pride of place in the first permanent exhibition of the Jewish Museum Berlin tells a similar story of the ambiguous uses of Christmas for groups seeking to resist racialized Christian hegemony. Choosing a Christmas tree to represent bourgeois family life among early-twentieth-century German Jews, the museum curators sought to raise questions about the ambivalences of assimilation, in this case through Jewish adaptations of Christian rituals of Christmas. Revealing some surprising twists and unexpected characters both showcased and hidden within the exhibit, Feller takes seriously the Christmas tree as a material witness that could evoke both warmth and violence in the museum context. Ultimately, he concludes, the Christmas tree in the Jewish Museum Berlin is (or now, was) a site of public memory that evoked conflicts over racialized religious difference in Germany's past and in the museum's present.

The ubiquity of Christmas remains a seasonal reality in multicultural cities, including Berlin. Sophie Reimers takes us into a Turkish-German family living in Berlin's Neukölln district to show how Christmas has been experienced there. Over the years, as children were born, grew up, and attended school, the family's attitude toward the holiday changed, but it remained a tension-laden litmus test of assimilation vs. maintaining family traditions. Schools and kindergartens become key sites in which this negotiation takes place, especially when, as in Neukölln, Muslim students make up upwards of 80 percent of the student body. In Germany, as a country only now coming to terms with the significance of immigration for its future national population, the education system is at the front line of struggles over how multiculturalism should be organized, and Christmas is one of its major touchstones.

With even greater focus on how schools are sites of Christmas contests, Helen Mo's chapter focuses on a swiftly moving conflict over the public acknowledgment of Christmas in an urban Canadian high school. When some of the students came to a misguided conclusion, aided by the internet, that the vice-principal had forbidden students to wish each other "Merry Christmas," the school was quickly flung into a very publicly mediated conflict about the role of "immigrants" (and people of colour) who were presumed to be non-Christian, and who were accused of "ruining" Christmas. Read alongside Isaac Weiner's reflections on the Grinch, Helen Mo's chapter is a lively and theoretically rich reflection on how stories about Christmas conflicts can be tinderboxes for racist or populist reactions that can have devastating consequences for all people involved in the conflict.

Taking us to a very different urban milieu, Katja Rakow describes the Christmas season in the shopping centres of Singapore, festooned for weeks in bright lights and decorations, milking the holiday for all it is worth. In spite of its apparent popularity among shoppers and merchants alike, Christmas also generates a certain amount of controversy with familiar patterns: just how Christian the holiday is, and how much of that religious narrative can be put on public display, is negotiated year after year. Rakow highlights in particular how Christian groups use the opportunity of this global holiday to position themselves firmly within the city's multi-religious environment, explaining the "reason for the season" in ways carefully crafted to conform to Singapore's specific brand of religious pluralism.

The final chapter, co-authored by Simon Coleman, Marion Bowman, and Tiina Sepp, brings us directly into a pulsing heart of Christian space – an urban cathedral in England for which the rituals marking Christmas are both an opportunity and a challenge. The authors examine how the Church of England, both blessed and saddled with the massive real estate responsibility of their cathedrals, is at once appreciative yet perplexed about how the aesthetics of Christmas – including the sounds of its music – offer a "periodic appeal" that draws a multicultural mix of people to churches every December. Focused on the "semiotic mediations" made possible by the affordances of a cathedral that is at once public and Christian space, the authors suggest that Christmas, even in this English Christian context, is a spectacle that is read as both secular and spiritual.

In his epilogue, Herman Bausinger reflects on further categories that these chapters evoke and possibilities for nuancing the category of "Christian" that underlies the holiday. Confessional, regional, and generational differences as well as the opposition of the "church" and the "world" – be that in the sense of the secular or the everyday, as well as between the emotional and rational – provide further lenses through which to contemplate the ways the holiday unfolds and is debated. Reminding his readers that Germany has not become a culturally diverse society only recently but has always been so, he observes that the appeal of Christmas stems to a large extent from its emotional quality, the mood of solemnity and ceremony it conveys, to which anyone – Christian or not – can be drawn.

In spite of resistance to its aggressive inclusivity, Christmas is also a beloved season among many Christians and non-Christians alike, in part because of its effects on public and domestic work. The holiday takes over city streets with both traffic and stillness: busy shoppers, Santa Claus Parades, and profusions of lights mark the city with a Christian ambiance, but for one or two days, or for the lucky people whose workplaces shut down for an entire week, Christmas also enforces the closing of the malls, shops, offices, and schools which had been running full-tilt in the preceding weeks.[11] This reliable calendrical closure brings a measure of calm and quiet for many, a clearly marked-off time of difference in which the incessant email correspondence of workplaces and the twenty-four-hour consumption of markets briefly stop. That said, the domestic work of Christmas, often highly gendered, intensifies for those who celebrate the holiday by baking, cooking, and decorating their family traditions into material form.

Part of the public work of Christmas, then, is to turn people to the space of the domestic, acting as an uncommon force that provides legitimation (or the illusion of such) for a brief collective respite from the incessant exchanges of modern work, communication, and consumption. In this book, Christmas is our holiday to think with, but other seasonal celebrations would provide equally fascinating axes of belonging and difference to explore. Religious holidays such as Eid or Rosh Hashanah also call forth public and domestic work for those who observe them, though in multicultural spaces shaped by Christian affordances (e.g. North America and Europe) these holy days have less collective force to shape the calendar. Taken together, however, religious holidays are a form of public memory strong enough to give pause to the relentless chronos of the marketplace and workplace, and thus to do the public work of making and remaking belonging and difference in multicultural societies.

Notes

1   See Bowler, *Christmas in the Crosshairs*.
2   See, for example, the report on the opening of a Christmas market in Bad Neustadt in the newspaper *Mainpost* or a sermon delivered in the Bavarian town of Taufkirchen in the Oberbayerisches Volksblatt. Nerche Wolf, "Auch Maria und Josef waren Flüchtlinge"; "Maria und Josef waren auch Flüchtlinge."
3   On habitus, see Bourdieu, *The Logic of Practice*.
4   Klassen, "Fantasies of Sovereignty."
5   See Monique Scheer's chapter in this volume for a brief overview.
6   Such as Miller, ed., *Unwrapping Christmas*, and Schmidt, *Consumer Rites*.
7   McNally, "Native American Religious Freedom."
8   Talal Asad, *Formations of the Secular*; Johnson et al., *Ekklesia*.
9   On the ways that multiculturalism has been transformed by neoliberal politics, see Kymlicka, "Neoliberal Multiculturalism?"
10 Boyte, "Constructive Politics as Public Work," 632.
11 Engelke, "Angels in Swindon."

Bibliography

Asad, Talal. *Formations of the Secular: Christianity, Islam, Modernity.*
Stanford, CA: Stanford University Press, 2003.

Bourdieu, Pierre. *The Logic of Practice.* Translated by Richard Nice.
Stanford, CA: Stanford University Press, 1990.

Bowler, Gerry. *Christmas in the Crosshairs: Two Thousand Years of Denouncing
and Defending the World's Most Celebrated Holiday.* New York: Oxford
University Press, 2016.

Boyte, Harry. "Constructive Politics as Public Work: Organizing the
Literature." *Political Theory* 39, no. 5 (2011): 630–60.

Engelke, Matthew. "Angels in Swindon: Public Religion and Ambient Faith in
England." *American Ethnologist* 39, no. 1 (2012): 155–70.

Hervieu-Léger, Danièle. *Religion as a Chain of Memory.* New Brunswick, NJ:
Rutgers University Press, 2000.

Johnson, Paul Christopher, Pamela E. Klassen, and Winnifred Fallers Sullivan.
Ekklesia: Three Inquiries in Church and State. Chicago: University of
Chicago Press, 2018.

Klassen, Pamela. "Fantasies of Sovereignty: Civic Secularism in Canada."
Critical Research on Religion 3, no. 1 (2015): 41–56.

Kymlicka, Will. "Neoliberal Multiculturalism?" In *Social Resilience in the
Neo-Liberal Era,* edited by Peter A. Hall and Michèle Lamont, 99–125.
Cambridge: Cambridge University Press, 2013.

"Maria und Josef waren auch Flüchtlinge." *Oberbayerisches Volksblatt.*
4 December 2015. https://www.ovb-online.de/muehldorf/waldkraiburg/
maria-josef-waren-auch-fluechtlinge-5927471.html.

McNally, Michael D. "Native American Religious Freedom Beyond the First
Amendment." In *After Pluralism: Reimagining Religious Engagement,* edited
by Courtney Bender and Pamela E. Klassen, 226–51. New York: Columbia
University Press, 2010.

Miller, Daniel, ed. *Unwrapping Christmas.* Oxford, UK: Clarendon Press, 1993.

Nerche Wolf, Karin. "Auch Maria und Josef waren Flüchtlinge." *Mainpost.*
26 November 2015. http://www.mainpost.de/regional/rhoengrabfeld/
Fluechtlinge;art765,9016150.

Schmidt, Leigh Eric. *Consumer Rites: The Buying and Selling of American
Holidays.* Princeton, NJ: Princeton University Press, 1995.

2

Tense Holidays:
Approaching Christmas through Conflict

Monique Scheer

Introduction

The Swedish ethnologist Orvar Löfgren is not one to mince words when it comes to Christmas in his home country: it is both a "dream" of family harmony and a "battlefield" in which the annual "Christmas quarrel" has become a tradition.[1] The holiday is the source of bitter disappointments and power struggles precisely because it is loaded with such high expectations. Through it all, memory runs deep. "Christmas for some people is an attempt to create a monument to a lost childhood," Löfgren writes, and it is always about identity: "micro-cultures of 'our own Christmas'" in this family, this region, this country[2] – which, like memories of childhood, are the source of strong but highly ambivalent feelings.

Löfgren's diagnosis is representative for his field and his generation. Research on Christmas in cultural anthropology since the mid-twentieth century has found the ambivalent nature of this holiday, its inherent contradictions and tensions, to be its most interesting feature, leading to a hermeneutic of binary oppositions: scholars try to understand how this festival not only survives but appears to thrive in paradoxes of familial intimacy and consumerism, local customs and global markets, tradition and modernity. These built-in tensions manifest themselves in the regularly occurring quarrels, struggles, and conflicts around this holiday.[3] Examining them can help us understand the cultural situations in which Christmas unfolds each year, providing researchers with a particularly rich site for investigating the ways public and private memory impinge upon each other.

In the following, I will sketch out the trajectories of a conflict-oriented perspective on Christmas in Germany and neighbouring countries with the occasional comparative glance across the Atlantic. Having begun in the dichotomies of the spiritual and material, tradition and modernity, local and global, the conflictual potential is now drawing its energy, I will argue, from changing understandings of the relationship of society and culture, and in particular, religion and culture. And just as the scholarship on Christmas has followed public debate in the past, so should it now make use of current conflicts to ask new questions about Christmas in multicultural societies.

Tensions in Classic Studies of Christmas

In his overview of anthropological research into contemporary Anglo-American Christmas written some twenty-five years ago, Daniel Miller outlines the main strands of inquiry as they stood then. First, there was the issue of Christmas's invention in the mid-nineteenth century by the Victorian middle class; second, whether the "spirit of Christmas" instituted at that time had succumbed to the forces of commercialization.[4] These two main pillars supported most of the research into contemporary German Christmas in the twentieth century as well, but it is interesting to consider the accents German researchers, especially in historical and cultural anthropology, have set. One is the desire to debunk the entire notion of "ancient folk tradition" with which Christmas customs are supposedly so deeply impregnated.[5] This urge to shine a light on their comparatively recent and middle-class origins was particularly strong in Germany since the tendency of late-nineteenth- and early-twentieth-century conservative folklorists to trace them back in vague genealogies to the shadows of medieval or even ancient history, developed from a nationalist to a racist (*völkisch*) agenda.

Hermann Bausinger exemplified this demystifying impetus when, in 1970, he published a study on the *Adventskranz*, the evergreen wreath with four candles, one for each Advent Sunday leading up to Christmas. He shows that the custom is neither old, nor of the "folk," but was in fact an upper-class innovation, an idea launched by pastors and teachers in the villages and often resisted by the local population.[6] Another accent was related to the division of Germany after the war and the competition between Marxist-Leninist and liberal ideologies, which also left their mark on academic work. The work of Ingeborg Weber-Kellermann, whose professional career spanned both East and West German academies, is an example: her pioneering study on German Christmas published in 1978 begins with the tension between the emotional meanings of Christmas and the engulfing power of commerce, but highlights the importance of class. She established for germanophone research the standard narrative of the holiday as the primary celebration of the newly created private sphere of the middle class, separate from the public sphere, and each specifically gendered. Children were placed at the centre of this celebration of home and family and showered with gifts. Weber-Kellerman's phrasing echoes Marxist orientations that scholars on both sides of the Iron Curtain could share: material concerns are not new to Christmas, threatening to submerge its religious contents, but were at the centre of it from the outset. "The holiday's religious cover should not make us blind to the effects of social class, which have always shaped the outer forms of this festival. The traditional differences between the urban and the rural, the externality of Christmas mummery in the village and the interiority of the bourgeois parlor ceremonies under the Christmas tree, are socially determined. Social backgrounds also underlie the confessional differences in the various regions of Europe and Germany, expressed in cultural signs such as the nativity scene and the advent wreath ... On this day, the gulf between the rich and poor opens up most shockingly, however, and has long been apparent in the amount and prestige of gift-giving."[7] For Weber-Kellerman, Christmas was an event which brought social injustice to light.

European ethnologists continued to work on Christmas in this critical vein in the decades which followed. Aside from debating genealogies of Christmas figures such as the *Weihnachtsmann* (Father Christmas), St Nicholas and Knecht Ruprecht, or the *Christkind* (an angelic bringer of gifts on Christmas Eve), Gottfried Korff was interested in their disciplinary functions for children in Wilhelmine households.[8] Utz Jeggle looked at mid-twentieth-century lower-middle-class settings, showing with data acquired among his students how the holiday was in the process of transformation, and at the same time acknowledging how much he personally hated its petty bourgeois atmosphere.[9] Deeply influenced by the work of the Frankfurt School, this body of German Christmas research seemed to revolve around the issue of authenticity: how real was Christmas? Was capitalism destroying its heart, or was it only ever about capitalism to begin with? Was it not, in fact, celebrating a myth – the myth of the happy, functional, nuclear family as the foundation of society? In 1974, Tübingen professor Martin Scharfe organized a student-run exhibition project called *Unbehagen an Weihnachten* (reminiscent of Freud's famous essay title, it could be translated as "Christmas and Its Discontents") which took this tack. The students claimed that Christmas, of all holidays, could best be used as a propaganda instrument, since as a national holiday it addressed everyone at the same time, constructing a falsely homogeneous "*Scheingemeinschaft*" (fake community), and its strong emotions preventing rational thinking. In the midst of the antiwar fervour of the 1970s, the students emphasized the duplicitous character of the seasonal message "peace on earth, goodwill to men," it being "a good opportunity to put the blame for a war on the enemy and present the intentions of the ruling class in one's own country as peaceful … Soldiers were reminded that they were at war in order to defend home and family. The holiday therefore had the function of boosting military morale … There was no room for social criticism."[10]

More strongly and directly than *Unwrapping Christmas*, the German literature of the same period tended to focus on the ways that Christmas has been politicized and ideologized,[11] a point the American historian Joe Perry noted and expanded upon in his recent study of German Christmas. Calling into question the public/private boundary the holiday so clearly transgresses, Perry's argument resonates strongly with the words of the Tübingen students written over thirty years prior as he looks at how politicians used Christmas to bring national ideologies into families and families used it to "embed themselves in political collectives."[12] The importance of the holiday for its potential to generate a strong sense of community and political purpose put it at the centre of constant political struggle: "By the twentieth century, Christmas, an invention of Germany's middle classes, had become an archetypal symbol of a German nation united above class, religion, region, or ideology – and therefore a tendentious site of political conflict. Competing groups struggled to define the holiday and control its observance. Social Democrats, National Socialists, Cold War liberals, and Communists – each appropriated German Christmas as a celebration of national harmony." Conflicts between the confessions – Protestant and Catholic as well as Jewish – were not far behind.

Research on Christmas has brought out how controversies over the way the holiday is celebrated grow out of broader conflicts in a society. At the same time, the questions applied to the object of research themselves emerge from those conflicts. Tensions within Christmas produced tensions in the research on Christmas. Either the holiday meant too much or it meant too little. Was it an instrument of oppression, disciplining children and emotionally manipulating adults into a false sense of communal harmony?

Or was it not really about anything at all anymore, other than spending lots of money on material goods? And was that spending inseparable from socio-economic injustice, or could it be re-interpreted as a culturally productive consumption, indeed a sacralization of materialism?[13]

Miller's introduction to *Unwrapping Christmas* sought to open up a new round of questions. His interest has been to explain the global success of Christmas, "which seems to grow in its accumulated rituals and the extravagance of the homage paid to it,"[14] while looking at the local ways in which the global themes have been taken up. In a later version of this text, which he prepared specifically for a German market,[15] Miller reiterates the point that "Christmas provides the vanguard for the now fashionable studies which come under the term 'local' and 'global.'" In spite of all the tendencies toward global spread and influence, its "easy syncretism" allows the local to triumph; its "arguments emerge from the strong sense that 'we' have always celebrated Christmas in this way, only to discover that the particular rite in question turns out to be the family tradition of watching Walt Disney cartoons."[16] By binding Christmas so tightly to local identity, this line of argument would seem to lead directly into the kinds of tensions and conflicts that "culture clashes" produce. Considering the particularly intense affective attachments Christmas engenders – for it does seem that it is hard to be indifferent to Christmas – these clashes will not be trivial. But Miller also points out that Christmas can, at the same time, link local communities to a global event. "The more people believe that their celebration is a token of a global action, a rite being repeated by millions across the world, the more Christmas is felt to establish a relationship between the celebrant and the world at large."[17]

German anthropologist Thomas Hauschild's recent monograph on the *Weihnachtsmann* tells a similar story, pointing at the subterranean connections, the universal truths embodied in this ancient figure and embedded in the holiday of which he is the main character. Hauschild begins, too, with tensions and conflicts around Christmas, especially those that emerge between religions. "Christmas polarizes us; some people insist on the Christian identity of the holiday, on its un-Islamic character. And that comes from both sides, from Islamists as well as Anti-Islamists, who have declared themselves protectors of Christianity, often without really believing in the Christian God themselves."[18] At stake are the children, their right to decide what and how they want to celebrate, without parents, educators, or politicians telling them one way or the other. Hauschild is convinced that debates over Christmas in Germany will increase in the coming years. "That is why I think it is important to point out that Father Christmas has Asian relatives, some of them older than Christianity."[19] For Hauschild, the globalization of Santa Claus is not new; it was there from the beginning, and this substrate is what he seeks to recover from myriad local appropriations. The fact that this mythical figure in each and every instance is a mélange of elements from diverse societies and religions points to the underlying universal themes he embodies, and these are what Hauschild teases out in his comparative study, hoping to provide a basis from which to stop quarrelling.

Hauschild's shift in perspective is indicative for the current situation in Germany. Issues around the materialism of Christmas and its being oppressively representative of middle-class values have certainly not lost their legitimacy; they come up in public discourse and private conversations year for year, having themselves become part of the ritual. Miller's point about Christmas's syncretic openness, the fusion of the global and the local, and the profusion of cultural forms it produces is also still relevant and helpful for understanding how Christmas can be attractive even beyond the borders of Christian territories. But mobility has also brought the world together into single spaces; migration brings many localities into close proximity. Christmas controversies are now getting pulled into broader concerns about local identity and how firmly boundaries around groups within a society should be drawn. Christmas, with its power to draw such boundaries, can be used to exclude, but also forcibly include, igniting a new round of debate. Löfgren's point that Christmas is always about "us" is back in the forefront: who gets to celebrate this holiday and who shouldn't have to be made to? How public should it be, and in what form? In Germany, a country that long attempted to ignore its attractiveness to migrants and to deny its character as a country of immigrants, this discourse represents a significant shift in the last decade. As public discourse reorients itself, so should the ethnographic research.

Christmas Controversies and the Religionization of Culture

The field on which debates and controversies over Christmas play out is being mapped by a new set of coordinates. While the axes created by the tensions between materiality and spirituality as well as ideology and authenticity have not disappeared, they are being overlaid and transformed

by new binaries. More than ever, I would argue, Christmas is being caught
in a tug-of-war between "religion" and "culture," with "culture" increasingly
understood as cultural heritage or public memory. More often than not, as
with the sacralization of the material, or the ideologization of authenticity,
this binary also collapses, producing a religionization of culture or vice
versa.²⁰ The axis between religion and culture is made more complex by the
fact that each of these is itself one half of a binary construct. Religion can
be opposed to the secular, invoking issues of public and private exercise,
and culture implies an opposition between self and other, "native" and
"foreign," and thus belonging and exclusion. These, too, are categories that
may have been discussed along with the others before, but in comparison
to the 1980s are now decisively at the forefront of conflicts in popular
debate over the "meaning" of Christmas and proper forms of observation in
societies discovering themselves as multicultural, local and global, "home"
and somehow "foreign" at one and the same time.

As my late colleague Utz Jeggle once observed: "Christmas always goes
beyond its current celebration and is at the same time: a celebration of the
memory of Christmas."²¹ Jeggle is arguing psychologically here, emphasizing the importance of past Christmases to explain the emotionalization
of the holiday, and that ethnographies should strive to reconstruct the
complexity of those feelings. But his argument also holds for Christmas
as a *lieu de mémoire* in Pierre Nora's sense, a site of public memory.²²
Memories of Christmases past are shared in public discourse and underpin
the emotions that feed into conflicts and struggles over the "true meaning"
of Christmas and how it should be staged in the public sphere.

For although the discourse on Christmas frames it as the most private of
holidays, celebrating the ideal middle-class nuclear family in their domestic
space, in practice, the holiday is *so very* public: decorations in the shopping
streets and malls, in public squares, train stations, and airports; municipal
Christmas trees, national Christmas trees; angels, stars, Nativity scenes;
Santa Clauses, elves, reindeer, and – where necessary – fake snow. It is
precisely because Christmas transcends the boundary between the material
and spiritual that it transcends the boundary between private and public.
As Leigh Eric Schmidt shows in his history of the Christmas market in the
United States, the merchants of food and drink as well as toys for the children took advantage of the season and decorated their shops accordingly
as early as the 1830s. And since the holidays also afforded more free time,
"venues of public amusement" such as "theaters, music societies, circuses,

and dance halls" saw fit to attract customers with seasonal decorations. Above all the museum, "natural-history exhibit, curiosity shop, art gallery, theater, menagerie, and side show all rolled into one," took part, festooning its halls and illuminating its facades.[23] From the beginning, the public wanted to take part in the celebration. In Germany, it was no different. Not only "under the sign of *Kauflust* [shopping craze]," as Joe Perry quotes from a Berlin newspaper in 1898,[24] but also by theming all kinds of entertainment, from orchestra concerts to vaudeville, *Panopticon* displays, dance balls, dinners, plays, and radio shows.[25] Not many generations have to pass before this kind of ubiquity in public spaces begins to feel natural and becomes a site of shared memories. As contested as the commercialization of Christmas was, its presence in the public square was not the issue. And insofar as it becomes associated with the way "we" have always done it, it can become elevated to the status of national or cultural heritage, giving it even more of a claim on public space.

The sorting out of the spiritual and the material at the heart of the struggle over Christmas in the marketplace did not imply that Christmas should be completely removed from the public sphere. Even if their proper domain was seen in the separate-spheres ideology of the nineteenth century as the home, the issue was whether the profusion of material pleasures of the feast degraded its religious meaning. Religion and culture were both on the same side of the spiritual/material binary. Cultural meanings did not harm the spiritual nature of the festival; it could be German as well as Christian. Perhaps that is why the "material" – always the provocateur of the Christmas spirit, from Ebenezer Scrooge to today – resonates on the one hand with the "secular" and on the other with the "foreign." This latter association became latent in the discourse on the commercialization of Christmas in Germany when it was associated with American influence, the Americanization of German culture – nowhere better encapsulated than in the continually repeated story that Santa Claus was the invention of an American soft drink manufacturer, intended to discredit this figure as inauthentic.[26] Santa is also somehow not religious, not part of the Christian story, not in the Bible; he evokes pagan or merely commercial associations. In this figure, the material, the secular, and the foreign flow together to form an opposition against the spiritual, German, and Christian embodied in traditional figures such as St Nicholas, the Holy Family, or the *Christkindl*.

Recent years have seen a re-sorting of these categories, as new "culture wars" overlap the older tensions between the global/Americanized and the local/national as well as the commercial and the spiritual. In the United States this manifests in discourse on a purported "War on Christmas" being waged by militant upholders of the First Amendment prohibition of a national religion, such as the American Civil Liberties Union. Conservative and radical right-wing commentators in the media have fanned the flames of this rhetoric, linking court disputes over the placement of Christmas decorations on government property or the singing of Christmas carols by public school choirs to a broader cultural agenda of "secular progressivism," epitomized in the use of the greetings "Happy Holidays" or "Season's Greetings" rather than "Merry Christmas."[27] In the interest of promoting the public affirmation of Christmas as a Christian holiday, these commentators criticize the decoupling of the commercial and the spiritual. Whereas earlier Christian conservatives railed against the appropriation of the religious holiday for marketing purposes, these new culture warriors demand it: calls to boycott the Starbucks coffee chain because its seasonal to-go cups do not use Christian symbols, or complaints that department stores avoid the word "Christmas" in their displays are prominent examples. In the process, symbols such as Santa Claus, reindeer, and elves – in the United States found to be useful as transdenominational, even secular signs of the season[28] – are re-encoded as accoutrements of a specifically Christian Christmas. The "we" being constructed here is "real America," to which atheists suing for the removal of Santa's flying reindeer from public schools do not belong. "Real" American culture is thus melded with Christianity in a kind of religionization of (national) culture and even of elements of the marketplace.

In Germany, a religionization of culture is also taking place and becomes apparent in Christmas controversies with slightly different accents, but with a very similar agenda. Absent a constitutional law forbidding a national religion, the claim that Christianity has a place in the public sphere is on different footing. Its proponents are less interested in demanding from private enterprise that they include Christian symbolism in their advertising and more interested in policing the presence of Christmas in public schools and day care as well as in official discourse. This push-back against efforts by educators and politicians to create a more inclusive environment in multifaith contexts is aimed at their "multiculturalist agenda." Rather than viewing these efforts as a clearer separation of religion and the state, or the creation of religiously neutral practices and spaces, right-wing populist groups re-interpret them as a creeping "Islamicization" of German society.[29] They view the "War on Christmas" in Germany as being waged by Muslims, aided and abetted (unwittingly or not) by multiculturalist do-gooders contributing to the country's cultural demise.[30] The melding of "German culture" with Christianity has become so commonplace in this discourse as to sometimes make "Christian" a general term for ethnic Germans, regardless of the level of their religious engagement. A leading member of the right-wing populist party *Alternative für Deutschland*, Alexander Gauland, stated in an interview that, though he is a member of the Protestant church, he considers himself to be a non-believing "cultural Christian," and claimed that his party "defends a cultural tradition against an alien (*raumfremde*) immigration, and this alien immigration comes from Islam ... We are not defending Christianity, but rather the traditional life-feeling (*Lebensgefühl*) in Germany, the traditional feeling of home (*Heimatgefühl*)."[31]

Local controversies in Germany over whether or not the term "Christmas" (*Weihnachten*, more literally Holy Night), the traditional seasonal greeting "*Frohe Weihnachten*," or the Christmas tree (*Christbaum* or *Weihnachtsbaum*) should be used in public spaces are not always forwarded by the radical right, nor do they always suspect a Muslim agenda behind inclusive language. Like the sensitivity that has arisen in North America over the use of "Happy Holidays" – which in the course of the religionization of culture is itself no longer viewed as neutral, as a marker of abstinence, but rather of conscious positioning as nonreligious or "politically correct" – sensitivity is perceptible in Germany over purported renamings of Christmas events and symbols. Christmas markets in Germany are becoming less overtly Christian in their symbolism, according to research by European ethnologist Gunther Hirschfelder: saints, angels, and scenes from Bethlehem are being replaced by winter symbols: snowflakes, evergreen trees, reindeer. The holiday is changing its character from commemorating an event in the narrative cycle of Christian mythology to becoming a winter party with carnivalesque elements (costumes, alcohol, pop music).[32] This may go more or less uncommented-on in many cities. The decision by merchants in Berlin-Kreuzberg in 2014 to name their new seasonal bazaar "Winter Market," however, was greeted with protest. "Why not *Weihnachtsmarkt*?" a reporter from the *Berliner Zeitung* asks, and suggests it is due to a "trend which is actively being promoted by politicians in Kreuzberg. They [the majority are from left-wing parties] don't like Christmas markets on public streets and squares because they display religious symbols … I know that most of the inhabitants in this neighborhood do not belong to any religion anymore. Fine. But why can't this unchurched society be more relaxed? Why do they try to remove the biggest holiday of the year out of the public space and out of people's minds?"[33] Like the saying "out of sight, out of mind" suggests, this commentator links public display directly with shared memory.

Memory is not always to be trusted, and will be negotiated in public conversations. In the winter of 2016, in the Catholic town of Rottenburg – seat of the diocese and therefore equipped with a large cathedral and bishop's palace – discussions over the naming of the tree that is placed at the centre of the marketplace each year during the pre-Christmas season started anew. Had it not been called a "Christmas tree" in the past? Why was the city now only referring to it as a "fir tree"? Could it possibly have to do with the presence of Muslims in the city – a presence which was felt to have noticeably increased in the course of taking in Syrian refugees? Two months later the emotions were still running high, begging to be satirized during the carnival season: the parish priest asked during his carnival sermon, "why not change the name of the 'St. Nicholas market' to 'Fir tree market'?" The town mayor and his deputies, in turn, came to the festivities dressed as fir trees with various name tags: "Christmas tree," "fir tree," "whatever."[34]

The "whatever" attitude becomes the habitus of a moderate position, and many in German multicultural cities and towns would likely subscribe to a "live and let live" motto when it comes to Christmas. The Kreuzberg merchants denied any attempt to hide religious symbolism, claiming the Winter Market was intended to offer "those who do not care for all the Christmas season hype" a place to shop.[35] The *Süddeutsche Zeitung* ran a series in 2011 on how well-known non-Christian Germans celebrated the holiday (or didn't), highlighting the hybridity and diversity of observances but also abstentions.[36] Ignoring Christmas, however, may be the most difficult option to realize, as Isaac Weiner argues in his chapter in this volume.

The change in Christmas decoration or labelling points to a shift in the meaning of secularization. Previously thought of as a process in which religion loses importance in the public sphere, it now points to just the opposite: symbols are understood to be disappearing from public spaces because religion has become *so* important. The religiously neutral public space no longer signifies a lack of interest in or open critique of organized religions, but rather an attempt to be inclusive of all belief systems – including nonbelief – and thereby attesting to their importance. Where it is not viewed as feasible to include symbols from all the relevant religious groups, it is better to include none rather than privileging a few. The more strictly secularist approach to the holiday emerging from an anti-religious attitude was at one time typical for some members of the 68er generation and later baby-boomers who were vocal in fighting the influence of the Churches in public life. Some of these very same people, however, are now shifting their target to non-Christian religions only, and are willing to accept Christianity as part of a European cultural heritage.

The culturalization of religion manifests ever more frequently as a heritagization of religion. Regina Bendix, among others, has used this term to denote the process by which certain objects, sites, and/or practices are selected for preservation and in this process are transformed.[37] Barbara Kirshenblatt-Gimblett has defined this process as "metacultural operations that extend museological values and methods" to present-day, lived practice, reconfiguring its relationship to the practitioners. Originally conceived as a term for (usually national) historical sites redesigned for purposes of commemoration and tourism (and thus discredited as commercially motivated), heritagization is now increasingly applied to cultural practices and knowledges, crafts and rituals, referred to as "intangible culture." Thus, as Bendix points out, heritage has a material and emotional pole, as they are "a set of accumulated communal experiences that are construed as a 'birthright.'"[38] This metacultural operation is increasingly applied to religion, in the process musealizing, secularizing, and construing it as threatened.[39]

An understanding of Christmas as a (perhaps endangered) cultural legacy becomes apparent in various bids to protect its traditions by registering them as official UNESCO Intangible Cultural Heritage. The German Christmas Museum in Rothenburg ob der Tauber launched an unsuccessful proposal in 2013 to register the *Weihnachtsmann* as German cultural heritage, and in the same year, the Netherlands sought this prestige for *Sinterklaas*, their version of St Nicholas who arrives by boat in mid-November accompanied by *Zwarte Piet* (Black Pete), a clown-like figure dressed like a courtly page, with black skin, a curly black wig, and bright red lips. When an official from the United Nations suggested this racist depiction should be eliminated from the custom, it triggered a sustained public debate that tapped into and was fuelled by the deeper political divides within the Netherlands.

St Nicholas has a squire or servant in most local iterations of this custom. In Germany, he is *Knecht Ruprecht* (Knave Ruprecht), tasked with punishing the naughty children and portrayed as a sort of wild man from the forest dressed in furs. Among the seafaring Dutch, the iconography of the rascally servant has been drawn from a context in which colonial power is made visible in the form of dark-skinned servants indentured to Dutch nobility or rich burghers. This was a stock figure in works of art and comic theatre in the seventeenth and eighteenth centuries, yet *Zwarte Piet* only crystallized as a standard element of the *Sinterklaas* custom in the mid-nineteenth century.[40] Both *Knecht Ruprecht* and *Zwarte Piet* have lost their menacing character in recent decades with shifts in child-rearing philosophies. Rather than carrying a switch with which to beat the naughty children or a big canvas sack in which to carry them away, they became more like clowns, running about, causing mischief. Unlike in Germany, where *Knecht Ruprecht* is considered antiquated and often ignored, *Zwarte Piet* has been viewed as essential to *Sinterklaas*, a feeling that has intensified for some of those involved in the debate. The subjective sense that dressing up and painting one's face black is not an act of discrimination or ridicule but of affection and fun, becomes implicated in a pattern of "us" and "them": non-Dutch people don't understand what it means to the Dutch, they are transferring American meanings of blackface onto something that has a whole different history. At the same time, the debate opened up a space for Dutch citizens of non-European heritage to be heard on their views of having this figure present as they grew up as Black in the Netherlands.

The Dutch debate has caused Catholic Germans to reconsider one of their beloved Christmas figures, the Black king of the Holy Magi. When Catholic children play their role as *Sternsinger* (Star Singers) on Epiphany, dressing up as the Three Kings who represent the three known continents of the world and go from house to house to sing songs, collect money for a good cause, and bless the home, then the most prestigious role is Caspar, because that person gets to paint his or her face black.[41] Since not only Black Pete, but a broader blackfacing debate, has reached German cities,[42] some children no longer feel comfortable with this practice.[43] As a reporter on *Vice* commented: "Traditions are valuable, but they can – and should – be questioned. In an age where the color of a person's skin no longer tells you anything about where they are from, *Sternsinger* with faces painted black or yellow are simply antiquated."[44] But an article in *Die Welt* responded to the idea of forgoing the makeup by claiming that it would "deny the diversity of the world, efface the memory that centuries ago, there was a special appreciation for different cultures with different gifts. Actually, that is what would be discriminatory."[45] These processes of negotiating a change in Christmas customs are evidence of how cultural practices are constantly in motion, acquiring new meanings. In this case, it is an awareness that comes from the context of a multicultural society that triggers new conversations about the way "we" have always celebrated Christmas.

The ubiquity of Christmas controversies would suggest that the holiday season always precipitates a kind of crisis. It is a time when the tensions come to the fore and demand our attention, in families as well as in societies at large. Because holidays, in spite of it all, do matter quite a lot, there is a great desire to resolve the conflicts and tensions around them. While they have always been there – tensions between the material and spiritual, the commercial and religious, as well as the legitimacy of customs and who determines what they are – they are also always undergoing change. Currently it appears that cultural and religious plurality are attracting the most attention and generating the most discourse. Christmas celebrations are taking place in spaces where multiple religious identities are situated – not only in religiously plural cities, but also in interfaith families.[46] More research on the perspective of how non-Christian or mixed-faith Germans experience the holiday can show how not only tensions and discontents but also pleasures and playfulness can emerge from this constellation. As the co-presence of multiple religious and holiday traditions invite new forms of celebration, commemoration, decoration, and consumption, Christmas appears – in public as well as scholarly discourse – to heighten the significance of "religion" as a force to be dealt with in the public sphere, with paradoxical effects. On the one hand, religion is subsumed under concepts such as culture, nation, heritage, or memory, and on the other, these concepts are in the process made equivalent to religion. The religionization of culture not only gives identitarian claims more force in public discourse (the "right" to religion is transferred to a "right" to national identity), but also provokes new debates over the meaning of Christmas.

Notes

1 Löfgren, "The Great Christmas Quarrel," 218–19.
2 Ibid., 231.
3 See also Nissenbaum, *The Battle for Christmas*, and Bowler, *Christmas in the Crosshairs*.
4 Miller, "A Theory of Christmas."
5 See Christian Marchetti's chapter in this volume for more on Christmas research in the context of early German *Volkskunde*.
6 Bausinger, "Der Adventskranz: Ein methodisches Beispiel."
7 Weber-Kellermann, *Das Weihnachtsfest*, 7.
8 Korff, "Hase und Co."
9 Utz, "Schöne Bescherung."
10 "Brochure for the Exhibit."
11 Explicitly the topic of the volume from Richard Faber and Esther Gajek; see Gajek, "Nationalsozialistische Weihnacht."
12 Perry, *Christmas in Germany*, 7.
13 This is the argument presented by Russell Belk; see Belk, "Materialism and the American Christmas."
14 Miller, "A Theory of Christmas," 5.
15 The original English manuscript on which the German book was based has since been published as Miller, "Christmas: An Anthropological Lens."
16 Miller, *Weihnachten: Das globale Fest*, 34. English quote taken from Miller, "Christmas: An Anthropological Lens," 426.
17 Miller, "A Theory of Christmas," 31.
18 Hauschild, *Weihnachtsmann: Die wahre Geschichte*, 24–5. My translation.
19 Ibid., 30.
20 See also Scheer, "Kultur und Religion."
21 Utz, "Schöne Bescherung," 22. My translation.
22 Christmas is included in the German publication that emulates Pierre Nora's project. See Foitzik, "Weihnachten."
23 Schmidt, *Consumer Rites*, 127.
24 Perry, *Christmas in Germany*, 143.
25 Ibid., 152, 153, 179.
26 That the story is far more complex and involves a great deal of transatlantic entanglement can be found in Bowler, *Santa Claus: A Biography*. In *Unwrapping Christmas*, Russell Belk remarks: "Sundblom's portraits [of Santa] for Coca Cola advertising beginning in 1931 were refinements on

[previously established] themes … [but] made clear that Santa dressed in red and white, and removed Santa's pipe (replacing it with a bottle of Coca Cola)." Belk, "Materialism and the American Christmas," 79.

27 See Stack, "How the 'War on Christmas' Controversy Was Created." At the time of this publication, there are also Wikipedia entries on "Christmas Controversies" in English, French, Czech, Finnish, Portuguese, Greek, and Malay.

28 Schmidt, *Consumer Rites*, 132–4.

29 The semantic mixture and overlap of religious, cultural, and national categories is perhaps nowhere more evident than in the name of the movement spearheading this rhetoric: *Patriotische Europäer gegen die Islamisierung des Abendlandes* (PEGIDA, Patriotic Europeans Against the Islamicization of the West), founded in Dresden in October 2014.

30 Cf. the title of a recent bestseller, which translates to *Germany Doing Away with Itself: How We Are Jeopardizing Our Country*; see Sarrazin, *Deutschland schafft sich ab: Wie wir unser Land aufs Spiel setzen*.

31 Löbbert and Machowetz, "Gehört die AFD auf den Katholikentag?"

32 Hirschfelder, "Kultur im Spannungsfeld," 29–31.

33 Schupelius, "Neue Idee aus Kreuzberg." My translation.

34 Bernhard, "Zunftmesse und Straßenfasnet."

35 As reported by Schupelius, "Neue Idee aus Kreuzberg." My translation.

36 "Prominente Nicht-Christen."

37 Bendix, "Heritage between Economy and Politics." See also Kirshenblatt-Gimblett, "World Heritage and Cultural Economics."

38 Peckham, *Rethinking Heritage*, 1. Cited in Bendix, "Heritage between Economy and Politics," 253.

39 See Hervieu-Léger, *Religion as a Chain of Memory*. A Horizon 2020 HERA Project titled "HERILIGION – The Heritagization of Religion and the Sacralization of Heritage in Contemporary Europe" began research in June 2016.

40 See Meertens Instituut, "Dossier: Zwarte Piet"; McGrane, "The Netherlands Confronts Black Pete."

41 This was what I heard from parents and children I spoke with, though this report claims just the opposite: Lichtenegger, "Blackface bei Sternsingern ist immer noch ein Problem."

42 The popular television show *Wetten, dass* caused an uproar in 2013 because the audience was asked to dress up as characters from a widely beloved series of children's books by Michael Ende, one of which is depicted in blackface. A debate which had begun a few years earlier over the decision

by the publisher of Pippi Longstocking books, Friedrich Oetinger in
Hamburg, to remove the N-word from the translation had sensitized the
public over the use of racist terminology and imagery in children's classics.

43 As indicated in this report from Moers, in the western Ruhr region:
Schwerdtfeger and Tress, "Sternsinger in NRW oft ohne schwarzen König."
My translation.

44 Lichtenegger, "Blackface bei Sternsingern ist immer noch ein Problem."
My translation.

45 Becker, "Warum wir wieder dunkelhäutige Sternsinger brauchen."

46 See, for example, Mehta, "Chrismukkah: Millennial Multiculturalism."
The mixing of the child-oriented Christmas and Hannukah celebrations
was also a known practice in Wilhelmine Germany; see Kugelmann,
Weihnukka.

Bibliography

Bausinger, Hermann. "Der Adventskranz: Ein methodisches Beispiel."
Württembergisches Jahrbuch für Volkskunde 21 (1970): 9–31.

Becker, Claudia. "Warum wir wieder dunkelhäutige Sternsinger brauchen." *Die
Welt*, 6 January 2017. https://www.welt.de/vermischtes/article160947125/
Warum-wir-wieder-dunkelhaeutige-Sternsinger-brauchen.html.

Belk, Russell. "Materialism and the American Christmas." In *Unwrapping
Christmas*, edited by Daniel Miller, 75–104. Oxford, UK: Clarendon
Press, 1993.

Bendix, Regina. "Heritage between Economy and Politics: An Assessment from
the Perspective of Cultural Anthropology." In *Intangible Cultural Heritage*,
edited by Laurajane Smith and Natsuko Akagawa, 253–69. London:
Routledge, 2009.

Bernhard, Dunja. "Zunftmesse und Straßenfasnet: Tausende kamen zum
ungeordneten Feiern in die Innenstadt." *Schwäbisches Tagblatt*, 7 February
2016. http://www.tagblatt.de/Nachrichten/Zunftmesse-und-Strassenfasnet-
Tausende-kamen-zum-ungeordneten-Feiern-in-die-Innenstadt-275844.html.

Bowler, Gerry. *Santa Claus: A Biography*. Toronto: McClelland & Stewart, 2005.

– *Christmas in the Crosshairs: Two Thousand Years of Denouncing and Defending
the World's Most Celebrated Holiday*. New York: Oxford University Press, 2016.

"Brochure for the Exhibit from December 1, 1974 to January 6, 1975
in Tübingen Castle." Library of the Ludwig Uhland Institute, n.d.
Sig. SDR 3394.

Foitzik, Doris. "Weihnachten." In *Deutsche Erinnerungsorte*, edited by Étienne Francois and Hagen Schulze, 154–68. Munich, Germany: C.H. Beck, 2009.

Gajek, Esther. "Nationalsozialistische Weihnacht: Die Ideologisierung eines Familienfestes durch Volkskundler." In *Politische Weihnacht in Antike und Moderne: Zur Ideologischen Durchdringung des Festes der Feste*, edited by Richard Faber and Esther Gajek, 183–216. Würzburg, Germany: Königshausen & Neumann, 1997.

Hauschild, Thomas. *Weihnachtsmann: Die wahre Geschichte*. Frankfurt, Germany: S. Fischer, 2012.

Hervieu-Léger, Danièle. *Religion as a Chain of Memory*. Translated by Simon Lee. Cambridge, UK: Polity Press, 2000.

Hirschfelder, Gunther. "Kultur im Spannungsfeld von Tradition, Ökonomie und Globalisierung. Die Metamorphosen der Weihnachtsmärkte." *Zeitschrift für Volkskunde* 110, no. 1 (2014): 1–32.

Kirshenblatt-Gimblett, Barbara. "World Heritage and Cultural Economics." In *Museum Frictions: Public Cultures/Global Transformations*, edited by Ivan Karp, Corinne A. Kratz, and Lynn Szwaja, 161–202. Durham, NC: Duke University Press, 2006.

Korff, Gottfried. "Hase und Co: Zehn Annotationen zur niederen Mythologie des Bürgertums." In *Soll und Haben: Alltag und Lebensformen bürgerlicher Kultur*, edited by Ueli Gyr, 77–96. Zürich, Germany: Offizin Verlag, 1995.

Kugelmann, Cilly. *Weihnukka: Geschichten von Weihnachten und Chanukka*. Hamburg, Germany: Nicolai Verlag, 2005.

Lichtenegger, Franz. "Blackface bei Sternsingern ist immer noch ein Problem." *Vice*, 5 January 2016. http://www.vice.com/de_at/article/sternsinger-blackfacing-384.

Löbbert, Raul, and Martin Machowetz. "Gehört die AFD auf den Katholikentag?" *ZEIT Online*, 25 May 2016. http://www.zeit.de/2016/23/leipzig-afd-katholikentag-streitgespraech.

Löfgren, Orvar. "The Great Christmas Quarrel and Other Swedish Traditions." In *Unwrapping Christmas*, edited by Daniel Miller, 217–34. Oxford, UK: Clarendon Press, 1993.

McGrane, Sally. "The Netherlands Confronts Black Pete." *The New Yorker*, 4 November 2013. http://www.newyorker.com/culture/culture-desk/the-netherlands-confronts-black-pete#entry-more.

Meertens Instituut. "Dossier: Zwarte Piet." *Meertens Instituut KNAW*, 23 October 2013. http://www.meertens.knaw.nl/cms/en/nieuws-agenda/nieuws-overzicht/202-nieuws-2013/144369-dossier-zwarte-piet.

Mehta, Samira. "Chrismukkah: Millennial Multiculturalism." *Religion and American Culture: A Journal of Interpretation* 25, no. 1 (2015): 82–109.

Miller, Daniel. "A Theory of Christmas." In *Unwrapping Christmas*, edited by Daniel Miller, 3–37. Oxford, UK: Clarendon Press, 1993.

– *Weihnachten: Das globale Fest.* Translated by Frank Jakubzik. Frankfurt am Main, Germany: Suhrkamp Verlag, 2011.

– "Christmas: An Anthropological Lens." HAU: *Journal of Ethnographic Theory* 7, no. 3 (2017): 409–42.

Nissenbaum, Stephen. *The Battle for Christmas: A Social and Cultural History of Our Most Cherished Holiday.* New York: Knopf, 1996.

Peckham, Robert. *Rethinking Heritage.* London: I.B. Tauris, 2003.

Perry, Joe. *Christmas in Germany: A Cultural History.* Chapel Hill, NC: University of North Carolina Press, 2010.

"Prominente Nicht-Christen über Weihnachten – 'Ich feiere mit.'" *Süddeutsche Zeitung,* 24 December 2011. http://www.sueddeutsche.de/leben/weihnachten-fuer-nicht-christen-ich-feiere-mit-1.1243206-8.

Sarrazin, Thilo. *Deutschland schafft sich ab: Wie wir unser Land aufs Spiel setzen.* Munich, Germany: DVA, 2010.

Scheer, Monique. "Kultur und Religion: Eine Unschärferelation mit Folgen." *Zeitschrift für Volkskunde* 113, no. 2 (2017): 177–99.

Schmidt, Leigh Eric. *Consumer Rites: The Buying and Selling of American Holidays.* Princeton, NJ: Princeton University Press, 1995.

Schupelius, Gunnar. "Neue Idee aus Kreuzberg: Weihnachtsmarkt soll 'Wintermarkt' heißen." *Berliner Zeitung,* 24 September 2014. http://www.bz-berlin.de/berlin/friedrichshain-kreuzberg/weihnachtsmarkt-soll-wintermarkt-heissen.

Schwerdtfeger, Christian, and Kilian Tress. "Sternsinger in NRW oft ohne schwarzen König." *RP Online,* 6 January 2014. http://www.rp-online.de/nrw/staedte/moers/sternsinger-in-nrw-oft-ohne-schwarzen-koenig-aid-1.3925278.

Stack, Liam. "How the 'War on Christmas' Controversy Was Created." *New York Times,* 19 December 2016. http://www.nytimes.com/2016/12/19/us/war-on-christmas-controversy.html.

Utz, Jeggle. "Schöne Bescherung." *Allmende* 1, no. 3 (1981): 1–23.

Weber-Kellermann, Ingeborg. *Das Weihnachtsfest: Eine Kultur- und Sozialgeschichte der Weihnachtszeit.* Munich, Germany: Bucher C.J., 1987.

3

"And *then*! Oh, the noise!
Oh, the Noise! Noise! Noise! Noise!"
or How the Grinch Heard Christmas

Isaac Weiner

Introduction

Nobody likes a grinch. First introduced in 1957, as the titular character in Dr Seuss's *How the Grinch Stole Christmas*, "grinch" has grown into a generalized epithet hurled at the most contemptible sort of person, one who, not content to wallow in their own misery, must do all they can to ruin the happiness of those around them. A killjoy, we might call them, or a spoilsport. A party pooper. However you name it, grinches are the worst.

The particular object of the original Grinch's disdain was, of course, Christmas. He hated the stockings, and he hated the presents. He hated the feasting, and he hated the ringing. He hated the noise ("Oh, the noise! Oh, the Noise! Noise! Noise! Noise!"), and he hated the singing ("They'd sing! And they'd sing! / AND they'd SING! SING! SING! SING!"). In fact, so consuming, so irrational, so incomprehensible was the Grinch's total contempt for Christmas that Dr Seuss could explain it only as an innate physical deformity, a biological defect rooted in the Grinch's malformed anatomy: "The Grinch *hated* Christmas! The whole Christmas season! / Now, please don't ask why. No one quite knows the reason. / It *could* be his head wasn't screwed on just right. / It *could* be, perhaps, that his shoes were too tight. / But I think that the most likely reason of all / May have been that his heart was two sizes too small."[1] A heart two sizes too small, Seuss speculates. What other reason could there possibly be for making such a fuss?

By the end of the story, of course, the Grinch's heart has grown three sizes larger. His plans to ruin Christmas are foiled by the residents of Whoville's unflappable good cheer. For even after he has stolen their "pop guns! And bicycles! Roller skates! Drums! / Checkerboards! Tricycles! Popcorn! And plums!"; after he has packed up "their presents! The ribbons! The wrappings! / The tags! And the tinsel! The trimmings! The trappings!"; after he has made off with all of the *stuff* that makes Christmas *Christmas* – he is stunned to discover that he has failed to put an end to the festive celebrations. "Every *Who* down in *Who*-ville, the tall and the small, / Was singing! Without any presents at all! / He HADN'T stopped Christmas from coming! IT CAME! / Somehow or other, it came just the same!" Chastened by the Whos' undaunted spirit, the Grinch learns that Christmas "*doesn't* come from a store," but that it might just mean "a little bit more." And with a newly enlarged heart, he returns all of the loot and carves the Whos' roast beast himself. The Grinch is a grinch no longer.

How the Grinch Stole Christmas has usually been read as a thinly veiled critique of the holiday's commercialization. As folklorist Thomas Burns pointed out in a 1976 article, "Underlying the Grinch's notion of the theft of Christmas is the assumption that Christmas is equated with its material manifestations. For the Grinch, Christmas is no more than a noisy material celebration."[2] Read thusly, the Grinch's antagonism toward the Christmas season stems from a simple misunderstanding, an inability to perceive what the holiday is really about. As the Whos so clearly manifest with their communal hand-holding and song, the "true" spirit of Christmas lies not in its outward manifestations, but in the humanitarian feelings of universal fellowship and goodwill that such practices are meant to engender. The Grinch's alienation from the broader Who community is a product of his failure to appreciate the properly spiritual basis of the holiday. Once he experiences Christmas for what it truly is, his resistance melts away and his conversion is immediate. Precisely because he has proven how unnecessary the material practices actually are, the Grinch learns to appreciate their value. By means of his enthusiastic participation, he escapes the isolation of his cave and pulls up a chair at the Whos' communal table.

On Dr Seuss's telling, in other words, the "authentic" meaning of Christmas is less about the Nativity of Christ as much as the need to integrate otherwise alienated individuals into the broader political community. This theme has been fleshed out more fully by recent scholarship that has taken interest in the civic ideology expressed through Seuss's writings.

Literary scholar Shira Wolosky, for example, has argued that even as Seuss "exuberantly endorses the individual in all his productions," he also grew "increasingly alarmed at individualism as a potentially devouring and anomic force." Approaching Seuss as a sophisticated commentator on American political life, she explores how his writings interrogate the "fault lines that threaten to undermine and destabilize" liberal democratic values. "What," she interprets Seuss's books as asking, "will prevent all the individual pursuits from disintegrating into contrary and contending self-interests, where community is not built out of individual energies but destroyed by them?"[3]

Through a close reading of selected stories, Wolosky demonstrates how Seuss celebrated unique individuals while simultaneously situating them within, and holding them accountable to, the broader society of which they were a part. "Dr. Seuss's is thus a vision not only of individuals," she explains, "but of community. It rests upon a faith that the exercise of individuality will build and strengthen social life."[4] Although Wolosky devotes little attention to *How the Grinch Stole Christmas*, children's literature scholar Julia Pond has more recently shown how Wolosky's argument works in the case of that story, too. "The Grinch must learn to respect and to understand the community as he remains in danger of self consumption," Pond writes. "His alienation from society engenders in him aggression and hatred for the group of which he cannot be a part. He transforms into a better version of himself through his recognition of support and joy originating in community, as depicted in the Whos' communal singing, the 'something / He liked least of all.'"[5]

On this reading, *How the Grinch Stole Christmas* becomes less a meditation on the authentic meaning of Christmas or the problem of over-rampant consumerism as it is a political allegory about the obligations of the individual to the community in liberal democratic societies. Yet in so doing, it reinforces the association of Christmas with communitarian values of consensus, inclusion, and social solidarity. It positions Christmas as a repository of shared civic virtues, as a locus around which potentially isolated or egoistic individuals might sublimate their self-centred pursuits and join together for a purpose greater than themselves (i.e. something "a little bit more"). To put it a bit too finely, Christmas becomes the glue that binds together the fragmented shards of a pluralistic society.

But can Christmas possibly bear the weight of this liberal democratic civic ideology? What are the conditions that allow an ostensibly Christian holiday to serve as a potent symbol of civic consensus and harmony? And how might we read *How the Grinch Stole Christmas* differently if we began with the presumption that Whoville was not a homogenous, monolithic community, but a multicultural, religiously plural society? What if we were to reread the story, in other words, with a more sympathetic ear to the Grinch's lonely and tragic predicament? How might that change the way we understand its message?

Although Seuss's story focuses almost entirely on the Grinch's activities, our sympathies are clearly meant to lie with the Whos, who are portrayed as victims of the Grinch's scorn and malice. And admittedly, the Grinch's strategy for solving his Christmas dilemma seems misguided at the least, if not outright dastardly. Yet what if we look for other ways to explain his actions, apart from his heart being two sizes too small? What if we grant that his motives stemmed from genuine feelings of alienation, isolation, and exclusion? Perhaps, we might speculate, the Grinch belonged to a minority religious community in a society whose members too often seemed to take their homogeneity for granted. Perhaps he was a marginalized dissenter, who, after being forced to endure the irritating racket of Whoville's seasonal festivities year after year, was sick of being made to feel as though he was ruining Christmas for everyone should he ever utter a word of complaint. In either case, what the Grinch objected to was not the spirit of Christmas itself but the presumption that that spirit was shared by all. In the noisy celebrations of Christmas ("Oh, the noise!"), he hears signals not of universal fellowship, harmony, and inclusivity, but of majoritarian dominance, exclusivity, and religious particularity. Read in this way, *How the Grinch Stole Christmas* takes on a more tragic tone, a tale of coerced assimilation. Confronted with the insistent sounds of the Whos' celebrations, he must ultimately join in or be vilified. The one thing the Grinch cannot do is doggedly maintain his difference.

My re-imagining of the Grinch story re-situates it within what Monique Scheer describes as a new agenda for Christmas studies.[6] I "shift the coordinates" of its conversation away from an intra-Christian dispute about the relationship between Christmas and commerce, or "the paradox between the spiritual values that the holiday is supposed to embody and the consumerist effects it causes," and toward instead a debate between Christians and "others" about the contested ways that Christmas is experienced in multi-religious contexts. On my reading, the Grinch story is less about the "authentic" meaning of Christmas and more about the "public work" Christmas does as a contested site of cultural memory, as a locus for political contests over inclusion and exclusion in a pluralistic liberal democracy.

Rather than castigate the Grinch, therefore, I want to consider why his options felt so limited in the face of the Whos' public festivities. Turning specifically to the celebration of Christmas in the United States, I want to interrogate why joining in seemed to be the Grinch's only viable choice, and what that might say about Christmas's hegemonic power. More broadly, I am interested in using the Grinch's dilemma as a case study for exploring the politics of pluralism and secularism in American society. I will explore how Christian privilege, or what the editors of this volume refer to as Christianity's particular "affordances," manifests itself both through the affective and sensory registers of public culture and through the power to name its public practices as alternately religious or secular. In either case, I suggest, the end result is the same: an ostensibly neutral public sphere shaped by distinctly Christian forms of material practice.

"And THEN they'd do something he liked least of all!"

The Grinch story centres on the sonic dimensions of the Christmas festival. The Grinch detests the noise of squealing children excitedly unwrapping and playing with their new toys. He despises the chimes of bells ringing in the holiday morning. And he cannot stand the sound of carolling, the joyous singing that finally drives him mad. Yet it is also these same carols that ultimately draw him in, when he hears the Whos' singing in place of the wailing "boo-hoo" that he expected. It is when he recognizes that their "sound wasn't *sad*! / Why, this sound sounded *merry*! / It *couldn't* be so! / But it WAS merry! VERY!" that he experiences his sudden growth of heart. The same sounds that once made him feel isolated and alone now encourage him to join in the fun.

Sounds appear in Seuss's story as both alienating and inviting, off-putting and delightful. They reach the Grinch in his isolation, and they envelop him in the fellowship of community. They remind him of the holiday he hates before they teach him to appreciate its "true" meaning. But the one thing they cannot be is ignored. Try as he might, the Grinch cannot block out their intrusions. Even holed up in his cave "just north of *Who*-ville," he cannot escape their call. By incorporating him into its acoustic territory, the Grinch feels as though Christmas has assaulted him, rather than the other way around.[7] And thus he feels compelled to respond, less out of spite, perhaps, than from necessity.

This emphasis on the sonic hardly seems a coincidence, for sound has long served as a critical site of public controversy and inter-religious negotiation. Church bells and prayer calls, public preaching and amplified music – each of these has generated conflict by eliciting complaint at various moments of US history. In fact, the Grinch's response fits with a broader pattern of how Americans have reacted to the sounds of religious difference reverberating throughout the shared spaces of common life. Whether experienced as harmonious or discordant, Americans have regularly described sound as particularly transgressive. They have noted the ways that sounds seem to spill over and across imagined boundaries between public and private, self and others, in ways that seem distinctly difficult to avoid.[8]

Whether accurate or not, this sentiment has been reinforced repeatedly by US legal authorities, who have distinguished between the ease with which one may close their eyes versus their ears. In a 1989 decision, for example, US Supreme Court Justice Anthony Kennedy described a Christmas crèche and Hanukkah menorah as "purely passive symbols" and emphasized that "passersby who disagree with the message conveyed by [them] are free to ignore them or even to turn their backs."[9] Seventeen years earlier, Justice John Marshall Harlan had argued even more strenuously that unwilling viewers were not "captive audiences" in the same way as unwilling listeners. In upholding Paul Robert Cohen's right to wear a jacket bearing the words "Fuck the Draft," Harlan made much of the fact that "those in the Los Angeles courthouse could effectively avoid further bombardment of their sensibilities simply by averting their eyes."[10] And as early as 1877, a Philadelphia judge had similarly elaborated the distinct threat posed by noise by succinctly explaining that "light may be shut out, and odors measurably excluded, but sound is all-pervading."[11]

For many unwilling listeners, however, the problem is not just that they cannot shut their ears, but that they might feel compelled to respond. Sonic displays are not "purely passive," as Justice Kennedy described the menorah and crèche, but stridently call out, breaking down one's defenses and inviting them not just to listen, but to participate. This was the anxiety expressed by many of the complainants in the call-to-prayer disputes that I have studied, who seemed concerned that merely listening to the *muezzin*'s

summons might signal their affirmation of its message.[12] Or consider
Immanuel Kant's complaint in his *Critique of Judgment* that "those who
have recommended the singing of hymns at family prayers have forgotten
the amount of annoyance which they give to the general public by such
noisy (and, as a rule, for that very reason, pharisaical) worship, for they
compel their neighbors either to join in the singing or else abandon their
meditations."[13] Religion out loud bothered Kant not merely because it
distracted him from his work, but because he found himself unwittingly
humming along. It impinged on his personal autonomy, leaving him no
choice but to join in. As the philosopher John Dewey once put it: "Vision
is a spectator; hearing is a participator."[14]

Many theorists have celebrated sound for precisely this reason, for
its potential to bridge boundaries by forging solidarity across religious,
racial, and ethnic divides. "The world we encounter at the level of sound
and acoustic experience is a new world of social experience and emotional
possibility," popular music scholar Josh Kun writes, "but it is also, necessarily, a strange world that we negotiate through listening." Listening to
the sounds and music of "others" can invite us to re-imagine our collective
identities and attachments, Kun suggests. It can open up new social spaces
in which diverse audiences confront and negotiate complex questions of
heterogeneity and difference.[15]

If Kun maintains an understanding of musical worlds as marked both
by familiarity and strangeness, then sociologist Emile Durkheim even more
strongly approached sound as a medium through which such differences
could be transcended and overcome. In his famous, if imagined, account of
Aboriginal totemic ritual practice in Australia, he emphasized the powerful
role that sound played in generating feelings of collective effervescence. In
vivid prose drawn not from experience but from his reading, he described
the "shouts, downright howls, and deafening noises of all kinds" that
would gradually coalesce "into rhythm and regularity, and from there
into songs and dances." He presented readers with "a scene of truly wild
frenzy," marked by clanging boomerangs, whirling bullroarers, and other
percussive accompaniment, culminating in the "echoing scream – actually
a howl" of "*Yrrsh! Yrrsh! Yrrsh!*"[16] Through their ecstatic noise, participants
in this ritual, at least on Durkheim's armchair reading of colonial accounts,
were transformed into something new, something outside of and greater
than themselves, something "a little bit more," to quote Dr Seuss. As with
Seuss's depiction of the Whos' communal carolling, Durkheim credits
sound with integrating discrete individuals into a collective social body.[17]

Yet I have also suggested that sound can function conversely as a force of dissension and discord. In complaints about religious noise, we find resistance to the idea that sound unites heterogeneous communities into a harmonious whole. Public sound is just as likely to be experienced as an unwelcome intrusion, as an aggressive and visceral violation of personal and communal boundaries. These different perceptions of sound hinge on different ways of evaluating sound's assimilating tendencies, whether it is understood as mitigating and overcoming differences or as effacing them altogether.

In this way, competing perceptions of sound resonate with broader debates about the meaning of Christmas in multicultural, religiously plural societies. To different audiences in different contexts, Christmas, too, can seem both universal *and* particularistic, inclusive *and* alienating, unitive *and* divisive. A similar ambiguity imbues debates about Christmas, hinging on whether it should be celebrated or condemned for its assimilating tendencies. As I have already suggested, this ambivalence can lead to different ways of reading the Grinch story, whether as extolling the virtues of humanitarian fellowship and goodwill or as a tragic reminder of the coercive effects of majoritarian dominance. But the one thing these readings share is the firm sense that Christmas, like sound, cannot simply be shut out. It cannot simply be ignored. Blocking it out, refusing to listen, failing to respond, are not viable options for a grinch, whether holed up in a cave just north of Whoville or residing today in the contemporary United States. Christmas is just too loud.[18] And so, we might ask, what other possibilities present themselves?

"The more the Grinch thought, 'I must stop this whole thing!'"

The Grinch, of course, responds by trying to "steal" Christmas, to mute its pervasive power by quieting down its public observance. He assumes that removing the holiday's material trappings will prevent the Whos from being able to celebrate quite so noisily. We might imagine that from his perspective, the Grinch feels less motivated by the need to ruin Christmas for others than by a fervent desire to not have to hear about it himself. Perhaps he could even learn to tolerate Christmas if the Whos would just try a bit harder to keep it to themselves.

On the one hand, then, the Grinch's objections to Christmas might have little to do with the holiday's ostensible religiousness. He might have claimed simply to be bothered by the noise. In this case, his arguments would resonate with those of countless other complainants throughout US history, including Vici and Stephen Diehl, residents of Antwerp, New York, who in 1994 had the audacity to seek a court order to stop a nearby Congregational church from blasting Christmas carols from its steeple four hours a day. "The sad thing is, I like listening to Christmas carols," Vici Diehl told a local newspaper. "But I don't like being forced to listen to anything for hours on end."[19]

On the other hand, the Grinch might have objected to Christmas celebrations precisely because they were religious. In that case, the Grinch's arguments might echo a rhetorical strategy that I have described elsewhere as "privatism."[20] This position assumes that in a radically heterogeneous society, religious differences are best kept quiet. It affirms an individual's right to believe and practise as they please, yet only to the extent that they can keep their personal piety properly contained. Privatists imagine a public sphere marked as secular, by which they generally mean devoid of any particularistic religious expression.

The privatist position, as I have outlined it here, presumes the *particularity* and *exclusivity* of celebrating Christmas. It regards noisy, public displays as inappropriate only if – or precisely because – they are not partaken in by all. Yet that is precisely what is at stake in Dr Seuss's story, which portrays the Grinch's effort to steal Christmas as an attack on the Who community itself. The Whos' actions are not presented as an importunate imposition, but as a collective expression of universal solidarity and goodwill. In fact, the Whos do not seem to understand what they are doing as a violation of privatism at all, for they regard Christmas as part of a commonly shared culture, not as a particularistic sign of religious difference. This is similar to how many Antwerp residents responded to the Diehls, in the Christmas carol dispute described above, including Helen Robbins, a local business owner, who said, "We're a little town, and we have nothing, not even street decorations, and the music is something that's inspiring and enjoyable. The consensus is, everyone who comes in here is in favor of the music."[21]

The Whos' (and Antwerp's) position that Christmas reflects the consensus of the community is bolstered by Dr Seuss's decision not to include any overt reference to Christ or the Nativity in his story. He deliberately frames Christmas as potentially, if not exclusively, secular, rather than religious. As folklorist Burns explains, "Boiled down to its didactic essence, the Grinch story suggests that the Christmas celebration *may* involve Christian religious belief but it need not do so to remain meaningful. So long as the material decoration, exchange, and feasting of Christmas remain linked to the social idea of humanitarianism, the festival of Christmas is socially significant and valuable. Viewed in this way, the Grinch story is itself a justification of the popular tradition which is non-religious."[22] And as a non-religious tradition, Christmas might presumably be shared and celebrated by all.

Seuss's approach resonates with a common rhetorical defense of public Christmas observances in the United States, which works to distinguish between the holiday's religious and secular dimensions. According to this logic, Christmas is assumed to have both religious and cultural significance, where the former is associated with those aspects deemed particularistic or potentially divisive, and the latter with that which is universal or commonly shared. Read in this way, Christmas can stand as both a distinctly Christian event and a decidedly secular one at the same time. As long as public celebrations emphasize the latter, as was the case with the Whos of Whoville, there should be no cause for concern.

Consider, for example, how this logic was deployed in a 1980 decision of the US 8th Circuit Court of Appeals to legitimate Christmas observance in the Sioux Falls, South Dakota, public schools. A group of residents had complained that such observances "constituted religious exercises," which ran afoul of the First Amendment's religion clauses, prohibiting state establishment of religion.[23] Writing for the court, however, Circuit Judge Gerald Heaney endorsed the lower court's view that Christmas had "acquired a significance which is no longer confined to the religious sphere of life. It has become integrated into our national culture and heritage." Turning specifically to the singing of carols, Heaney emphasized how widespread was its practice. "Carols were banned for a period in the New England Colonies by the Puritans," he wrote, "but they have been sung in homes, schools, churches, and public and private gathering places during the Christmas season in every section of the United States since that time. Today, carols are sung with regularity on public and commercial television and are played on public address systems in offices, manufacturing plants and retail stores in every city and village." In this way, Heaney concluded, they had clearly "achieved a cultural significance that justifies their being sung in the public schools."[24] Because Christmas could be said to have both religious and cultural bases, that is, because it was as much a part of a common heritage as a feature of particularistic religious expression, then its public acknowledgment could not be deemed problematic.[25]

The very obviousness of this claim warrants further scrutiny. As Lori Beaman has explained in a different context, religion is understood here as having "two faces" – one that preserves religion as a space of particularity and difference and another that offers "a broader imagining of religion" by "fold[ing] it into culture and render[ing] it part of who 'we' are."[26] Christmas is presented as something that "we" all share, an integral component of our national heritage and identity, even as it remains at the same time a distinctly Christian holiday. And the court advances this claim by pointing to precisely that aspect of the holiday that bothered the Grinch the most. As Heaney explained, it was the rampant pervasiveness of Christmas music, its ubiquitous presence across multiple arenas of American social life, or even its very *unavoidability*, that served, in part, as sign of its secularity – and thus, ironically, its permissibility. Because one could not help but hear the sounds of Christmas wherever one might go, Christmas had become a part of who "we" are.

What is so significant about this, of course, is not only how such an argument might seem unintelligible to members of minority religious traditions – for whom having to listen to Christmas music in so many other arenas of everyday life might offer precisely the justification for *not* having to do so within the particular context of the public schools – but, even more crucially, how such an argument could not possibly be extended to their own practices in the same way. By appealing to factors such as history and ubiquity, the court ensures that the logic of its decision could only be extended to majoritarian practices, for minority practices could not possibly be regarded as similarly widespread. Only majoritarian practices could be understood as having "both religious and secular bases," as the court defines it, and thus only majoritarian practices could claim a place in the public schools without disrupting their purported secularity. Put differently, the secular functions here not as a sign of religious neutrality or absence, but as a way of making space for the observances of the dominant majority, now marked as cultural or commonly shared. In this way, a school policy designed to protect minority students from majoritarian dominance ends up doing precisely the opposite. A school policy designed to protect the rights of a grinch, we might say, ends up forcing him to join in.

We find similar logics and effects at work in disputes about the public display of crosses and crucifixes. In a 2010 case, for example, concerning an eight-foot white cross in the Mojave Desert, the US Supreme Court was divided over the question of how to interpret the public meaning of this ostensibly Christian symbol. For the more liberal justices, the cross could only be understood in narrowly sectarian or particularistic terms. "The cross is not a universal symbol of sacrifice," Justice John Paul Stevens wrote, in dissent. "It is the symbol of one particular sacrifice, and that sacrifice carries deeply significant meaning for those who adhere to the Christian faith."[27] But for the more conservative justices, part of the cross's appeal lay precisely in its capacity to "transcend" its Christian context and speak to values of a more universal nature. "Although certainly a Christian symbol," Justice Anthony Kennedy acknowledged in his plurality opinion, "the cross was not emplaced on Sunrise Rock to promote a Christian message." Instead, he explained, the Mojave Desert cross was intended to honor "the noble sacrifices [of fallen soldiers] that constitute our national heritage."[28] In language directly reminiscent of that used by Judge Heaney in the Sioux Falls Christmas case, Kennedy interpreted the cross as *both* a Christian symbol *and* a part of our shared cultural heritage, as both religious and secular, that is, and therefore potentially universal and inclusive.[29]

In the 2011 *Lautsi* case about the display of crucifixes in Italian state schools, the Grand Chamber of the European Court of Human Rights confronted a similar set of arguments about history, culture, and national heritage.[30] While acknowledging that "the crucifix is above all a religious symbol," the Grand Chamber gave due regard to the Italian government's contention that the cross was also "a cultural and identity-linked symbol, the symbol of the principles and values which formed the basis of democracy and western civilization."[31] It also considered an Italian administrative court ruling that described the cross as a "universal sign of the acceptance of and respect for every human being as such" and "a reflection ... on Italian history and the common values of our society."[32] Here, again, we find majoritarian symbols subsumed into the category of culture, understood as transcending their sectarian religious connotations and speaking instead to a set of purportedly universal or commonly shared values.

In its actual judgment, the European Court avoided having to decide whether the crucifix was essentially a religious symbol or not. Its ruling left ambiguous the question of whether the crucifix could transcend its Catholicity and stand also for "secular" values, such as liberty, human rights, and democracy. Yet even so, what was most revealing about the Court's thinking was how hard it worked to distinguish the Catholic crucifix from a Muslim headscarf. In a previous decision, the Court had upheld a measure prohibiting a Muslim teacher from wearing her headscarf in the classroom by characterizing it as a "powerful external symbol," which was impossible not to notice and therefore violated the principle of state neutrality. At the time, it had suggested that a crucifix might be understood in the same way.[33] Yet in *Lautsi*, the Grand Chamber reversed course by describing the crucifix as "an essentially passive symbol," which could not "be deemed to have an influence on pupils comparable to that of didactic speech or participation in religious activities."[34] For this reason, the crucifix was found to have no necessary impact on the principle of neutrality. The upshot of the Court's decision, in other words, was that minority religious symbols had to be closely monitored and carefully regulated while majority symbols could be essentially ignored. Or, as legal scholar Lorenzo Zucca puts it, "we could conclude that some symbols are more neutral than others."[35]

At the same time, the Grand Chamber emphasized that Muslim *students* enjoyed a right to wear headscarves in the classroom and offered this as evidence for the openness of Italian state schools to religious diversity.[36] When teachers wore apparel identified as Islamic, it was found to violate the principle of neutrality, yet when students did so, it was embraced in the name of tolerance and religious freedom. In either case, the headscarf was marked as inescapably and incontrovertibly *religious*. Whether prohibited in the name of secularism or celebrated in the name of pluralism, the headscarf was regarded as an expression of religious *difference* and particularity. The crucifix, however, could be understood differently. The crucifix, a symbol of the dominant majority, could be regarded as an expression of commonality and universality, as a critical element of a shared national culture and heritage. The majoritarian symbol could transcend its religious particularity while the minority symbol could not.

I found a similar, though not identical, dynamic at play in American disputes about the Islamic call to prayer. Again and again, unwilling listeners would complain about the *adhan* as unwanted religious noise while ignoring the chimes of nearby church bells. The former was attacked as an inappropriate auditory intrusion while the latter went unmarked and unnoticed, not perceived as disrupting the normative secularity of public space. In many of the cases I studied, neighbours would even describe the sounds of church bells as themselves secular. The sounds of a minority religious community would thus stand out as a particularistic expression of difference while the sounds of the socially dominant would fade to the background, seeming so ubiquitous and pervasive as to hardly warrant comment. In fact, their power seemed to emerge precisely from this *failure* to attract much attention at all. In their very ubiquity and familiarity, or perhaps in their very unnoticeability, they could even more readily become a part of who "we" are. They could even more insistently demand our participation – or, to paraphrase Immanuel Kant, become those sounds to which we unwittingly find ourselves humming along.[37]

All of this speaks to what we might describe as the politics of ambient faith. In *God's Agents*, his incisive ethnography of biblical publicity in England, anthropologist Matthew Engelke uses the category of ambience to describe the British and Foreign Bible Society's efforts to inject its faith into the public culture, not in a loud or boisterous way (as with some of the groups I have studied), but by trying to make it "part of the background noise of daily life."[38] Yet there is a politics to the possibilities of ambience, for not all groups seem equally capable of making their sonic (or symbolic) expressions part of the "background culture." Not all sounds, that is, can similarly escape notice or critique. For even when celebrated in the name of pluralism, minority practices inexorably stand out as *different*.

"He HADN'T stopped Christmas from coming! IT CAME!"

I have suggested that we might interpret the Grinch's effort to "steal" Christmas as a well-intentioned, if ill-advised, response to how he experienced the holiday's pervasiveness as a religious "other." He aims to mute Christmas's public power by calling attention to its particularity and exclusivity, by contesting the presumed consensus on which its public observance was predicated, thereby refusing to let it fade unnoticeably into the background. The Whos, by contrast, continue to imagine their observance as a collectively shared cultural practice, engaged in by all members of the Who community. As members of the dominant majority, they enjoy the privilege of recasting their celebrations as secular, not religious, offering them an effective strategy for combatting the Grinch's efforts. On their (or really Seuss's) rendering, Christmas stands for universal values of humanitarian fellowship and collective solidarity, to which any member of Who society could theoretically subscribe. The upshot of such an approach is that majoritarian practices are protected under the rubric of culture while minority practices stand subject to special scrutiny as religious intrusions – or, put differently, it helps to construct and maintain a secular public sphere marked by distinctly Christian forms of material practice.

But if it can be useful for religious majorities to describe their practices as cultural, then it can prove equally valuable to classify them as religious. In the case of the British and Foreign Bible Society, for example, it was important that the group sought to inject religion, qua religion, into a public sphere presumed to be hostile to overtly religious discourse. While part of the organization's success undoubtedly emerged from the intimate association of Christian "religion" with British "culture," its leaders would not have been satisfied to fully collapse the categories into each other.

We find this dynamic illustrated even more vividly in conservative allegations of a liberal "War on Christmas." Such rhetoric constitutes a different kind of response to Grinchian efforts to mute Christmas's public power, treating them more as discriminatory attacks on Christians' religious rights than as challenges to the collective consensus of the community as a whole. In the case of carolling in the public schools, for example, its defenders might argue not that such practices constitute part of our national heritage, but that silencing them would deprive Christian students of their right to practise their religion as they please. In this guise, Christmas's advocates understand themselves not as standing in for the dominant culture, but as standing apart from it, constituting an embattled minority within a rapidly secularizing social environment.[39]

This line of argument expresses a real ambivalence about Christmas's place in American culture. Even as its observance remains ubiquitously pervasive and widespread, the rhetoric of a "War on Christmas" reflects a deeper underlying anxiety about Christianity's shifting position in a multicultural, religiously diverse society. When confronted with the particularity and contestability of their traditions, Christians find themselves forced to defend practices that they had long been able to take for granted. What might be intended as an effort to place members of the majority on the same footing as everyone else can be perceived as a powerful sense of displacement.

There is an important tension here, however. By trafficking in the language of religious embattlement and persecution, the "War on Christmas" rhetoric relies, in large part, on the presumed *religiosity* of Christian symbols and practices. It refuses to represent such displays as merely cultural or secular. This discourse thus relies on precisely that which was downplayed or even denied in the public school cases discussed above. In one context, Christmas is defended as an integral part of who "we" are, as embodying universal, commonly shared values, while in the other, Christmas is presented as a particularistic religious tradition that warrants special protections and privileges. Secular on the one hand and religious on the other, but in either case the result is the same: making space for the practices of the majority while de-legitimizing the objections of the minority.

My point here is not to argue that Christmas is actually religious or secular, nor is it to affirm the notion that Christmas has discrete religious and secular dimensions that can be neatly distinguished. Rather, I want to underscore how Christmas can be framed as either religious or secular depending on context, in ways that tend to be of value to those doing the framing. Defining Christmas as religious or secular is a strategic or political distinction, in other words, not an essential one. Rhetoric about Christmas is malleable, not fixed, and can be employed in a variety of ways for a variety of purposes, always shaped by the needs and interests of those doing the deploying.

Taking this point seriously directs our attention not just to the impossibility of drawing bright lines between religious and secular but also to who has the power to draw such lines in the first place. As I have tried to show through my disparate examples, American Christians often enjoy the right to frame their practices as alternately religious or secular, particularistic or universal, in ways that are not as readily available to religious minorities. Christians are able to dart back and forth across the line as necessary, representing themselves at times as the guarantors of a commonly shared national culture and at other times as members of an embattled and besieged religious subset.[40] In either case, the end result is a public sphere rendered more hospitable to the practices of the dominant majority. Christian privilege is manifested here, then, not by its pervasiveness or power to force others to listen, but by its power to lay claim to the categories of religious and secular themselves, to construct their meanings and demarcate their boundaries as politically useful.

Legal scholarship has tended to treat the categories of religious and secular as essentially fixed. It has approached the distinction between Christmas's religious and secular dimensions as relatively stable or self-evident. Typical are statements such as this one, from a 1992 law review article, that "Christmas rituals can only be reasonably understood as religious because such rituals can never be truly divorced from the broader religious context in which they arose."[41] Such assertions, whether arguing for Christmas's inherent religiosity or secularity, imply that adjudicating Christmas's proper place in American life is simply a matter of drawing the right lines. They assume that our political conflicts over Christmas observance stem from a fundamental misrecognition of what the holiday is really about. To resolve them, therefore, all one need do is look back to history or doctrine to determine the holiday's essential nature.

My point, by contrast, is not that such determinations are wrong but that they are not natural. It is not that we cannot or should not draw distinctions between religious and secular, but that we must always be attentive to how the very act of line drawing *itself* cannot be divorced from the broader political context in which it arose. The question of Christmas's secularity arises not in the abstract, that is, but within the context of particular disputes and controversies. Its ambiguous nature does not cause political conflicts as much as it is a product of them. We might even say that Christmas is not religious or secular until particular social actors find value in naming it as such, for particular reasons and toward particular ends.

In that case, the task for scholars is to interrogate why naming Christmas as religious or secular is useful, whose interests are served by defining Christmas in this way, and to what ends. We should not take such distinctions for granted, but interrogate instead why they seem so obvious and even necessary to draw. As Hussein Ali Agrama has argued, in fact, secular governance often seems defined less by the need to separate religious from secular than by making such a distinction politically salient and significant in the first place.[42] In so suggesting, I am following the work of other scholars who have pursued similar questions in other contexts, showing how the distinction between religious and secular is itself the product of particular contests over public power and limited social resources.[43] I am directing our attention to how "religion" is produced *through* public controversy, rather than existing prior and giving rise to it.[44] In short, I want to suggest that political conflicts over the public observance of Christmas are not just about whether religion should be performed in public, but about the power to define the very nature of such performances in the first place.

Again, to be clear, my argument is not that Christmas is essentially religious, secular, or both, but that the very act of drawing such distinctions is political, not natural. And I believe this helps us to understand why the Grinch's options must have felt so limited in the end. As I have suggested, the Whos' raucous celebrations could not be easily tuned out or ignored.

Some kind of public response must have seemed in order. Yet the Grinch found himself unable to mute their good cheer – and not only because he discovered that Christmas was about more than presents. Enjoying the affordances that come with belonging to the dominant majority, the Whos could frame any attack on their Christmas observances *either* as a threat to their religious freedom *or* as a challenge to the presumed consensus of the community as a whole. In either case, the Grinch would be exposed as a pitiable malcontent, an unsympathetic deviant, whose actions appeared motivated more by anatomical perversity then by "genuine" feelings of alienation and isolation.

But if inclined instead to proudly sing out his own tune, the Grinch would discover that participating publicly was not available to him on the same terms, for the privileges afforded to the majority could not be extended to religious minorities in the same way. The Grinch's own public performances would inexorably be marked as particularistic displays of difference, as setting him apart from the broader community rather than locating him squarely within it, and thus subject to either celebration or suspicion, but never simply taken for granted. In the end, then, finding himself unable to ignore, silence, or participate on his own terms, the Grinch must have felt stuck. Lacking other options, he chooses to make the best of a difficult situation – by merrily joining in the fun.

Conclusion

In this chapter, I have offered an imaginative rereading of the Grinch story, one that clearly departs from the plain meaning of the text, yet that I think is nonetheless supported by it. By shifting our perspective from that of the Whos to the Grinch, and by recasting him as a member of a minority group, I have found that Dr Seuss's tale offers a useful case study for thinking through some of the inherent tensions of pluralism and secularism in the United States. On my reading, the story is less about the dangers of commercialization and consumerism as much as about questions of national belonging and citizenship in a multicultural society and how these issues are expressed through the affective and sensory registers of public culture. Who defines the boundaries of communal consensus in such contexts, and on what terms? What are the hidden or not-so-hidden costs of public participation? By interpreting Seuss's story in this way, I have considered why Christmas's public meaning has grown increasingly contested in a religiously heterogeneous American context and how it has emerged as a locus for a broader set of debates about the political incorporation of religious minorities. More specifically, perhaps, I have tried to make audible what anthropologist Birgit Meyer describes as the "politico-aesthetics" of public religious expression, or the particular legal regulations and social norms that govern who can make themselves heard and how, and that shape our assumptions about who and what belongs in public.[45]

So, given all of these tensions, what is a grinch to do? It might seem that his best strategy is to challenge majoritarian norms by participating on his own terms. He might strive to follow Rabbi Mordecai Kaplan's advice, for example, who in 1948 asked: "Why should Jews consider it a good American practice for Christians to display Christmas trees and sing Christmas carols in public, while feeling too inhibited to display the Hanukkah lights publicly and to sing Hebrew hymns in the streets?" He might contest Christian dominance, that is, by injecting his own public practices into the background culture. Indeed, such particularistic displays of difference are probably a necessary step on the way to what we might describe as normalization. Yet even so, we should remain sensitive to how such inclusion can often seem possible only on terms dictated by the majority and, in that case, can look little different from the Grinch's decision to join in. We must remain alert to the possibility that participation, even in one's own key, can come to resemble just another form of assimilation.

Therefore, we should also consider the possibility that the Grinch's initial instinct may have been right all along. Recall that the story does not begin with his efforts to "steal" Christmas but with his desire not to be bothered by it at all. Holed up in his cave to the north, he seems content simply to do his own thing until he is driven mad by the noise ("Oh, the noise!"). Only when he can no longer block it out does he feel compelled to respond in some way. This suggests that what the Grinch really wanted most of all was not to be included, but to be left alone. What alternative practices of pluralism might such an acknowledgment entail?

Notes

1 Quotes taken from Dr Seuss, *How the Grinch Stole Christmas*.
2 Burns, "'How the Grinch Stole Christmas': Its Recent Acceptance," 198.
3 Wolosky, "Democracy in America," 167.

4   Ibid., 173.

5   Pond, "A Transformative Biblical Encounter."

6   Scheer, "Shifting the Coordinates." See also her chapter in this volume.

7   LaBelle, *Acoustic Territories.*

8   Weiner, *Religion Out Loud.*

9   County of Allegheny v. ACLU, 492 U.S. at 664 (Kennedy, J., concurring in part and dissenting in part).

10 Cohen v. California, 403 U.S. at 21.

11 "Report of [George L.] Harrison et al. vs. St. Mark's Church, Philadelphia," 490.

12 Weiner, "Calling Everyone to Pray."

13 Kant, *The Critique of Judgment*, 196. By dismissing "noisy" ritual as "pharisaical" worship, Kant suggests that true religion ought to be concerned with inward dispositions rather than external forms. In so doing, he echoes a classic Christian theological (and supercessionist) critique of Jewish law, thus demonstrating how arguments about religion out loud can serve to legitimate underlying assumptions about religion and religious difference.

14 Dewey, *The Public and Its Problems*, 219.

15 Kun, *Audiotopia*, 12. Also see Kapchan, "The Promise of Sonic Translation."

16 Durkheim, *The Elementary Forms of Religious Life*, 218–19.

17 It is interesting how central a place sound occupies in Durkheim's account, especially because he never experienced it himself. Perhaps he had a closer, more familiar soundscape in mind as he wrote? I am grateful to Pamela Klassen for suggesting this possibility.

18 On the impossibility of blocking out Christmas, consider also Rabbi Mordecai Kaplan's argument that, for economic reasons, Christmas had become more important for many American Jews than the Jewish holidays: "Thus the economic life requires Jews to cooperate with non-Jews to an immeasurably larger extent than was formerly the case ... The holidays are striking examples of this. Christmas and Easter have acquired an important industrial significance in modern times, and the industries affected are largely those – the personal-articles industries – in which Jews are heavily involved ... It does not matter that Jews do not, on the whole, observe Christmas and Easter; it is significant that such occasions have come to be among the most important in their year." Kaplan, *Judaism as a Civilization*, 29–30.

19   Gramza, "Stop the Carols, Antwerp Couple Plead."

20   Weiner, *Religion Out Loud*, 177.

21   Gramza, "Stop the Carols, Antwerp Couple Plead."

22   Burns, "'How the Grinch Stole Christmas': Its Recent Acceptance,"
     200. Julia Pond argues that Dr Seuss's story is replete with Christian
     symbolism, though none relating specifically to Christmas. See Pond, "A
     Transformative Biblical Encounter."

23   Florey v. Sioux Falls School District, 619 F.2d at 1313.

24   Ibid. at 1316.

25   Two notable US Supreme Court cases addressing the constitutionality of
     Christmas displays draw similar distinctions between the religious and
     cultural dimensions of Christmas. See Lynch v. Donnelly, 465 U.S. 668
     (1984), and County of Allegheny v. ACLU, 492 U.S. 573 (1989). On *Lynch*,
     also see Sullivan, *Paying the Words Extra*, and Smith, "God Save This
     Honourable Court."

26   Sullivan et al., "Beyond Establishment," 214.

27   Salazar v. Buono, 559 U.S. at 748 (Stevens, J., dissenting).

28   Ibid. at 715–16.

29   For incisive commentary on the Court's decision, see Sullivan, "The Cross:
     More than Religion?" The title of Sullivan's essay is a reference to Justice
     Kennedy's assertion that "one Latin cross in the desert evokes *far more than
     religion.*" In this claim, I cannot help but hear echoes of the Grinch, who
     learns that Christmas, too, is about something "a little bit more."

30   Lautsi v. Italy, Judgment.

31   Ibid., para. 36.

32   Ibid., para. 15.

33   Ibid., para. 73.

34   Ibid., para. 72.

35   Zucca, "Lautsi: A Commentary," 221.

36   Lautsi v. Italy, Judgment, para. 74.

37   Weiner, *Religion Out Loud*; Weiner, "Calling Everyone to Pray."

38   Engelke, *God's Agents*, 52.

39   On American Christian use of the tropes of victimization and persecution,
     see Bivins, "Embattled Majority."

40   Winnifred Fallers Sullivan makes a similar point in Sullivan, *Prison
     Religion*. In narrowly jurisprudential terms, we might say that they present
     Christmas as secular or cultural in establishment clause contexts and
     religious in free exercise cases.

41   Hartenstein, "A Christmas Issue," 1000.

42　Agrama, "Sovereign Power," 181–99.
43　Curtis, *The Production of American Religious Freedom*; Wenger, *We Have a Religion*.
44　Johnson, *Sacred Claims*; Weiner, "The Corporately Produced Conscience."
45　Meyer, "Lessons from 'Global Prayers,'" 597.

Bibliography

Agrama, Hussein Ali. "Sovereign Power and Secular Indeterminacy: Is Egypt a Secular or a Religious State?" In *After Secular Law*, edited by Winnifred Sullivan, Robert A. Yelle, and Mateo Taussig-Rubbo, 181–99. Redwood City, CA: Stanford University Press, 2011.

Bivins, Jason. "Embattled Majority: Religion and Its Despisers in America (Or: The Long-Lurching Wreck of American Public Life)." *Religion in American History*, 6 November 2012. http://usreligion.blogspot.nl/2012/11/embattled-majority-religion-and-its.html.

Burns, Thomas A. "'How the Grinch Stole Christmas': Its Recent Acceptance into the American Popular Christmas Tradition." *New York Folklore* 2, no. 3 (1976): 191–204.

Cohen v. California, 403 U.S. 15 (1971).

County of Allegheny v. ACLU, 492 U.S. 573 (1989).

Curtis, Finbarr. *The Production of American Religious Freedom*. New York: New York University Press, 2016.

Dewey, John. *The Public and Its Problems*. New York: H. Holt and Company, 1927.

Dr Seuss. *How the Grinch Stole Christmas*. New York: Random House, 1957.

Durkheim, Émile. *The Elementary Forms of Religious Life*. Translated by Karen E. Fields. New York: Free Press, 1995.

Engelke, Matthew. *God's Agents; Biblical Publicity in Contemporary England*. Oakland, CA: University of California Press, 2013.

Florey v. Sioux Falls School District, 619 F.2d 1311 (United States Court of Appeals for the Eighth Circuit 1980).

Gramza, Janet. "Stop the Carols, Antwerp Couple Plead: The Pair Seeks Court Order against Church's Playing of Holiday Songs from Its Steeple." *The [Antwerp, NJ] Post-Standard*, 18 December 1994.

Hartenstein, John M. "A Christmas Issue: Christian Holiday Celebration in the Public Elementary Schools Is an Establishment of Religion." *California Law Review* 80, no. 4 (1992): 981–1026.

Johnson, Greg. *Sacred Claims: Repatriation and Living Tradition.*
Charlottesville, VA: University of Virginia Press, 2007.

Kant, Immanuel. *The Critique of Judgment.* Translated by James Creed
Meredith. Oxford, UK: Oxford University Press, 1952.

Kapchan, Deborah A. "The Promise of Sonic Translation: Performing
the Festive Sacred in Morocco." In *Practicing Sufism: Sufi Politics and
Performance in Africa,* edited by Abdelmajid Hannoum, 150–74. London:
Routledge, 2016.

Kaplan, Mordecai. *Judaism as a Civilization: Toward a Reconstruction of
American-Jewish Life.* New York: T. Yoseloff, 1957.

Kun, Josh. *Audiotopia: Music, Race, and America.* Berkeley, CA: University of
California Press, 2005.

LaBelle, Brandon. *Acoustic Territories: Sound Culture and Everyday Life.*
New York: Continuum, 2010.

Lautsi v. Italy, Judgment (European Court of Human Rights 2011).

Lynch v. Donnelly, 465 U.S. 668 (1984).

Meyer, Birgit. "Lessons from 'Global Prayers': How Religion Takes Place in
the City." In *Global Prayers: Contemporary Manifestations of the Religious
in the City,* edited by Jochen Becker, Katrin Klingan, Stephan Lanz, and
Kathrin Wildner, 590–601. Zürich, Germany: Lars Müller Publishers, 2014.

Pond, Julia. "A Transformative Biblical Encounter: The Garden of Eden in
How the Grinch Stole Christmas." *The Looking Glass: New Perspectives on
Children's Literature* 14, no. 1 (2010).

"Report of [George L.] Harrison et Al. vs. St. Mark's Church, Philadelphia:
A Bill to Restrain the Ringing of Bells so as to Cause a Nuisance to the
Occupants of the Dwellings in the Immediate Vicinity of the Church."
Philadelphia, PA, 1877.

Salazar v. Buono, 559 U.S. 700 (2010).

Scheer, Monique. "Shifting the Coordinates of Research on Christmas."
Presented at the Workshop on Christmas in the Multicultural City,
University of Tübingen, 10 December 2015.

Smith, Jonathan Z. "God Save This Honourable Court: Religion and Civic
Discourse." In *Relating Religion: Essays in the Study of Religion,* 375–90.
Chicago, IL: Chicago University Press, 2004.

Sullivan, Winnifred. *Paying the Words Extra: Religious Discourse in the Supreme
Court of the United States.* Cambridge, MA: Harvard University Press, 1994.

– *Prison Religion: Faith-Based Reform and the Constitution.* Princeton, NJ:
Princeton University Press, 2009.

– "The Cross: More than Religion?" *The Immanent Frame*, 5 May 2010. http://blogs.ssrc.org/tif/2010/05/05/more-than-religion/.

Sullivan, Winnifred, Elizabeth Shakman Hurd, Saba Mahmood, and Peter Danchin. "Beyond Establishment." In *Politics of Religious Freedom*, 207–19. Chicago, IL: Chicago University Press, 2015.

Weiner, Isaac. "Calling Everyone to Pray: Pluralism, Secularism, and the Adhān in Hamtramck, Michigan." *Anthropological Quarterly* 87, no. 4 (2014): 1049–77.

– *Religion Out Loud: Religious Sound, Public Space, and American Pluralism.* New York: New York University Press, 2014.

– "The Corporately Produced Conscience: Emergency Contraception and the Politics of Workplace Accommodations." *Journal of the American Academy of Religion* 85, no. 1 (2016): 31–63.

Wenger, Tisa Joy. *We Have a Religion: The 1920s Pueblo Indian Dance Controversy and American Religious Freedom.* Chapel Hill, NC: University of North Carolina Press, 2009.

Wolosky, Shira. "Democracy in America: By Dr. Seuss." *Southwest Review* 85, no. 2 (2000): 167–83.

Zucca, Lorenzo. "Lautsi: A Commentary on a Decision by the ECtHR Grand Chamber." *International Journal of Constitutional Law* 11, no. 1 (2013): 218–29.

4

"Stille Nacht" Time and Again: Christmas Songs and Feelings

Juliane Brauer

Introduction

In his novel *Buddenbrooks* (1952), Thomas Mann erected a monument to bourgeois Christmas festivities.

> She [the Frau Consul] finished, and from the pillared hall came a trio of voices: "Holy night, peaceful night!" The family in the landscape room joined in. They did so cautiously, for most of them were unmusical, as a tone now and then betrayed. But that in no wise impaired the effect of the old hymn. Frau Permaneder sang with trembling lips; it sounded sweetest and most touching to the heart of her who had a troubled life behind her, and looked back upon it in the brief peace of this holy hour ... Now the Frau Consul rose. She grasped the hands of her grandson, Johann, and her great-granddaughter, Elisabeth, and strode across the room ... The whole great room was filled with the fragrance of slightly singed evergreen twigs and glowing with light from countless tiny flames ... And a row of smaller trees, also full of stars and hung with comfits, stood on the long white table, laden with presents, that stretched from the window to the door ... Large objects, too large to stand upon the table, likewise adorned with tiny trees and covered with gifts for the servants and the poor, stood on either side of the door.[1]

This scene encapsulates all of the key elements of bourgeois Christmas festivities: Christmas was a family holiday. Around the Christmas tree, the gathering and unity of the family were celebrated as the nucleus of private interiority. But Christmas was and remains a celebration of charity and goodness, too. Thus, the servants and the poor are invited, taken into the family on Christmas Eve and given gifts. The key symbols of the festivities are the decorated tree with gifts beneath its boughs, the scent of singed fir branches, the shining of candles, and the music, namely the collective singing of Christmas songs. In this snapshot, Thomas Mann focused above all on the emotional power of song. Frau Permaneder sang "with trembling lips"; the singing of "Stille Nacht, heilige Nacht" ("Silent Night, Holy Night") sounded "sweet" and "touching" to the heart of her "who had a troubled life behind her."

Taken together, these things contribute to the specific German "Christmas mood,"[2] whose ideal type was developed in the time of the German Empire. "Christmas turned the German lands into the Heimath der Innigkeit und Gemütlichkeit," writes Joe Perry in his cultural history of German Christmas.[3] In doing so, he makes a simple yet poignant insight: the history of German Christmas festivities is a history of emotions. German Christmas festivities are coloured by a specific set of emotions that includes interiority and "Gemütlichkeit" (warmth, friendliness, homeliness), as well as a yearning for solace, peace, and harmony. This particular composition of emotions unified the German bourgeoisie as an "emotional community, rooted in feelings of family love, joy, and concern for others."[4] It was an expression of German bourgeois culture and thus served as a driving force for the growing German national consciousness of the nineteenth century. Taking up perspectives from the history of emotions, I would like to take a closer look at how Christmas emotions came to take on their specific form and ask what precisely constitutes them. How and why are they conserved in such a way that they can seemingly always be called forth at will during the holidays? In particular, I would like to work out a better understanding of the collective singing of Christmas songs: after all, the scene from *Buddenbrooks* describes such singing in detail, and it seems to have functioned as a key emotional component of Christmas festivities.

The Christmas tree, family gathering, singing, candles, the scent of homemade cookies, gifts, and charitable giving remain parts of German Christmas festivities today, essential for evoking that special Christmas feeling on Christmas Eve. Among these diverse elements which, over the last two centuries, were assembled to shape Christmas festivities, the practically obligatory, often quite sentimental, singing of carols, particularly those deemed somehow folkloric, is particularly prominent. It is a rather recent

development; around 1800, this item was still absent from Protestant bourgeois Christmas rituals. E.T.A. Hoffmann's Christmas tale "The Nutcracker
and the Mouse King" (1816) contains no reference to collective song.[5]
The people described in Friedrich Schleiermacher's "Die Weihnachtsfeier"
("The Christmas Fest," 1809) sang church chorales in their living room,
extending the solemnity of church services into a private space.[6] These
seem to be very different from the "sweet" and "touching" singing of
"Stille Nacht" by Frau Permaneder. Only in the course of the nineteenth
century was the wealth of Christmas songs composed that still make up
the repertoire of Advent and Christmas singing today. Among them are
the so-called "popular Christmas songs"[7]: "Morgen Kinder wird's was
geben" (circa 1810), "Oh Du fröhliche" (1818), "Süßer die Glocken nie
klingen" (1826), "Am Weihnachtsbaume die Lichter brennen" (1841), "Alle
Jahre wieder" (1842), "Kommet, Ihr Hirten" (1847), "Kling Glöckchen,
klingelingeling" (1850). Like these, "Stille Nacht, heilige Nacht" (1818) was
a new Christmas song of the nineteenth-century bourgeoisie, characterized
by scenes evocative sometimes of the Christian narrative but often merely
of seasonal customs.

The Christmas song repertoire was influenced by the social developments of the nineteenth century, with its new definition of Christmas as
a private family celebration in addition to its being a church festival. This
development was a symptom of the bourgeois longing for harmony and
their withdrawal from the "outer world."[8] Perry sees this development as a
transatlantic phenomenon "closely tied to the emergence and consolidation
of the nation-state."[9] The child came to stand at the centre of familial happiness. It is not for nothing that the nineteenth century is often seen as the
"century of the child," as it was the period when childhood was first defined
as a separate phase of life.[10] Accordingly, bourgeois Christmas festivities
also came to focus on the fulfilment of children's wishes. This increased
care for the child reflects the nostalgia for an idealized family life and
the purity and innocence of private happiness that the child symbolized.
Thus, Christmas was to become a "culmination of bourgeois yearnings for
security, well-being, and comfort."[11] Drawing on the Christmas liturgy of
the church, a private ritual came into being that sought to performatively
reproduce an "island of feeling in a world increasingly determined by
sobriety and rationality."[12] The happiness of the private sphere, a yearned-
for familial harmony, and sentimental comfort and interiority could be
relived and felt in the Christmas festivities. Christmas was thus one way

that the bourgeois milieu of the nineteenth century constituted itself as an "emotional community."[13] This emotional community was defined not only by a shared Christmas feeling, but also by a clear notion of who was allowed to partake in the Christmas festivities and who wasn't. In line with Barbara Rosenwein's concept, the bourgeois emotional community was constituted not only by a collective understanding of which emotions were appropriate for the occasion, but also by shared values and opinions.[14] For this reason, the development of German Christmas festivities has been viewed through the lens of the rise of the nation-state in the nineteenth century.[15] The Christmas feeling, as Thomas Mann artfully described it, was seen as something characteristically German. As such, Christmas became, in a sense, the German national holiday.[16]

The fact that collective singing came to occupy such a prominent position in the Christmas ritual was also the product of parallel developments. First, music and song were needed to recreate the private-sphere version of church rituals. A plenitude of new, popular Christmas songs were composed to fulfil this need. Second, in the course of the nineteenth century, collective singing had taken on a new significance for the ascending German bourgeoisie; it had become a common cultural practice in various social and political groups of the era. Members of the workers' education unions of the *Vormärz* period sang together, and workers' choirs became popular. Middle-class men sang at the so-called *Liedertafel* (choral societies), choirs that demonstrated belonging and moral strength through collective song.[17] Following the motto "Where people are singing, you can be at peace; bad people don't have songs," German men used song as a way to forge political and social ties. It is no coincidence that the movement for a nation-state in the nineteenth century went hand in hand with the notion that German music and German song were profound, good, and thus morally superior. Singing Christmas songs combined the message of the birth of Christ with the self-image of the warm-hearted, music-loving, well-educated German, the symbol of German morality.

Third, singing Christmas songs in the home became popular at the same time as domestic music was blooming. Learning a musical instrument was an integral part of a good bourgeois upbringing. Growing enthusiasm for domestic music was spurred by the mass production of small pianos. To satisfy this market, music publishers printed song books with easy-to-play popular Christmas songs. By 1900, collective singing of popular Christmas songs had become one of the most important parts of German

Christmas festivities, nearly always culminating in the performance of the most important song, "Stille Nacht, heilige Nacht."

The emotional power of Christmas songs is still regularly invoked. Asked during an interview how he prepares for Christmas, the famous tenor Rolando Villazón praised the emotional power of Christmas songs:

> My wife loves Christmas songs, but more because they evoke such a joyful ecstasy. I like that too. This music can make us generous or empathetic and make us think: Yes, we can open our door to others … Sometimes music does that. It puts us in such a spirit of sharing and embrace.[18]

The collective singing of a specific repertoire of Christmas songs seems to be more popular than ever, whether it be beneath the Christmas tree at home, in kindergartens and schools, at Christmas parties put on by work or clubs, at Christmas markets, or at grand events, such as the Christmas singing of the football team 1. FC Union Berlin, which "goes beyond generational and team barriers," drawing about 28,000 participants to the stadium Alte Försterei.[19]

Why has the collective singing of Christmas songs had uninterrupted success since the nineteenth century? To those who have known them for a long time, perhaps since childhood, and sing them regularly as part of the seasonal ritual, Christmas songs would appear to store the specifically bourgeois family Christmas feeling, bringing together interiority, warmth, closeness, and a yearning for harmony, peace, and belonging. The claim, therefore, that this chapter seeks to substantiate is that songs are a medium that connects memories and emotions with one another, which can then be called up in the practice of singing. This claim can be perhaps most effectively demonstrated by looking at those situations in which most of the other elements of Christmas cheer are missing, and the song alone is implemented to evoke the desired feelings.

Thus, I will look at some moments of this kind in the two-hundred-year history of the song "Stille Nacht, heilige Nacht," among them the trenches of the First World War and the parade grounds at the Sachsenhausen concentration camp. This will demonstrate that singing can be defined as an emotional practice[20] that enables practitioners to reactivate and reshape particular feelings.

Music, Emotions, and Memory

Music is "embodied experience."[21] Contrary to a claim widely held among psychologists of music, music has no universal meaning. Rather, it acquires meaning through the concrete situations in which it is performed. This process is dependent upon multiple factors, including the individual experiences, perceptions, and needs of listeners and performers.[22] With the help of music, emotions can be managed. Musicologist Tia DeNora calls this "emotion work," because music is "part of the reflexive constitution of that [internal emotional] state."[23]

In order to better illustrate the relation between music, emotion management, and memory, we might refer to the space in which music and emotions come together as a contact zone. It is a zone between inside and outside, the self (or the mindful body[24]) and society. The mindful body, the concrete conditions of performance, and the musical material (composition) constitute the three pillars of this "contact zone" that is musical perception. A crucial aspect of this model is that music acquires its meaning in this triangular contact zone.[25]

That certain music evokes different emotions in individual people is popular knowledge.[26] It is precisely these reactions that the contact zone model is capable of explaining. The song "Stille Nacht, heilige Nacht" has the potential to evoke happiness, comfort, and Christmas feelings because it is regularly sung at Christmastime on the streets, in Christmas markets, and in department stores. People who heard the song sung throughout their childhood while sitting around the Christmas tree with their family will most likely associate it with feelings of security, home, and joy. However, it is also conceivable that people will associate it with memories of conflict and disappointment that are poignant precisely because they occurred during Christmastime. Finally, these feelings can be overwritten or altered through new situations and experiences that come to be associated with the song later in life.

Thus, the perception of music is guided by embedded knowledge, expectations, memories, and emotions. In this *contact zone*, described above as a triangle, listeners perceive or remember music, and this perception is conditioned by individual experiences and associations. The mindful body has learned to attribute to certain music certain emotions. Thus, perceiving music is at once an act of cultural self-confirmation and an act of identity construction. Emotions, identity, and memories are connected with one another through the medium of music.[27] Following the model developed above, we might say that the contact zone is the site where "emotion work" takes place. Moreover, performing emotions through the medium of music allows listeners and performers to ascribe new emotions to perceived music. This conception of experiencing music fits well with praxeological conceptions of emotions, such as that of Monique Scheer. According to Scheer, emotions are no doubt something we experience. But they are also something that we "do": "emotions are something people experience and something they do. We have emotions and we manifest emotions."[28] As such, Scheer conceives of emotions as a practice that is both inscribed into the body and acted out through it ("[a] bodily act of experience and expression").[29] This perspective seems particularly well-suited for describing collective song as an emotional practice. Important here is that the perception and performance of music are practices of modulating emotions within the above-described contact zone. In contrast to listening to music, singing is a more intense form of grappling with memories and emotions, because as a form of emotion management, it involves the body in a much more active fashion.

Beyond that, collective singing not only enables participants to navigate their inner experience of memory and present – it also enables them to establish connections with others and create a feeling of community.[30] Kay Kaufman Shelemay calls such communities "musical communities":

a collectivity constructed through and sustained by musical processes and/or performances. A musical community can be socially and/or symbolically constituted; music making may give rise to real-time social relationships or may exist most fully in the realm of virtual setting or in the imagination.[31]

To conclude these theoretical considerations and summarize the conception of singing used in the following analysis, singing is an emotional practice that enables practitioners to reactivate, communicate, and regulate feelings. On the one hand, it serves to strengthen conceptions of self through the evocation of memories, and on the other, it serves to constitute a feeling of belonging to a "musical community." The concept of the contact zone makes clear how dynamic and fluctuating the relation between memory and music is, and helps demonstrate how this connection can be bolstered through repetition.

"The Most Famous of All Christmas Songs"[32]

The original composition of the song is ambivalent. On the one hand, it is inconsistent, and on the other, it is catchy.[33] Its catchiness derives from the repeated phrase whose rhythm and melody is varied throughout the song. Rhythmically, it contrasts lightness, movement (dotted eighth note / sixteenth note / eighth note), and calm (quarter note / eighth rest). The light-footed feeling is recognizable in the 6/8 time signature. The inconsistency of the original is produced through the way this rhythmic phrase is forced onto the rhythm of the vocals.[34] Unusual here is the way the first syllables of "stille," "alles," "einsam," etc. are artificially extended over two notes (dotted eighth and sixteenth). Remarking that the rhythm "takes some time to get used to," Grunewald writes that it reminds him more of a "decampment song" than a lullaby.[35] Harmonically and melodically, the song seems to oscillate. The melody of the one-measure phrase – two-measure in the middle section – briefly ascends before reliably falling back to the tonic. The song primarily uses whole steps and thirds. Only at the transition to the middle part is there a minor seventh, and, in the transition to the third part, a fourth. The phrases are separated through eighth rests. Harmonically, the song is very conventional, using authentic cadences with constant return to the tonic. As such, the song evokes the impression of a constant swinging, and the repetitions, sequences, and simple variations make it easy to learn and sing.

The origins of the song are easily recounted, and have been discussed in films, stories, research literature, and popular literature.[36] The assistant pastor Joseph Mohr composed the text in Mariapfarr in Austria's Lungau region in 1816. At Christmas 1818, Mohr gave the text to the teacher and organist Franz Gruber and asked him to compose a melody for two solo voices, a choir, and guitar accompaniment, as the organ was out of commission.[37] The song only became widely known beyond the Salzburg area because non-church choral groups performed it for an "audience interested in popular music."[38] In the wake of the late Romantic interest in folk music, the song as an "authentic Tirol folk song"[39] was widely distributed. The complicated third, fourth, and fifth stanzas were left out and the inconsistencies between the rhythm of the lyrics and the music were smoothed out by the Zillertaler singers. Grunewald claims that in the three-stanza version sung today, the "Christmas story is transformed into a sentimental idyll." However, abridging, smoothing, and thus sentimentalizing the song are what made it into an international and

Figure 4.1   "Kirchenlied auf die heilige Christnacht," circa 1855.

commercial success.[40] Only then could it become the most well-known and successful of all Christmas songs. Thus, it was the song "Stille Nacht, heilige Nacht" that, in being sung again and again, retained its feeling of reliability.

The 1914 Christmas Truce

When the First World War began in 1914, German propaganda claimed that the men would be home before Christmas. As Christmas came, it was clear that the end of the war was nowhere in sight; instead of returning husbands, sons, and brothers, relatives received news of their deaths. But German propaganda did not want to let feelings of depression and despondency get the upper hand. The 1914 Christmas holidays were used to reactivate long-accustomed Christmas feelings both in the trenches and in living rooms at home where men were absent, as these

Figure 4.2   Postcard dated 12 December 1914.

feelings bespoke happiness, content, harmony, and thus resilience for what was to come. Family members and others sent soldiers on the front miniature decorated Christmas trees. People mailed care packages and a large number of Christmas postcards. These postcards tailored the old Christmas feeling to the new conditions of December 1914. Men sent postcards from the front with the words "Herzliche Weihnachtsgrüße und baldiges Wiedersehen" ("Loving Christmas Greetings and See You Soon"). One of these cards preserves the sentimental idyll of the "Stille Nacht."[41] It depicts soldiers sitting, standing, and lying around a Christmas tree in an otherwise empty building, which might be seen as a modern stable. They open presents and read books. One plays the accordion, another seems to sing while looking off into the distance. A small image of a mother with her three children around the Christmas tree in the upper right corner of the postcard suggests that the men are thinking about being with their families. The mother is reading a letter and is also looking off into the distance. The song "Stille Nacht" is evoked by a sign in the middle of the postcard. The lighted Christmas tree and the song "Stille Nacht" were supposed to unite the families separated by hundreds of kilometres into an "emotional community."

The idyll of a peaceful, quiet Christmas cast an illusion over the suffering, the dangers, and the fears on both sides. Such cards helped reactivate well-known Christmas feelings and drowned out destructive feelings and thoughts; they helped transmit the illusion of security and made tangible confidence, hope, and strength.

It is impossible to say how effective this strategy of emotion management was in individual cases. However, letters and memories of soldiers vividly recount how Christmas songs helped evoke Christmas feelings, if only for short periods, between the fronts in the most literal sense. The most well-known example is the so-called Christmas Truce.[42] During the 1914 Christmas holidays, soldiers on the fronts in Belgium and northern France spontaneously engaged in gestures of camaraderie. Multiple witnesses attest to the fact that – without command or permission – German, French, and Scottish soldiers put down their weapons and celebrated Christmas together. Drawing on the memories of his great-grandfather William Wood, David Burgess tells the following story of the Christmas Truce:

> On Christmas Eve of 1914, soldiers across both fronts slept in their trenches awaiting the end of the war. They were told it'd be over by Christmas. Some German soldiers decided to sing hymns, in this case the most notable is 'Silent Night' or 'Stille Nacht.' As they did so, soldiers across the allied side began to listen, and some began to sing along with them.[43]

In this case, too, the by then internationally known song served to help create an emotional community that transcended the frontlines. Many letters, diary entries, and memories tell of the camaraderie between soldiers of opposing forces during Christmas 1914. Interestingly, it seems that it was often the German soldiers who made audible peace offerings by singing not only Christmas songs, but also patriotic songs such as "Die Wacht am Rhein" ("The Watch on the Rhine").[44] The choice of the song "Stille Nacht" was not just a matter of chance, as the singers most likely presumed that the song would be known to the soldiers of other nations. Here, too, the song functioned as a medium of memory and emotion management. By singing the song, the soldiers would have been able to evoke Christmas feelings long practised in their living rooms at home, reactivating memories of security, belonging, and the peaceful message of Christmas in the midst of the horror of trench warfare. If this had not been the case, the song could not have functioned as a temporary olive branch. In line with the bourgeois conviction "Where one sings, you can be at peace; bad people don't have song," trust in the Christmas Truce was forged through singing Christmas songs as a collective. It seems that singing together and shooting at one another are mutually exclusive. Viewing collective song as an emotional praxis can help explain this. Following the theory of performativity, singing the song produces the reality referred to in its lyrics: peaceful camaraderie. By singing Christmas songs, an emotional community was temporarily brought into being. Its key point of reference was the feeling of Christmas, shared by soldiers from all nations. This Christmas ritual does not represent something desired and given. Rather, the act of celebration itself produced the Christmas feeling referred to in the song.[45] Thus, in line with Kaufman's insights, the soldiers constituted a "musical community" that allowed itself, however temporarily, to forge social and emotional ties.

Trusting in these bonds, the men celebrated Christmas together. They exchanged food and alcoholic drinks, played soccer, and sang Christmas songs. It sounds like a Christmas fairy tale and is ripe for mythologizing, as was done in the international film production *Merry Christmas*.[46] A key difference between the films based on the event is interesting here. One of the most emotional scenes in *Merry Christmas* depicts a German tenor who is a soldier singing the internationally known songs "Stille Nacht" and "Adeste Fideles." This singing breaks the ice between the two sides and initiates the Christmas Truce. The film was based on memories, just as was an earlier film made in 1969.[47] However, the 1969 film only depicts the soldiers eating and drinking together, talking, exchanging gifts, and taking pictures. Singing does not play in at all. In all likelihood, the co-production from 2005 exaggerated the significance of music for emotional effect. Thus, the film probably says more about the particular emotional resonance of music in the early twenty-first century than it does about the actual significance music had during the 1914 Christmas Truce.

Christmas in the Sachsenhausen Concentration Camp

Memories of survivors of the Sachsenhausen Concentration Camp evidence that the Christmas song "Stille Nacht, heilige Nacht" left its traces at places of great human suffering during the Second World War as well. In 1948, the Norwegian survivor Eric Gunnar Auster recalled the Christmas celebrations of 1941 or 1942:

Suddenly, as we were standing there [on the parade grounds],
18,000 men with their caps in their hands, we heard an orchestra
playing the old Christmas song "Stille Nacht." Complete silence
came over the grounds. I noticed that most of us were very touched.
Our thoughts wandered from the camp, away from all the evil and
sadness. We were back at home with our loved ones, celebrating
Christmas ... Had the SS-men forgotten the times when prisoners
were being executed and we had to march past the executed men
to marching music? And at Christmas they allowed themselves to
play "Stille Nacht" on the same parade grounds. Had we landed in a
madhouse? It seemed that way. Then maybe a few days later another
person was executed there.[48]

"Stille Nacht" represents here Christmas songs in general. It was certainly
known to many of the nearly 20,000 prisoners from multiple nations.
Above all, Auster emphasizes the contradictory effect that the song had
on him. On the one hand, it evoked familiar memories of an earlier
period of his life, memories of warmth and comfort among family. The
emotions were particularly strong; most were "very touched." The song
helped the prisoners to escape the reality they were confronted with and
imagine they were at home with their families. On the other hand, they
felt the contrast between these positive memories and the situation there
on the parade grounds at Sachsenhausen. The 20,000 prisoners stood
in ice-cold weather with insufficient clothing on the parade grounds,
exhausted from performing daily forced labour, and were forced to watch
the Christmas show of the camp guards. The Christmas tree was there
where the gallows stood, and Christmas songs were played by the prison
orchestra, which otherwise played loud marching music while prisoners
marched past the executed.[49] This set-up derided the positive Christmas
memories that the song "Stille Nacht" evoked. But to what extent were the
emotions the prisoners associated with this song changed by the experience?
How much did it determine their future memories of the song? Could
it still serve as a medium that transported comforting Christmas feelings
after the experience of the camp? Unfortunately, the available sources offer
no answer to these questions. However, the memories of musicians who
survived the concentration and extermination camps demonstrate that
the connection between memory, emotion, and music heavily depends on
individual personality. There were musicians who continued to play music

as a form of survival until old age, just as there were musicians who could no longer play or sing after their experiences in the camps.[50]

One can only speculate as to why the camp commanders of Sachsenhausen staged this Christmas festival with an accompanying concert every year. Maybe it was simply the habit of singing around the Christmas tree, independent of the situation. On the other hand, the camp SS had their own Christmas celebration in the officers' casino. It is more likely that the Christmas fest, which reminded Auster of a "madhouse," served as a display of power, conceived as a way to further torture and demean prisoners, making real the hopelessness of their situation. At the same time, the Christmas ritual allowed the camp commanders to put their cultivated German civility on display. The music almost certainly was there to symbolize their moral superiority. In contrast to this self-construction of the morally good and civil German, the suffering, ragged bodies of the prisoners could be easily depicted as unfit, immoral, and bad. In this scenario, the Christmas songs did not serve to produce emotional community, but rather emotional exclusion. It served to position those who found themselves on the side of the choreographed Christmas feelings, namely the SS guards, against those who suffered under the contrast between happy memories and their horrific situation. This double-sided constitution of emotional communities was produced through the staging of the Christmas ritual on the parade grounds of Sachsenhausen.

However, after the evening roll call, while the SS commanders celebrated their Christmas in the officers' casino, the prisoners themselves secretly organized their own Christmas festivities in their barracks. Multiple memories and preserved Christmas programs testify to this fact. The sources show how important the various national celebrations were for the prisoners' conceptions of self, and make clear the significance that these Christmas rituals and songs had.

In particular, there is a considerable amount of material on the experience of the French prisoners. The Christmas celebrations within the barracks were well-prepared by the prisoners. Participants and audience members were all prisoners in a single group. For instance, in 1943, 300 French prisoners celebrated their first Christmas in captivity in Staaken, a satellite camp of Sachsenhausen. For Andre Picart, the celebrations signified the first reunification of all French prisoners, and thus appeared as a demonstration of patriotism.

Depuis quelques temps, avec plusieurs camarades, nous avions l'intention de réunir tous les Français du camp et d'organiser une première manifestation patriotique: la fête de Noël pouvait en être l'occasion, il s'agissait de la réaliser.[51]

Some French prisoners also organized a traditional Christmas celebration with concert for the 180 Frenchmen held at Falkensee, most of whom were from Marseille. On 25 December 1943, the French met for a two-hour program at Block 1 of the Falkensee camp. They heard strong, patriotic songs, newly composed songs, and classic national Christmas songs. Among them was "Minuit, Chrétiens" (1847), which was written down on the back of a form dated 1944.[52]

Puis le concert se déroula, comme tous les concerts où chacun fait de son mieux pour distraire ses camarades. Nous avions entre autres deux excellents chanteurs de Marseille qui s'étaient déjà produits à la radio, notre camarade Jean d' Ouzouer-le-Marché, dans 'Ca c'est Paris', notre Kid Francis, ex-champion de France et d'Europe de boxe qui devait mourir da veille de la libération, d'autres encore … Bientôt, il fut cinq heures, l'heure de la distribution du pain et l'on chantait en chœr – les Montagnards-, la chanson 'A Compiègne' et pour clôturer 'Le chant du départ'.[53]

In their memories, survivors have written that the primarily emotional effect of the Christmas festivities stood at the foundation of the French prisoners' shared consciousness. Songs strongly associated with French identity and patriotism gave credence to this view of the celebrations. The act of presenting themselves as a singing community helped give individual prisoners confidence and hope. Thus, Jean Melai wrote:

Pour la première fois, les «Franzouse» em force, s'étaient fait connaître; chacun ressentit au fond de lui même l'impression de n'être plus isolé, d'appartenir à une collectivité, d'avoir retrouvé la notion de la Patrie, et de la France … Noël 1943? Un rayon de lumière au fond du gouffre.[54]

The Christmas celebrations of the French prisoners helped them grapple with the emotions associated with captivity. Thus, Daniel Moresmau

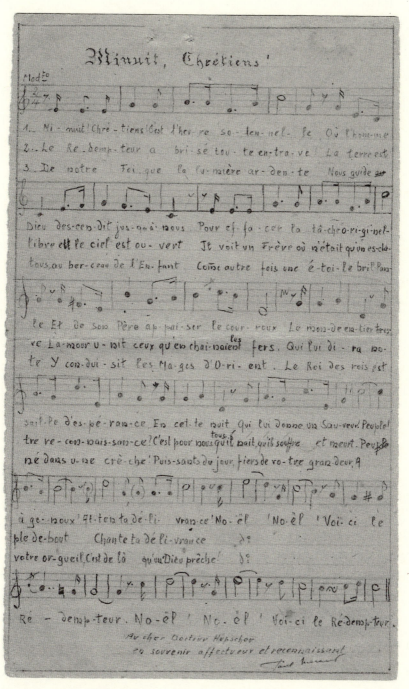

Figure 4.3 "Minuit, Chrétiens."

recalls: "Our minds wandered back home. The magic of the melody was a way to escape the prison."[55] The notion of the "magic of the melody" refers again to the strong connection between memories and emotions in the medium of song. These memories were mobilized and communicated in the emotional praxis of collective singing. Norwegian, Czech, and Polish prisoners also celebrated their own national Christmas festivities. All of these national Christmas celebrations at Sachsenhausen show that Christmas played a significant, twofold role in giving prisoners emotional strength. First, collective singing in the context of nationally specific rituals reminded prisoners of a time before their captivity. Feelings of happiness, security, trust, and memories of normality served as an important antipode to the everyday loneliness, anxiety, and despair in the camp. Second, celebrating Christmas rituals in a small group, hidden from the sight of the guards, gave prisoners the chance to feel a sense of belonging to a community and thus allowed them to participate in the use of important resources for survival, both immaterial and material.

"Sing That Old German Folk Song": *Ringsendung* of the German Radio

"Attention everybody," exclaimed the moderator of the Christmas program of the *Großdeutscher Rundfunk*, Werner Pflücker, shortly before nine o'clock on the evening of 24 December 1942. The program began with a nearly one-and-a-half-hour exchange of Christmas greetings between the front and the homeland and then moved to conversations with soldiers on the Arctic Ocean, the Atlantic coast, the Black Sea, in Crete, in the Caucasus, and in Stalingrad. For the grand finale, the moderator at the central radio in Berlin asked soldiers at approximately twenty radio stations on the front: "With the fresh impression of these hours that we have spent together, all our comrades in the farthest reaches should call in and report that they heard our program."[56] Like a teleconference today, this "broadcast" closed the 1942 Christmas program with the purportedly spontaneous appeal:

"Here is the Black Sea port on Crimea. We ask all our comrades to sing along to the old German Christmas song 'Stille Nacht.'" Then one heard men singing with piano accompaniment, after which soldiers from all the other stations began singing along. Pflücker commented: "Now all stations are fulfilling the wish of

our comrades way down south on the Black Sea ... Now they are
singing on the Arctic and in Finland. And now they are singing
on the battlefields near Rzhev. And now we can hear all the other
stations: Leningrad. Stalingrad, and now France, Catania and Africa
are singing. And now all are singing along. Everybody sing with us
in this moment the old German folk song."

These words are progressively drowned out by the crescendo of the men's
voices, even when Pflücker, ever more moved, raises his voice above the
singing. The recording ends after the three traditional stanzas of the song
are sung.[57]

Media experts agree that the supposedly live broadcast was a "grandiose
fabrication of the National Socialist rulers," staged in order to "feign
authenticity to the public."[58] Whether it was a "sound construction" or
a "radiophonic orchestration"[59] is here less important than the way the
radio program and the collective singing of "Stille Nacht, heilige Nacht"
produced the illusion of a community that overcame thousands of kilometres of distance. That is, the "effect of authenticity"[60] is here more
important than the program's actual authenticity. The radio program seems
to have succeeded in producing the imaginary construction of a family
Christmas evening, the illusion of being close to one's family or close to
the soldier off fighting thousands of kilometres away:

The sound of the technology – crackles, rasping, echo – along with
the montage and the way the radio personalities spoke were essential
means for producing the mood: the program worked, had an effect,
precisely because the technology was audible.[61]

Who knows how many women and children sat in front of their
Volksempfänger on this Christmas Eve and really felt nearness to their
husbands and fathers? Who knows how many men on the multiple fronts
listened to the radio and felt closer to wintry Germany, or how many
actually joined in to sing the most famous Christmas song, and in doing
so felt a sense of belonging to an emotional community? They could
reactivate memories of Christmas during times of peace and the feeling
of Christmas, along with the yearning for peace and harmony, without
being suspected of "undermining military morale" or "subversion of the war
effort." Supporting this is the fact that the popular version of "Stille Nacht"

sounded over the airways, and not any one of the National Socialist adaptations.[62] This is remarkable, as the National Socialist–influenced Christmas festivities became prominent in 1942 at the latest, when an indirect ban on all Christmas songs with Christian content came into effect.[63] It was also not the very successful Christmas song of National Socialist domestic music composer Hans Baumann, "Hohe Nacht der klaren Sterne,"[64] but the popular song that had been sung for over a century, "Stille Nacht, heilige Nacht."

Conclusion

In 2002 Esther Gajek counted about fifty German-language adaptations of "Stille Nacht."[65] In 2011, it was declared an intangible cultural heritage in Austria by UNESCO.[66] Since its composition two hundred years ago, this Christmas song continues to be sung by many during the Christmas season. In a letter to the initiative "Halleiner Stille Nacht-Orgel," world-famous tenor Placido Domingo wrote: "I think 'Stille Nacht, heilige Nacht' was predestined to be a song of world peace in a way like no other song on earth!"[67] Domingo may be right, at least if one considers the examples taken from the extreme situations from both World Wars analyzed here. Like no other song, it seems to function as an imaginary island beyond space and time that continues to promise harmony, warmth, comfort, and happiness.

If one were to write a history of "Stille Nacht, heilige Nacht," one would encounter the song in the snow-covered valleys and mountains of the Austrian Alps, at the Christmas celebrations of bourgeois Hanseatic families, in the trenches of the nineteenth and twentieth centuries' wars, and on the parade grounds and in the barracks of the concentration camps. In divided Germany, one could hear the song sung at company Christmas parties and in youth groups of all political circles. Today, one still hears it at one of Berlin's largest soccer stadiums. People sing it at Christmas Mass; children play it on their recorder or piano next to the Christmas tree. It is sung in at least three hundred languages and dialects by people who live in conditions good and bad. Singing this song seems to have been invested with so much emotional weight and positive Christmas feelings over the past two hundred years that it still has the potential to have a "sweet and touching" effect on the hearts of those who hear it, whether young or old. Innocence and the yearning for harmony and peace seem to have crystallized in this song in a singular way, and for this reason it will probably continue to be sung for years to come. It seems to contain in condensed form the Christmas feelings that were established in the nineteenth century and have been rehearsed ever since.

Notes

1 Mann, *Buddenbrooks*, 453–4.
2 Perry, *Christmas in Germany*, 4.
3 Ibid., 18.
4 Ibid., 5. Perry borrows the concept of "emotional community" from the historian of emotions Barbara Rosenwein. See Rosenwein, "Worrying about Emotions in History."
5 Hoffmann, *Nussknacker und Mausekönig*.
6 Schleiermacher, *Die Weihnachtsfeier: Ein Gespräch*.
7 These should be distinguished from the "old church Christmas songs" such as "Es ist ein Ros entsprungen," as well as from the "church songs with Biblical content." The classification comes from Helmut Loos: see Loos, *Weihnachten in der Musik: Grundzüge der Geschichte weihnachtlicher Musik*, 40.
8 Foitzik, "Weihnachten," 157.
9 Perry, *Christmas in Germany*, 3.
10 Key, *The Century of the Child*.
11 Foitzik, *Rote Sterne, braune Runen: Politische Weihnachten zwischen 1870 und 1970*, 28. All German and other foreign-language sources cited here were translated by Adam Bresnahan, unless otherwise noted.
12 Foitzik, "Weihnachten," 157.
13 Perry, *Christmas in Germany*, 5. "When Germans talked about or experienced the Christmas mood, I suggest, they joined an emotional community rooted in feelings of family love, joy, and concern for others."
14 Rosenwein, *Emotional Communities*, 24. "Emotional communities are groups in which people have a common stake, interest, values, and goals."
15 Perry, *Christmas in Germany*, 3. Perry writes that the (re)discovery of Christmas was "closely tied to the emergence and consolidation of the nation-state."
16 Ibid., 4. "Emotions, too, had national characteristics. At the heart of German Christmas was what celebrants called the Weihnachtsstimmung,

or Christmas mood, a feeling that only Germans experienced during
their semi sacred moments of family festivity. Observers ... pondered the
mysteries of ... 'this great and untranslatable German word' [Stimmung]."

17 See Klenke, *Der singende "deutsche Mann": Gesangvereine und deutsches
Nationalbewußtsein von Napoleon bis Hitler.*

18 Lauer and Wilton, "Interview with Rolando Villazón."

19 "Gänsehaut-Atmosphäre im Stadion."

20 In accordance with Monique Scheer's characterization of emotional
practice in Scheer, "Are Emotions a Kind of Practice?"

21 Corness, "The Musical Experience," 21.

22 Hesmondhalg, "Towards a Critical Understanding," 329. "Music often
feels intensely and emotionally linked to the private self."

23 DeNora, *Music in Everyday Life*, 57.

24 The concept of the "mindful body" comes from the anthropology of the
body; according to it, the body is a product of biological and cultural
factors, seen as the conceptual unity of body, mind, and society. See
Scheper-Hughes and Lock, "The Mindful Body." The concept is worked
out more concretely in Scheer, "Are Emotions a Kind of Practice?"

25 See also Brauer, "How Can Music Be Tortuous?"

26 Thus, music is often seen as a "tool for coping with life." See Kristen and
Römer, "Emotional Besetzte Musik Als Werkzeug Der Erinnerung: Eine
Empirische Musikpsychologische Studie," 243.

27 DeNora, *Music in Everyday Life*, 63. Tia DeNora calls this mechanism
"emotion work." Music can be used to manage one's own feelings by
evoking certain memories: "remembering / constructing who one is."

28 Scheer, "Are Emotions a Kind of Practice?" 195.

29 Ibid., 209.

30 See Hesmondhalg, "Towards a Critical Understanding," 341.

31 Kaufman Shelemay, "Musical Communities," 364.

32 Taken from Straßer, "Bekannte Weihnachtslieder und ihre Entstehung:
Vor 182 Jahren entstand das Lied 'Stille Nacht, Heilige Nacht," 375.

33 See the illustration at "'Stille Nacht!'- Fassung - Autograph VII."

34 For more detailed analyses, see Grunewald, "In der heiligen Nacht," 85–6.

35 Ibid., 81.

36 "Silent Night Society."

37 See Gassner, *Franz Xaver Grubers Autographen von Stille Nacht Heilige
Nacht mit der Geschichte des Liedes.*

38 Grunewald, "In der heiligen Nacht," 86.

39 Ibid.

40 Ibid., 95.

41 "Herzliche Weihnachtsgrüße und baldiges Wiedersehen - Stille Nacht."

42 See the more extensive account in Crocker, *The Christmas Truce*. For Michael Jürrgs's literary version see Jürgs, *Der kleine Frieden im großen Krieg: Westfront 1914, als Deutsche, Franzosen und Briten gemeinsam Weihnachten feierten*.

43 "Christmas Truce of 1914."

44 See also the memoirs of 2nd Lieutenant Albert Brainerd Raynes; Raynes, "Letter Home."

45 Fischer-Lichte, *Performativität: Eine Einführung*, 43–4.

46 Carion, dir., *Merry Christmas*.

47 Ibid.

48 Auster, "Leben in einem Konzentrationslager."

49 See also Brauer, *Musik im Konzentrationslager Sachsenhausen*.

50 Brauer, "How Can Music Be Tortuous?" 9–10.

51 Picart, "Noël 1943 au 'Kommando de la Mort,'" 95.

52 "Minuit, Chrétiens."

53 Melai, *De Moutiers à Oranienburg*, 146.

54 Ibid., 146–7.

55 Moresmau, "Letter to Juliane Brauer."

56 *Christmas Program of the Großdeutscher Rundfunk*. While the original recording is preserved at the Deutschen Rundfunkarchiv, the last minutes of the program can be heard on YouTube (https://www.youtube.com/watch?v=nOZZkYrFl6I). One can also listen to a selection of the program, presented as a form of propaganda, at the Documentation Centre Nazi Party Rally Grounds.

57 According to the production plays, the program was supposed to conclude with the chorale "Und wenn die Welt voll Teufel wär," and then the most well-known Luther chorale "Eine feste Burg ist unser Gott." However, these songs are not heard on the available recordings. See Diller, "Die Weihnachtsringsendung 1942: Der Produktionsfahrplan der RRG," 51.

58 Ibid., 47–8. Diller discusses the program production plan.

59 Schrage, "'Singt alle mit uns gemeinsam in dieser Minute.'"

60 Ibid., 272.

61 Ibid., 281.

62 See Foitzik, *Rote Sterne, braune Runen: Politische Weihnachten zwischen 1870 und 1970*, 119.

63 This is the estimate of Esther Gajek; see Gajek, "Wilde Nacht! Streikende Nacht! Politische Weihnacht im 20. Jahrhundert und ihre Relevanz für ausgewählte 'Stille Nacht'-Umdichtungen," 214.

64 See further Gajek, "'Hohe Nacht der klaren Sterne' und anderer 'Stille Nacht' der Nationalsozialisten."

65 Gajek, "Wilde Nacht! Streikende Nacht! Politische Weihnacht im 20. Jahrhundert und ihre Relevanz für ausgewählte 'Stille Nacht'-Umdichtungen," 209.

66 UNESCO, "Intangible Cultural Heritage."

67 See "Das Welt-Friedenslied."

Bibliography

Auster, Eric Gunnar. "Leben in einem Konzentrationslager." *Norsk-Vanforetids-Skrift*, 1948. 134/15. Archiv Sachsenhausen [AS].

Brauer, Juliane. *Musik im Konzentrationslager Sachsenhausen*. Berlin: Metropol Verlag, 2009.

– "How Can Music Be Tortuous?: Music in Nazi Concentration and Extermination Camps." *Music and Politics* 10, no. 1 (2016): 1–34.

Carion, Christian, dir. *Merry Christmas*. 2005.

Christmas Program of the Großdeutscher Rundfunk. N.d. https://www.youtube.com/watch?v=nOZZkYrFl6I.

"Christmas Truce of 1914 – Grandad William – His Story." Collections. *Europeana 1914–1918*. Accessed 11 October 2016. http://www.europeana1914-1918.eu/de/contributions/4296.

Corness, Greg. "The Musical Experience through the Lens of Embodiment." *Leonardo Music Journal* 18 (2008): 21–4.

Crocker, Terri Blom. *The Christmas Truce: Myth, Memory, and the First World War*. Lexington, KY: University Press of Kentucky, 2015.

"Das Welt-Friedenslied." *Stille Nacht Gesellschaft*. Accessed 11 October 2016. http://www.stillenacht.at/de/welt-friedenslied.asp.

DeNora, Tia. *Music in Everyday Life*. Cambridge: Cambridge University Press, 2000.

Diller, Ansgar. "Die Weihnachtsringsendung 1942: Der Produktionsfahrplan der RRG." *Rundfunk und Geschichte: Mitteilungen des Studienkreises Rundfunk und Geschichte* 29, no. 1/2 (2003): 47–511.

Fischer-Lichte, Erika. *Performativität: Eine Einführung*. Bielefeld, Germany: Transcript, 2012.

Foitzik, Doris. *Rote Sterne, braune Runen: Politische Weihnachten zwischen 1870 und 1970*. Münster, Germany: Waxmann, 1997.

– "Weihnachten." In *Deutsche Erinneringsorte*, edited by Etienne François and Hagen Schulze, 154–68. Munich, Germany: C.H. Beck, 2001.

Gajek, Esther. "'Hohe Nacht der klaren Sterne' und anderer 'Stille Nacht' der Nationalsozialisten." In *175 Jahre "Stille Nacht! Heilige Nacht,"* edited by Thomas Hochradner and Gerhard Walterskirchen, 101–28. Salzburg, Austria: Selke Verlag, 1994.

– "Wilde Nacht! Streikende Nacht! Politische Weihnacht im 20. Jahrhundert und ihre Relevanz für ausgewählte 'Stille Nacht'-Umdichtungen." In *"Stille Nacht! Heilige Nacht!" Zwischen Nostalgie und Realität: Joseph Mohr - Franz Xaver Gruber - ihre Zeit*, edited by Thomas Hochradner, 209–23. Salzburg, Austria: Verein "Freunde der Salzburger Geschichte," 2002.

"Gänsehaut-Atmosphäre im Stadion." *Frankfurter Allgemeine Zeitung*, 23 December 2015. http://www.faz.net/aktuell/sport/fussball/1-fc-union-berlin-traditionelles-weihnachtssingen-bei-kerzenschein-13983087.html.

Gassner, Josef. *Franz Xaver Grubers Autographen von Stille Nacht Heilige Nacht mit der Geschichte des Liedes*. Oberndorf, Germany: Verkehrs- und Verschönerungsverein, 1968.

Grunewald, Eckhard. "In der heiligen Nacht mit allem Beyfall produzirt: Anmerkungen zur Entstehungs- und frühen Wirkungsgeschichte des Stille Nacht-Liedes." *Lied und populäre Kultur* 56 (2011): 79–95.

"Herzliche Weihnachtsgrüße und baldiges Wiedersehen - Stille Nacht." 133/191. 13.4.1 Bildpostkarten. Accessed 11 October 2016. http://www.bildpostkarten. uni-osnabrueck.de/displayimage.php?pos=-7735.

Hesmondhalg, David. "Towards a Critical Understanding of Music, Emotion and Self-Identity." *Consumption, Markets and Culture* 11, no. 4 (2008): 329–43.

Hoffmann, Ernst Theodor Amadeus. *Nussknacker und Mausekönig*. Frankfurt am Main, Germany: Insel-Verlag, 2004.

Jürgs, Michael. *Der kleine Frieden im großen Krieg: Westfront 1914, als Deutsche, Franzosen und Briten gemeinsam Weihnachten feierten*. Munich, Germany: Bertelsmann Verlag, 2003.

Kaufman Shelemay, Kay. "Musical Communities: Rethinking the Collective in Music." *Journal of the American Musicological Society* 64, no. 2 (2011): 349–90.

Key, Ellen. *The Century of the Child*. New York: G.P. Putnam's and Sons, 1909.

Klenke, Dietmar. *Der singende "deutsche Mann": Gesangvereine und deutsches Nationalbewußtsein von Napoleon bis Hitler*. Münster, Germany: Waxmann, 1998.

Kristen, Susanne, and Gabriele Römer. "Emotional Besetzte Musik Als Werkzeug Der Erinnerung: Eine Empirische Musikpsychologische Studie." *Lied Und Populäre Kultur* 59 (2014): 243–51.

Lauer, Céline, and Jennifer Wilton. "Interview with Rolando Villazón." *Welt Am Sonntag*, 29 November 2015.

Loos, Helmut. *Weihnachten in der Musik: Grundzüge der Geschichte weihnachtlicher Musik*. Bonn, Germany: Gudrun Schröder Verlag, 1992.

Mann, Thomas. *Buddenbrooks*. Translated by Helen Tracy Lowe-Porter. New York: Random House, 1952.

Melai, Jean. *De Moutiers à Oranienburg*. N.d.

"Minuit, Chrétiens." 1944. IV 172. Depot of the Sachenhausen Memorial.

Moresmau, Daniel. "Letter to Juliane Brauer." 25 April 2006.

Perry, Joe. *Christmas in Germany: A Cultural History*. Chapel Hill, NC: University of North Carolina Press, 2010.

Picart, Roland. "Noël 1943 au 'Kommando de la Mort.'" *La France du Centre*, 31 December 1945.

Raynes, Albert Brainerd. "Letter Home Written by 2nd Lt Albert Brainerd Raynes about the Christmas Truce of 1914, 4." *First World War Poetry Digital Archive*. Accessed 5 November 2018. http://www.oucs.ox.ac.uk/ww1lit/gwa/document/9133/4614.

Rosenwein, Barbara. "Worrying about Emotions in History." *American Historical Review* 107, no. 3 (2002): 821–45.

– *Emotional Communities in the Early Middle Ages*. Ithaca, NY: Cornell University Press, 2006.

Scheer, Monique. "Are Emotions a Kind of Practice (And Is That What Makes Them Have a History?): A Bourdieuian Approach to Understanding Emotion." *History and Theory* 51, no. 2 (2012): 193–220.

Scheper-Hughes, Nancy, and Margaret M. Lock. "The Mindful Body: A Prolegomenon to Future Work in Medical Anthropology." *Medical Anthropology Quarterly* 1, no. 1 (1987): 6–41.

Schleiermacher, Friedrich. *Die Weihnachtsfeier: Ein Gespräch*. Halle, Germany: Schimmelpfennig & Co, 1806.

Schrage, Dominik. "'Singt alle mit uns gemeinsam in dieser Minute' – Sound als Politik in der Weihnachtsringsendung 1942." In *Politiken der Medien*, edited by Daniel Gethmann and Markus Stauff, 267–85. Berlin: Diaphanes, 2005.

"Silent Night Society." N.d. *Stille Nacht Gesellschaft*. http://www.stillenacht.at/en/.

"'Stille Nacht!'- Fassung - Autograph VII." N.d. *Stille Nacht Gesellschaft.*
http://www.stillenacht.at/de/text_und_musik.asp.

Straßer, Willi. "Bekannte Weihnachtslieder und ihre Entstehung: Vor 182
Jahren entstand das Lied 'Stille Nacht, Heilige Nacht." *Die Oberpfalz:
Heimatzeitschrift für den ehemaligen Bayerischen Nordgau* 88 (2000): 374–5.

UNESCO. "Intangible Cultural Heritage in Austria: 'Silent Night' –
the Christmas Carol." *Austrian Commission for* UNESCO. Accessed
11 October 2016. http://nationalagentur.unesco.at/cgi-bin/unesco/element.
pl?eid=68&lang=en.

5

Situating German *Volkskunde*'s Christmas: Reflections on Spatial and Historical Constructions

Christian Marchetti

Introduction

Christmas as a complex of popular customs, rites, and beliefs falls into the academic domain of German *Volkskunde*,[1] a discipline that developed from nineteenth-century romantic folklorist roots into the study of those dimensions of culture taken as traditional, vernacular, and ethnic in the early twentieth century. In this canonical understanding of Volkskunde, Christmas forms the most dense and productive period in the annual cycle of customs. From the beginning of the discipline's history, Volkskunde's actors engaged in collecting, interpreting, and also popularizing the customs and rituals, figures and objects, and material and linguistic utterances of the festive Christmas season. As it developed into an institutionalized academic discipline with severe nationalist tendencies, for German Volkskunde – especially in the Weimar Republic and during National Socialism – Christmas meant first and foremost *Deutsche Weihnacht* (German Christmas), thought of as a specific and special manifestation of German *Volkstum* or *Volksgeist*.[2]

The main goal in the following chapter is not to delineate or deconstruct the "Christmas ideology" of German Volkskunde by analyzing the historical and political infusions and derivations of this ideology's theories and interpretations. Instead, Volkskunde's engagements with Christmas will be examined as a kind of "public work," in the sense proposed by this volume, on an object which presents itself as kind of a historical field, which can be explored in a historical ethnography.[3] Or perhaps the spatial metaphor of the "site of memory" or historical landscape is more apt: long-term historical structures, contemporary frameworks and conjunctions, institutional and political economies, and hegemonic discourses form this landscape's substructure, on which the various encounters between Christmas as an object of knowledge and Volkskunde as a practice of knowledge took place. By taking Christmas as kind of a critical junction, one is able to identify significant communications, divides, or breaches that would otherwise be difficult to see.

Therefore this chapter's purpose is to engage in an exploration of the spatial and temporal dimensions of this landscape, outlining its central orientations but also wandering through its border zones and peripheries, following traces that earlier exploration have left behind and in doing so coming to a more diverse and multifaceted understanding of what Volkskunde's Christmas was.[4]

Cardinal Directions

This chapter first focuses on the interwar era, as it is the period in which Volkskunde first managed to become an institutionalized and approved academic discipline in Germany. At the time, Christmas was not only the subject matter of a number of monographic publications,[5] but also a standard item in most of the numerous compendia and handbooks on *Deutsche Volkskunde* that were being published.[6] Out of this body of literature, it is Adolf Spamer's work on Christmas that is this chapter's chosen point of departure. His work provides a fitting starting point, as Spamer, the first professor of Volkskunde at the Friedrich Wilhelm University in Berlin, was without a doubt at both the institutional and political centres of the young discipline.[7]

Spamer's slim 1937 book *Weihnachten in alter und neuer Zeit* (*Christmas in the Past and Present*) and the corresponding paragraphs of his comprehensive two-volume handbook on *Deutsche Volkskunde*, published in 1934, elaborate on the development of Christmas, which can be unravelled mainly along a spatial-symbolic framework provided by the four cardinal directions or, more precisely, by the cultural divides that they demarcate. The history of Christmas as Spamer and many of his contemporaries wrote it was one of East versus West and of North against South.

The North/South divide in particular was of crucial importance, as it divided the Christmas customs inherited from the heathen Germanic

North from those inherited from Mediterranean antiquity. Spamer, more a typical bourgeois scholar than a militant Nazi, offered up impressive evidence for the foundations of the Christmas cults of light and of family, of the rituals of presents and decoration, and also of the more "magical" practices of ancestor worship and divination found in rural Christmas folklore, in Roman customs of the Saturnalia, and in other ancient celebrations. At crucial points, however, he paid tribute to the other strain of Christmas theory, that of it being rooted in heathen northern European midwinter sun cults.

It was this northern theory in particular that expanded Christmas into a twelve-day festive season that corresponded with the allegedly pre-Christian midwinter season of "Jul," a liminal time in which the divisions and borders between the realms of the living and the dead, between past, present, and future, and between the natural and the supernatural became porous and transparent. Spamer participated in this primitivist discourse by way of ethnological comparison. According to him, the demon world of Germanic midwinter lived on in the harmless figures of *Krampusen*, *Zwetschgenmanderln*, *Feuerrüpeln* or *Pflaumentoffeln*, *Pelzrupprichen*, and various little mythical figures made of moss and pine cones that populated contemporary *Weihnachtsmärkte*, just like pre-Columbian demons lived on in contemporary *Naguales* figures in Mexico.[8]

Theories about heathen cults of light and trees played a central role here; one of the leading pieces of evidence used in the pre-Christian northern Germanic theory was the *Julblock*, a wooden log, preferably from the roots of a tree, that burned in an open fire all through the festive season, forming the centre of the Germanic household's midwinter festivities.[9]

The roots of most of the folk elements of Christmas festivities were traced to a contact zone between Mediterranean antique culture and northern Germanic primitive culture. While Spamer navigated along this divide by tracing the lineages of many folk elements into both spheres, many of his predecessors and contemporaries took a much more distinct and militant northern stance when identifying the sources of the special German quality of Christmas.[10]

In this discourse, North and South were not just cultural areas, but symbolic and temporalized spaces. The South – or the oriental-antique world – signified the historical origin of Christian religion whose apperception by Germanic peoples was the key process of German cultural development. When examined through the lens of the South, Christmas

Abb. 26. Christgeburt mit Engel= und Königsscharen.
Gedrechselt und geschnitzt zu Seiffen (Erzgebirge). 1935

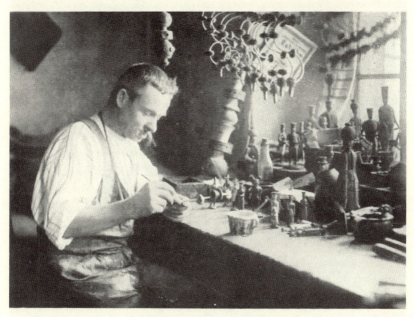

Abb. 27. Der Arnsfelder „Männelmacher" bei der Arbeit

Figure 5.1   Christmas decoration and carver from the Erzgebirge.

customs were seen to have developed out of antique continuities or through the transformation of original Germanic forms into Christian ritual. The North, in contrast, signified the source of a pre-historical – and, in a sense, timelessly preserved – primitive heathen Germanic heritage, survivals of which were to be found underneath a Christianized surface. In a more liberal reading, "German Christmas" as a ritual and symbolic complex could integrate the Christian religious holiday with the Germanic primitive within.[11]

The other great Christmas divide ran right through the Christian religious quality of Christmas and, in a first cut, separated East from West. Establishing the ecclesiastical celebration of Christ's birth on the night of 24 December as opposed to the celebration of Epiphany on 6 January was, according to Spamer, "a full victory" of Rome against the Eastern Church and a significant and enduring demarcation in the Great Schism of the Christian Church.[12] This religious segregation between Roman Catholicism and Byzantine Orthodoxy, between the Romanic sphere and the Slavic world, corresponded with the East-West divide deeply inscribed into mental maps of European culture.[13]

On German ground, the corresponding intra-Christian divide was that between the Catholic and Protestant denominations. For German Volkskunde, Christmas customs articulated this divide in a complex and historically dynamic interaction. While Protestantism's ritual purism displaced many of the popular – and sometimes quite crude – customs, it also contributed greatly to the special emotional keynote of German Christmas that was created by its family-focused, inward orientation, its close-to-kitsch decorations: in short, its *Besinnlichkeit*.

Spamer found that by pulling all of this together, German Christmas could form a unique and cohesive emotional *"Erlebnisgemeinschaft,"*[14] a social group held together by communal cultural practices and experiences, the best living example of which he himself had found in the Protestant crèches-carving villages of the middle German *Erzgebirge*.

The Centre

This more centrist Christmas discourse of German Volkskunde aimed at defining a central place for German culture in a European cultural landscape and bridging the internal denominational and social divisions of the German nation. One element of Christmas festivities in particular

Vom Himmel hoch da komm ich her...

Abb. 33. Erfatzweihnachtsbaum aus Swakopmund

Figure 5.2 Substitute Christmas tree from Swakopmund (German colonial town in present-day Namibia).

whose triumph would effectively break down these internal borderlines was the Christmas tree, the *Weihnachtsbaum*. "That on German territories the split between urban and rural Christmas customs isn't as apparent as it is in other countries is due first and foremost to the Christmas tree's triumphant transformation into the unifying communal symbol of the German Christmas experience."[15] Researchers did not consider it problematic that the Christmas tree was a relatively young invention (it was first documented in the sixteenth century); indeed, it was seen to open up a new field for symbolic speculation, albeit one in which scholars were wildly reaching for any clues as to the trees' origins that would support their pet theories. As a composed symbolic arrangement, the Christmas tree could be deconstructed into its basic components; each single component could then serve as a link in any constructed chain of lineage. Viewed in this way, the Christmas tree was a tree, a conifer, a composition of green twigs, an adorned object, a triangular wooden construction, and a candle-holding device. This complex arrangement could be taken as the outcome of a complex history, but more often than not, one element or a certain combination was privileged in order to support an author's standpoint in the discourse outlined above. While religious Volkskunde interpreted candlelight as symbolizing the light of Jesus Christ,[16] other authors preferred to highlight the green tree as the core characteristic, relating it either to the (Indo-)Germanic "tree of life" or to the use of 'living' green twigs for midwinter's apotropaic magics.[17]

Perhaps it was this symbolic polyvocality that was the Christmas tree's recipe for success; in any case, it became the core element of *Deutsche Weihnacht*, facilitating a united national *Weihnachtserlebnisgemeinschaft*. This community was potentially global as it included the *Auslandsdeutschtum*, Germans abroad, who performed their participation with acts of botanical Christmas colonialism, turning any wooden substitute at hand into "*Ersatzweihnachtsbäume*": "And where the fir tree is missing, substitute Christmas trees are improvised. Lights are placed on the cedars of Lebanon, hung with oranges in place of apples, and on Javanese palm trees, Japanese Cryptomeria, Chilean Araucaria, arctic Andromeda tetragonia, Mexican cactus, and Arabian coffee trees. One conjures up cotton snow for Brazilian pine trees and, deeply touched, sings the Christmas carols of childhood, even though the candles are quickly melting in the heat of high summer."[18] Under this global Christmas tree the atmosphere was still sentimental and inherently peaceful.

Territorialization

In the interwar period, the rise of German Volkskunde to a fully institutionalized discipline was driven by three big science projects: the *(Internationale) Volkskundliche Bibliographie* (*International Folklore Bibliography*), the *Handbuch des Deutschen Aberglaubens* (*Encyclopedia of German Superstition*), and the *Atlas der Deutschen Volkskunde* (*Atlas of German Folklore*).[19] These projects were thought to provide a bibliographic, encyclopedic, and territorial inventory of German folk culture; mapping the cultural geography of Christmas was one of their core goals.

In the *Internationale Volkskundliche Bibliographie*, Christmas entries found their proper place in chapter X, "Sitte, Brauch, Fest, Spiel / Manners and Customs, Festivals, Pastimes / Usage et coutumes, fêtes, jeux"; partition B, "Einzelnes / Special subjects / Sujets particuliers"; number twelve, "Kalenderbräuche / Calendar Customs / Coutumes saisonnières"; subsection b, "Winterbräuche / Winter Customs / Coutumes hivernales."[20] In general, the majority of the articles on Christmas are located in this subsection, but Christmas-related entries are also to be found in the sections on arts and crafts, popular belief, and popular speech.

In the ninth volume of the *Handbuch des Deutschen Aberglaubens*, published in 1941, the entry "Weiher s. See" (pond, see lake) is followed by the reference "Weihnacht s. Nachtrag" (Christmas, see addendum), followed by a twenty-six-column-long entry on "Weihnachtsgebäck" (Christmas baked goods). The author of the entry on Christmas, Lily Weiser-Aal, like a number of her colleagues, missed the deadline, so her 101 columns were printed after the section on "Wechselbalg" (changelings) in the addendum printed at the end of the last volume.

"Questionnaire No. 3," sent out in 1932 to gather data for the *Atlas der deutschen Volkskunde*, dedicated ten paragraphs containing forty-four individual questions to Christmas customs and figures and produced maps showing the spatial distribution of the use of the *Adventskranz* (Advent wreaths) (Map 36), children's beliefs about the gift-bringers (Map 37), and the names for the Christmas tree (Map 38). Five maps dealt with the "twelve nights" (Maps 44–9), three with the names of the evenings of 24 December and 31 December (Maps 50–3), and two more with the special food served on these occasions. The *Nikolaus* alone took up five maps (Maps 56–61), and three more maps charted the habitats of numerous other figures of the Christmas festive season (Maps 62–5).

German Christmas was now at the institutional centre of German Volkskunde, and the celebration's rich and diverse customary practices were territorialized into a specifically German Christmas culture. This mapping of German folk culture did not stop at Germany's borders.[21] While the German state had lost large parts of its eastern territories after 1918, the German public and politicians were discovering its "lost diasporas" abroad. The discipline of Volkskunde in particular engaged in the project of *Sprachinselforschung*, the exploration of German-speaking settler groups in eastern and southeastern Europe, who were thought to have been living in isolation among alien nations and therefore to have preserved traces of a more authentic heritage.[22] Some of these groups were only just about to learn that they belonged to the German *Volkstum*.[23]

Extreme Positions

In 1944 the publishing house *Grenze und Ausland,* an agency of the *Volksbund der Deutschen im Ausland* (VDA), printed and distributed a small brochure entitled *Weihnachten der Volksgemeinschaft*.[24] This collection of *Durchhaltepropaganda,* recipes for baked goods, instructions for handcrafted gifts, non-biblical theatrical plays, a short text on World War I and the "*Kriegsweihnacht,*" descriptions of exemplary family festivities, and newly composed Christmas carols such as "Hohe Nacht der klaren Sterne"[25] is representative of National Socialist Christmas propaganda. The brochure's content was extracted from the volume *Deutsche Kriegsweihnacht,* issued by the *Kulturamt der Reichspropagandaleitung* of the NSDAP.

This particular brochure was mainly aimed at the "*deutsche Volksgruppen im Ausland,*"[26] especially the political organizations of Germans abroad. In 1933, the German-speaking minorities in the post-Habsburg nation-states, which had served as compensatory objects in the Weimar Republic for territories lost after World War I, became the particular targets and tools of Third-Reich political influence and manipulation. With World War II entering into its final phase in Europe, or, in the diction of National Socialist propaganda, in the face of enemy forces of "plutocratic and bolshevist nature," the editors evoked the "*urhafte Kraft,*" the primeval force of the pan-German "*Volksgemeinschaft*" gathered around the "*brennenden Holzstoß,*"[27] the burning log (recall the northern *Julblock*).

Aside from being a telling example of National Socialist Christmas propaganda, the small booklet *Weihnachten der Volksgemeinschaft,* of which only the German National Library in Leipzig holds a copy, wouldn't attract much attention today if it weren't for its editor, Dr Inge Kellermann, at the time a twenty-six-year-old female scholar and practitioner of Volkskunde and *Sprachinselforschung* and a former student of Spamer. After working as a conscripted telephone operator for the *Luftwaffe,* she found another duty essential to the war effort as a *Kulturreferent für auslandsdeutsche Schulen* at the VDA office in Berlin, where she edited and distributed teaching material for German schools and kindergartens abroad.[28] Kellermann's biography and further scientific endeavours will be addressed in more detail below.

During National Socialism, Volkskunde scholars and practitioners actively participated in the construction of a politically and ideologically radicalized Christmas.[29] Central components were its radical de-Christianization and re-interpretation in line with National Socialist cults of motherhood and race. Up until World War II, the political aim of this reconstruction was the creation of a racially defined *Volksgemeinschaft* and the incorporation of Germans outside the German Reich into this ideological body.[30] During the war, the emotional resources provided by Christmas were served up as antidotes to hardships at home and on the frontlines.

The scholarly side to this was the now fierce and often counterfactual emphasis placed on Christmas's allegedly heathen Germanic or "northern" origin and nature. For Volkskunde this was no newly invented theory; giving Christmas a Germanic undertone was deeply rooted in the discipline's DNA. Most of the elements of the Christmas season that were not obviously Christian had been readily attributed to the Germanic pantheon or a rather indefinite "Indo-Germanic" historical stratum, but with the rise of National Socialism, the Germanic nature and appearance of German Christmas became the essence of the holiday's brand. As this racial essence had to be pure, mixed and unclear elements such as the Christmas tree had to be scrupulously Aryanized. Interestingly, given the variety of speculations and theories about the Christmas tree's origins, there was one particular possible lineage that no *Volkskundler* had taken into consideration before 1933.

In his book on the tree of lights in Germanic myth and German folk custom, published in 1938, Otto Huth, a religious scholar and Volkskundler working mainly in Strasbourg and Tübingen, showed a series of photographs of large medieval seven-branched candelabra from churches in Germany and Austria.[31] Two years earlier the Viennese Volkskundler and museum curator Arthur Haberlandt had published his symbolic analysis of one of these lampstands in an article titled "Christmas Tree – Tree of Life – Tree of Lights."[32] Both accepted that the medieval creators of these lampstands might have been unwittingly influenced by biblical models, but the two authors, each affiliated with rival Volkskunde organizations inside the Third Reich, were at odds about the lampstands' original symbolic meaning. Haberlandt, who had collaborated closely with the *Amt Rosenberg*, had studied the detailed artwork of the lampstand in the Stift

Klosterneuburg near Vienna *in situ*. He concluded that because the object was a formal emulation of the seven-branched candelabra from the "Old Testament," it did not represent a tree at all. In contrast, Huth, who was a member of the *SS-Ahnenerbe*, argued that more or less all of the lampstands were survivals of the Germanic "tree of life." Thus, its "Indo-Germanic" origin had priority over the seven-armed biblical lampstands which formed a branch, so to speak, from the same root, but weren't forerunners of the medieval lampstands. It was Haberlandt who addressed the elephant in the room directly, stating that it was most certain that those church stands could not be progenitors of the German Christmas tree.[33] Arbitrary arguments and semiotic selectivity, as seen above, were used to make the case: the Germanic Christmas tree could find its roots in anything but the Jewish menorah. It was with ideological contributions such as this that Volkskunde, now a political and militant discipline, reached a central position in the Nazi system of power.

Borderlands

Having traced the creation and propagation of "German Christmas" by the central actors and agencies of German Volkskunde and the political payoff of their actions, we will now decentre these narratives, as we move into Volkskunde's peripheries. The key stories at the discipline's centre needed to be told first; upon departing the well-trodden centre for the intellectual and temporal margins of German-speaking Volkskunde, however, lesser-known trails and back paths come into view. These less visible pathways allow a more multifaceted narrative to emerge than the one sketched out above, a narrative that may provide better insight into more culturally diverse ways of dealing with Christmas. To this end, small excursions will be made. It is not by chance that all of them lead to the late Habsburg Empire or its post-imperial legacy.

A Bosnian Muslim Christmas

The first detour will go via Vienna to Sarajevo, Bosnia. Volkskunde in the Habsburg Empire developed simultaneously with Volkskunde in the German Reich; they were interconnected in many ways, but, being situated in a multi-ethnic empire, Austrian Volkskunde developed a specific interest in and sensibility for cultural diversity and comparative methods.

German-speaking Austrian Volkskunde was, in addition, far from alone within the Habsburg Empire; from the late nineteenth century on, an ample array of national ethnologies emerged.[34]

One of the test sites of Austrian Volkskunde was the Habsburg Empire's quasi-colony of Bosnia-Hercegovina, acquired in 1886 and annexed in 1906. It was a truly multi-religious and multi-ethnic society consisting of the traditional urban and land-owning Muslim upper strata, Catholic/Croatian and Orthodox/Serbian peasants, Sephardic Jews, and the *kuferašen*, an invasive, actually rather diverse caste of Habsburg bureaucrats and military and civil officials.[35] Here, as one central representative phrased it, on the "dividing line between West and East,"[36] Habsburg's proximate colonialism[37] was said to create "an enchanting mixture."[38]

In this situation, local intellectuals adopted the concept of a *Bosnische Volkskunde* that concentrated on the Muslim part of the population. One important protagonist here was the female owner and editor of the German-language daily paper *Bosnische Post*, Milena Preindlsberger-Mrazovic (1868–1924).[39] On 24 December 1913, this periodical published an interesting article titled *Ein Weihnachtsbrauch der bosnischen Muslims* (A Bosnian Muslim Christmas custom). It described a local "trick or treat"–style custom performed by Muslim youngsters among not only the Muslim, but also the Catholic households of their villages. The very same custom had attracted scientific attention nearly twenty years before when it had been reported by Sadik Effendi Ugljen, a local sharia judge, in the prestigious *Wissenschaftliche Mitteilungen aus Bosnien und Herzgovina*, the mouthpiece of Austro-Hungarian science on Bosnia.[40] While Ugljen deferred to the theory that the Bosnian Muslims were the descendants of certain medieval Christian heretic groups in order to explain the custom's origins,[41] the author of the 1913 article in the *Bosnische Post* interpreted it as an example of interreligious exchange, something not uncommon in a country where different communities historically lived close together and intermingled with one another.

In defiance of k.u.k. (*kaiserlich und königlich*, imperial and royal) nostalgia, it must be said that national quarrels, supremacist ideologies, and racist theories were alive and kicking in the Habsburg Empire and that Bosnia and Hercegovina, on the brink of World War I, were strained by social tensions and ethno-political unrest. But nevertheless, in settings such as this, the science of Volkskunde had to create approaches that could deal with the presence of cultural difference, interrelations, and exchange on a much more daily basis than in purportedly culturally homogeneous Germany. This imperial legacy would not vanish completely with the dissolution of Habsburg rule.

Selling Transylvanian Christmas in Germany

The next field trip starts with a travel magazine. In 1903, the readers of *Wandern und Reisen*, a short-lived illustrated magazine dedicated to tourism, Volkskunde, arts, and sports, could immerse themselves in the picturesque scenery of "Christmas with the Saxons in Transylvania."[42] The nameless village and its surrounding mountains were "[a]s snowy as a fairy tale,"[43] and the Christmas folk life staged there was also frosted with a layer of romanticism. The magazine paints a charming picture: Christmas preparations involve all members of the peasant community. The rustic but studious schoolchildren work hard to learn a Latin carol. The young men form a squadron, riding into the woods to collect fir twigs for the traditional Christmas crowns, which will be decorated by the young girls. The women reorganize their labour in the fields and their domestic workload in anticipation of the upcoming feast, turning from braking and hackling to cleaning and baking. Everyone is firmly bound by pious Protestantism, peasant work and tradition, and starched linen caps and underskirts. Even the young people's dancing on the second day of celebrations, accompanied by "gypsy" fiddlers, is a form of work, a highly regulated performance. The focal point of the Christmas proceedings is the Protestant pastor and the staged family life showcased in his living room. As the Saxon peasant is too sober, prosaic, and conservative for something so "modern" it is here that the only Christmas tree in the village is displayed. Its "warm lights" project "true Christmas feelings" on the peasant children's faces as they stain the furbished floorboards with their snow-encrusted boots.

The author of this literary-ethnographic account was Regine Ziegler (1864–1925), the daughter of just such a Transylvanian Saxon pastor; at the time, however, she was living as an author in Berlin. Ziegler published several articles on seasonal customs in her home region, profiting from her family experience and the fairytale quality these accounts from the European periphery evoked in the metropolis of Berlin. To enhance this quality, Ziegler sprinkled the scenery with germanophile characteristics: she gave the Saxon peasants the features of "pithy Teutons"[44] when they sang "Stille Nacht" in church, and she described the young lads' squadron

Abb. 25. Weihnachtspyramide in Neppendorf (Siebenbürgen).

Figure 5.3 Transylvanian-German Christmas pyramids.

riding off into the snowy woods as "the Wild Hunt," a generic folk myth associated with Odin and his crew or other Nordic mythologies. Despite Ziegler's efforts, the German quality of the ethnographic scenery is disputable: her object of description is a germanophone Protestant peasant community living in the Hungarian part of the Habsburg monarchy – but what qualifies groups such as these as "German"?[45]

The Transylvanian Saxons, who have no relation whatsoever to the inner-German Saxons, had been settling in the southeastern European region of Transylvania since medieval times. Thanks to legal privileges granted to them by the Hungarian kings and their economic preponderance in the local towns, they had consolidated a privileged life space for themselves. The Protestant Reformation had both reinforced the German-speaking population in Transylvania in number and deepened the divides between them and the other populations. Although they organized and presented themselves as a closed community, the Saxons were also embedded in this multi-ethnic region. The region's history was filled with conflict and deeply marked by a century of tensions with the Ottoman Empire. In Saxon villages the Protestant churches were heavily fortified against the invasions and incursions that threatened from the east, but many of them also housed precious collections of oriental carpets that the Saxons had traded in from Istanbul.[46] In the modern period, the Saxons lived mainly in mixed villages, and their Transylvanian towns had ceased to be purely "German." Hungarians, Saxons, Székelys, Romanians, Jews, and Roma ('Gypsies') formed a regional society of complex interdependencies and hierarchies. Religious, social, and linguistic divides cemented segregation; the Saxons maintained their habitual pride, but had to exploit new resources to maintain their Saxon identity. Around the end of the nineteenth century – not much later than in Germany – Volkskunde became *en vogue* among the Transylvanian Saxons.

From the beginning, Transylvanian-Saxon Volkskunde was well positioned to achieve certain benchmarks such as ethnographic collections and museum expositions. Having studied in German universities, Saxon students, usually Protestant theologists, brought Volkskunde back to their home region where they occupied multiple central positions in the strictly organized political/religious/ethnic community. They applied Volkskunde in troubled times, particularly when traditional Saxon privileges came under pressure and crumbled due to Habsburg neo-absolutism and Hungarian nationalism. Even though Transylvania did not have its own

German-speaking university, Volkskunde was done in the quasi-academic environment provided by the *Siebenbürger Verein für Landeskunde*.

When Transylvania became part of Romania after World War I, the Saxons sought to take advantage of this change with tactical political flexibility and opportunism, but their hopes of successfully acting as a national minority were disappointed. Nevertheless, Saxon Volkskundler collaborated with Romanian ethnographers and scholars, though they also used Volkskunde as a means to explore and relate to the other germanophone populations in Greater Romania, in the Zips region, and in the Banat. In these interwar years Transylvanian-Saxon Volkskunde became more professional and productive.[47] And it sold itself well, especially in Germany, as Regine Ziegler had tested out. Transylvanian Saxon Volkskunde items, such as the typically decorated "Christmas crowns," became a standard feature in German Christmas volumes.

Transylvanian Saxons embraced their "Germanness," and practitioners of Volkskunde played a large part in popularizing and furnishing this concept. Some Christmas writings reveal that the Germanness of Christmas in Transylvania was something to be actively vernacularized. As one Saxon Volkskundler wrote in the popular almanac *Sächsischer Hausfreund* in 1911, "For many of us, the German Advent and Christmas carol is still a buried treasure of nearly inexhaustible wealth. How worthwhile it is to naturalize the customs of the advent tree or the advent crown among our selves. It's the best way to prolong and internalize the joy of Christmas … Give German advent customs a place and sing only our loving and profound Christmas carols."[48]

In a way, Volkskunde was one of the most important conveyors of Germanness to the Saxons. But Transylvanian Saxon Volkskunde was not only an admittedly successful supplier of idealized conservative scenes transported from faraway Transylvania to Germany to represent a paragon of *Auslandsdeutsche* culture; nor was it just an ideologically blindfolded propagator of German *Volkstum* to a German-speaking minority abroad. Volkskunde was also a way to produce both knowledge and interpretations of the self in a given local situation. For example, one central topic of the time, the question of the historical region of origin of the Transylvanian Saxons, could be settled by means of comparative dialect analysis, an innovation of Saxon science.[49]

The historical appearance of the Christmas tree in Transylvania was also diligently investigated and some Saxon Volkskunde activists cherished

Fällen des Badnjaks in Topola. (Zu S. 17)

Figure 5.4   Logging the 'badnjak' in Central Serbia.

those older local customs endangered by this new one.[50] Other observers, namely the Volkskundler and folk art collector Emil Sigerus (1854–1947), remarked that the Christmas tree had not found its way directly from German Protestant lands, but had arrived in Transylvanian towns via Vienna.[51] Sigerus was one of the Saxon Volkskundler who had an open and skilled eye not only for cultural influences reaching Transylvania from the East and the West, but also for the manifold cultural interferences between the Transylvanian nation and the unique cultural style of the region. This Transylvanian Volkskunde was thought to be a distinct and unique approach, investigating the culture of the Saxons as the product of a few survivals from the region of origin, a good share of actively adopted and appropriated German national culture, and the profound historical experiences and influences acquired through living in a multi-ethnic region for centuries.[52]

Southern Slavic Comparisons

The third excursion follows a young Austrian scholar on his explorations of the close European other of German Volkskunde, the Slavic culture. Austrian Volkskunde itself had a slavophile branch; the influential Viennese Slavicist Vatroslav Jagić (1838–1923) was a long-term member of the board of the *Verein für Österreichische Volkskunde* (Austrian Society for Volkskunde). Vienna was also an important stopover for Volkskundler and Slavicists who for various reasons followed the call of southeastern "wild Europe" and sometimes ended up joining the Serbian ethnographic school around Jovan Cvijić (1865–1927).

In 1925, while lecturing at the University of Belgrade, Edmund Schneeweis (1886–1964) published a book on "Serbo-Croatian Christmas Customs."[53] The book was financed by the Austrian society for Volkskunde; its president, Michael Haberlandt, promoted it as a fine example of the benefits of transnational collaboration and comparative methods for European Christmas research.

Schneeweis's interpretation of the ample material he had collected from southern Slavic ethnographers and his own fieldwork resembled – or even exactly mirrored – the German Volkskunde model of Christmas, minus the Germanic heritage theory. Christmas appeared as a powerful, magnetic ritual complex, absorbing and appropriating seasonal customs. He concluded that Slavic Christmas had, therefore, mainly perceived and absorbed the antique Roman customs of the Calends, mixing and blending them with heathen Slavic traditions.[54] Schneeweis's primary evidence for the persistence of Roman tradition, prominently displayed in the frontispiece of the book, was, ironically, the *badnjak*, a ritually harvested and burned log, identical to the allegedly *"urgermanische Julblock."*

Devoted to comparative ethnography, Schneeweis presented his ethnographic material strictly separated from his interpretations because "experience has taught us that only the material collected has persistent value, while our interpretations will be revised by the progress of science."[55] Obviously Schneeweis extended this rule not only to his own, but to all interpretations of Christmas ethnography.

From Budapest to Europe: Translating Christmas

The fourth excursion begins in Budapest and interwar Hungary. Here, Volkskunde had flourished as a scientific practice among German-speaking[56] academics from the late days of the Habsburg Empire into the interwar period. These local scholars developed their specific approach towards their German heritage in a highly politically controversial situation. The postwar order had turned them from subjects of a multi-ethnic empire into members of a national minority in a country reduced by war to a nation-state. While the German-speaking populations in Hungary became an object of discovery for German Volkskunde's *Sprachinselforschung*, at the local level the so-called "Suabian" peasants were highly integrated into the rural multi-ethnic landscapes that the internal colonization of the Habsburg emperors had created in southern Hungary. Up to World War I these peasants did not have any sense of community with the German-speaking small-town population, which itself lived as part of a multicultural symbiotic urban culture. Large parts of the more educated and upward-oriented strata of these *Deutschungarn* (German-Hungarians), just like the similar strata of the Jewish population, assimilated themselves by changing their names and language preference to form the backbone of the emerging Hungarian bourgeois society.[57]

While much of the Volkskunde research in Hungary was done as part of Hungarian-German philology, the only professorship for Volkskunde was held by Elmar (Elemér) von Schwartz (1890–1962), a Catholic academic and member of the Order of Cistercians born in western Hungary.[58] Schwartz promoted linguistic, onomatologic, and folkloristic research among the German-speaking populations in interwar Hungary, but he did not overemphasize the importance of language or nationality. Instead, Schwartz promoted a specific German-Hungarian identity, separate from and independent of the 'greater German nation.' Among his colleagues and students such a hyphenated self-understanding of belonging to a political Hungarian nation and to a cultural – and maybe also racial – German *Volk* was also not uncommon. Schwartz claimed that inside the Hungarian state the interrelation of Germans and Hungarians not only had a political and cultural character, but was also an emotional matter.[59]

Moreover, as a proponent of religious Volkskunde, at times he emphasized denominational divides over ethnic or national ones. Looking beyond religious divides, he also saw religious practices and customs as vivid fields of exchange between different language groups.[60] Consequently, he dedicated his own *Institut für Deutsche Sprachwissenschaft und Volkskunde* at the Pázmány-Péter-University in Budapest to Christmas research; the study of the trans-ethnic diffusion and translation of the carol "Stille Nacht, heilige Nacht" became his personal pet project.[61]

Schwartz supervised three dissertations on the carol[62] and planned to cover not only its Hungarian (*"ungarische"*) versions, but also those in all of the other languages spoken in the country (*"ungarländische nicht-ungarische"*), which were Croatian, Slovak, Slovene, Ruthenian, and Romanian. After losing his professorship in 1948, Schwartz moved to the University of Leuven, Belgium, to continue his academic work and also his research on the world-renowned carol. The culmination of this research was the collection *Europa singt "Stille Nacht, heilige Nacht..."* posthumously published in 1963.[63] Here, variants of the song not only in the major European languages, but also in Hebrew or Latin and in minor tongues such as Faroese, Esperanto, Manx Gaelic, or *"Eskimoisch"* were printed together with re-translations of the texts into German.[64]

Schwartz ascribed the global success of the carol to the catchiness of its simple and appealing tune. According to Schwartz, Christian missionaries with their translation experience played a larger role in spreading the content of the carol than the *Auslandsdeutschtum*. In the "Christmassy Europe" Schwartz presented in his posthumous book, intercultural translation took place at the level of popular festive singing and, in the best case scenario, as an act of spiritual and emotional empathy or understanding (*"seelisches Einfühlen"*) that revealed basic characteristics of giving and receiving in folk culture.[65]

Hiking the Contact Zone

The end of World War II put an end to Inge(borg) Kellermann's engagement with Third Reich science; even before the end of the war, her
experiences had begun to alienate her from its ideology. What remained
was her interest in Volkskunde, and luckily Spamer, already retired, was
able to place her in the new Institute for Volkskunde in (East) Berlin.
Now called Weber-Kellermann after a short-lived marriage, she kept on
travelling the inter-ethnic landscape of southeastern Europe.

One of the first projects she took up when she returned to her former
field was the study of folklore about a strange magical practice: the so-called
Luzienstuhl (St Lucy's chair).[66] Starting on St Lucy's Day, 13 December, an
adept is supposed to construct a small wooden chair out of the wood of seven
(or twelve) different trees or bushes. Sitting on that chair in church during
the Christmas Eve service, he or she will be able to identify the witches
living in the community. Descriptions of the practice were provided by
numerous sources but varied significantly, especially regarding instructions
about what one has to do to escape the witches' deadly wrath afterwards.[67]

Weber-Kellermann's interest in the custom was sparked by a Hungarian-
German peasant woman in Mösz in southern Hungary who attributed the
name *Luzienstuhl* to a wicker whip used for the traditional whipping of
children on Christmas. Obviously, in the multi-ethnic village, exchange in
folklore and folk customs and beliefs produced complex and complicated
entanglements. Thus in her article Weber-Kellermann set out to "pace out
the geographical extension and cultural historical depth" of the custom's
elements and variations. This undertaking was "*eine weite Wanderung*," a
long hike that concluded with the conviction that the *volkskundliche* or
ethnographic exploration of the great contact zones ("*Kontaktlandschaften*")
at the eastern and southeastern borders of the German language zone
could only be successful when carried out in collaboration with scholars
and scientists from neighbouring countries. Furthermore, she concluded
that the "reality of folk life" for "our southeastern Germans" could only
be understood in relation to and in interaction with the cultures of their
neighbours.[68] The following year she published her paradigmatic article
on inter-ethnic relations in the research of language islands in the *Journal
of Austrian Volkskunde*.[69]

Ingeborg Weber-Kellermann was the first German Volkskundler who
more or less explicitly criticized the discipline's ideological implications

and its involvement in the southeast during the Nazi occupation in particular. Her development of the concept of "interethnics," or social and cultural exchange between different ethnic groups in multi-ethnic spaces, emerged from her (self-)critique of the ethnocentric approach of *Sprachinselvolkskunde*, of which she, as a young student of the discipline, had been part. It was an ideological as well as a theoretical and methodological critique that reframed German Volkskunde's entanglement with southeastern Europe on intercultural terms. It also contributed profoundly to critical assessment of the discipline's involvement and collaboration with National Socialism in general and to the re-imagining of Volkskunde as a European ethnology. That the first empirical testing ground for this new understanding of Volkskunde was an admittedly rather crude and even marginal custom from the wide field of Christmas folklore fits perfectly into Weber-Kellermann's further career. She did away with not only the ideological axioms of *Sprachinselvolkskunde* – namely the superiority and insularity of German culture in eastern and southeastern Europe – but also a number of ideological theories on Germanic continuities in Christmas customs.[70]

The Return

Decentring the history of German Volkskunde's Christmas does not provide a completely different or alternative narrative. The historic-ethnographic approach tested here was an admittedly extensive and eclectic one. The spatial-symbolic order deployed above served to navigate Volkskunde's Christmas discourse, but it did not serve as an instrument for in-depth analysis or critique. Nor can the rather short visits paid to various sites of Volkskunde practice here replace detailed, close, and differentiated studies of these practices' respective formations, achievements, and shortcomings. Nevertheless, revisiting the borderlands and peripheries of the disciplinary discourse, following less-trodden paths, and exploring dead ends proves to be a telling and productive undertaking; outside of the centre of the discipline, marginal, alternative, and dissenting approaches are to be found, namely among ethnographic actors living, travelling, and researching in southeastern Europe.

Doing Volkskunde proves to have been a travelling practice. Southeastern Europe wasn't only the imagined anti-modern counter-world where a more authentic German folk culture waited to be discovered and explored by professional German Volkskundler. The historical post-imperial legacy of this area provided it with a religious, cultural, and ethnic diversity, which made it a significant and at times provocative "other" for German Volkskunde and its project of representing a homogenized German folk culture.

For most ethnographers of one or another Habsburg nationality, German-speaking science had been both a model for and the counterpart to their own development. Volkskunde could therefore serve as a field of exchange or a zone of contact. Intellectuals and activists of the local German-speaking minority groups actively appropriated its practices, methods, and theories, adjusting them to their specific historically checkered experiences and their changing political and social situations and highly culturally heterogeneous life-worlds. The settings of cultural diversity in which they formulated and enacted specific approaches can be regarded as laboratories for the study of ethnographic knowledge production.

As "being German" in southeastern Europe was a complicated and ambivalent matter that required actors to make an effort to both perform and explain it, Volkskunde as a cultural practice was able to contribute to the ongoing process of "doing German." This could result in unreflective navel-gazing that reproduced and superimposed the theories at the ideological and geographical centre of the discipline onto other contexts. But when Volkskunde was performed as an ethnographic practice with reference to a heterogeneous life-world, it could also produce a respectable stock of knowledge on cultural diversity. Consequently, the ethnographic exploration of southeastern Europe repeatedly contributed to the reorientation of the discipline.

The "public work" of searching for the Germanness in Christmas was one of the central questions that contributed to the development of Volkskunde as a discipline. This search wasn't necessarily an ideologically blindfolded or scientifically futile one, but just as Volkskunde never did and never could fully explain Christmas, one can't explain or understand the history of Volkskunde only by reference to its Christmas research. Nevertheless, with its highly performative customs, its pervading atmosphere, and the wide range of religious and profane, private and public activities attached to it, Christmas provided an important field of research to explore cultural practices that transcended social, political, and symbolic divides and borders.

By exploring the triangular interrelations and interconnections of the discipline of German Volkskunde as a translocal practice of knowledge, the particular cultural complex of Christmas, and the specific historical and spatial relationship between German culture and southeastern Europe, one emerges with a more complex and perhaps more telling picture of all three of them.

Notes

Research for this article was funded by the German Federal Government Commissioner for Culture and the Media (BKM), supported by the German parliament.

1   Starting at the beginning of the 1970s, the discipline of *Volkskunde* underwent programmatic self-critique, reorientation, and renaming. This process was initiated by the Tübingen Ludwig-Uhland-Institut für Volkskunde, which replaced its technical name with "*Institut für Empirische Kulturwissenschaft*" in 1971. Other institutes in German-speaking countries renamed themselves as *Europäische Ethnologie*, *Kulturanthropologie*, or *Populäre Kulturen*. See Dow, *German Volkskunde: A Decade of Theoretical Confrontation, Debate and Reorientation (1967–1977)*, and Korff, "Change of Name."

2   Perry, *Christmas in Germany.*

3   Wietschorke, "Historische Ethnografie: Möglichkeiten und Grenzen eines Konzepts."

4   Bausinger, "Das Weihnachtsfest der Volkskunde. Zwischen Mythos und Alltag."

5   Meyer, *Das Weihnachtsfest*; Weiser-Aall, *Jul, Weihnachtsgeschenke und Weihnachtsbaum*; Schneeweis, *Die Weihnachtsbräuche der Serbokroaten*; Spamer, *Weihnachten in alter und neuer Zeit*; Huth, *Der Lichterbaum*; Strobel, *Bauernbrauch im Jahreslauf.*

6   Meier, ed., *Deutsche Volkskunde*; Spamer, *Die Deutsche Volkskunde*; Beitl, *Deutsche Volkskunde*; Spieß, *Deutsche Volkskunde als Erschließerin deutscher Kultur*; Naumann, *Grundzüge der deutschen Volkskunde*; Wrede, *Deutsche Volkskunde auf germanischer Grundlage*; Peßler, *Handbuch der Deutschen Volkskunde.*

7   Jacobeit et al., eds., *Völkische Wissenschaft.*

8   Spamer, *Weihnachten in alter und neuer Zeit*, 92–3.

9 See Mackensen, *Volkskunde der deutschen Frühzeit*, 37.

10 See Strobel, *Bauernbrauch im Jahreslauf.*

11 The way in which a radicalized reading turned this contact zone into a battlefield on which the Germanic primitive was bound to throw off its imposed Christianity is still visible in the pencil underlining, corrections, and comments in the copy of Spamer's Christmas book in the Tübingen Volkskunde library.

12 Spamer, *Weihnachten in alter und neuer Zeit*, 27.

13 Wolff, *Inventing Eastern Europe*; Kaser et al., eds., *Europa und die Grenzen im Kopf.* For Volkskunde's engagement in this discourse see Johler, "Eine 'Ost/West'-Ethnographie. Volkskundliche Perspektiven auf Europa."

14 Spamer, *Weihnachten in alter und neuer Zeit*, 48.

15 Ibid., 94. My translation.

16 Boette, *Religiöse Volkskunde*, 131.

17 Strobel, *Bauernbrauch im Jahreslauf.*

18 Spamer, *Weihnachten in alter und neuer Zeit*, 94. My translation.

19 Hoffmann-Krayer, ed., *Volkskundliche*; Hoffmann-Krayer and Bächtold-Stäubli, eds., *Handwörterbuch des Deutschen Aberglaubens*; Zender, *Atlas der deutschen Volkskunde.*

20 The bibliography was started in 1917 and became international and trilingual when it was restarted after World War II.

21 While the maps themselves only covered Germany's interwar borders and Austria, the additionally published text volumes included the German-speaking populations of eastern and southeastern Europe. The organization Atlas had corresponding bureaus in places such as Sibiu/Hermannstadt (Romania), Timișoara/Temeschwar (Romania), and Budapest (Hungary). See Schmoll, *Die Vermessung der Kultur.*

22 Kuhn, *Deutsche Sprachinsel-Forschung.*

23 Penny and Rinke, "Germans Abroad."

24 Weber-Kellermann, *Weihnachten der Volksgemeinschaft.*

25 Composed by Hans Baumann (1914–1988), who had also written "Es zittern die morschen Knochen," one of the most popular National Socialist marching songs.

26 Weber-Kellermann, *Weihnachten der Volksgemeinschaft*, 5.

27 Ibid., 5–6.

28 Weber-Kellermann, "Erinnern und Vergessen: Selbstbiographie und Zeitgeschichte," 21–2.

29 Gajek, "Nationalsozialistische Weihnacht: Die Ideologisierung eines Familienfestes durch Volkskundler."

30 Even before the war, symbolic Christmas greetings were used as a
    propaganda tool to bind German communities abroad to inner German
    politics. Every year in December the *Volksbund der Deutschen im Ausland*
    sent out vast numbers of blue candles to Germans all over the world.

31 Huth, *Der Lichterbaum*.

32 Haberlandt, "Weihnachtsbaum - Paradiesbaum – Lichterbaum."

33 "In gewachsenem lebensfrischem Tannengrün von Lichtern erstrahlenden
    deutschen Weihnachtsbaum"; see ibid., 162.

34 Baskar, "Small National Ethnologies"; Johler, "European Ethnology."

35 Kamberovič et al., eds., *"Nijemci" u Bosni i Hercegovini*.

36 Kállay, *Die Lage der Mohammedaner in Bosnien*, 6.

37 Donia, "The Proximate Colony."

38 Kállay, *Die Lage der Mohammedaner in Bosnien*, 5.

39 Sparks, "The Good Woman of Sarajevo."

40 Effendi Ugljen, "Etnographische Varia."

41 Kállay, *Die Lage der Mohammedaner in Bosnien*.

42 Ziegler, "Weihnachten bei den Sachsen in Siebenbürgen." Quotes are also
    taken from a largely corresponding article Ziegler published the same year
    in a journal of the German Association for Rural, Social and Regional
    Welfare (Deutscher Verein für Ländliche Wohlfahrts- und Heimatpflege).
    See Ziegler, "Weihnachtsfeier im siebenbürgischen Sachsendorf." Ziegler
    also published articles on Carnival, Easter, and Pentecost in Transylvania.

43 Ziegler, "Weihnachtsfeier im siebenbürgischen Sachsendorf."

44 "*markige Germanengestalten*," in Ziegler, "Weihnachten bei den Sachsen in
    Siebenbürgen," 722.

45 Judson, "When Is a Diaspora Not a Diaspora?"

46 Sigerus, *Siebenbürgisch-sächsische Burgen und Kirchenkastelle*; Schmutzler,
    Altorientalische Teppiche in Siebenbürgen.

47 Schullerus, *Siebenbürgisch-sächsische Volkskunde im Umriß*.

48 Herfurth, "Unsere Weihnachtsbräuche." Herfurth also recommended
    certain collections in a footnote: "Very much recommended:
    H. Pfannenschmidt: Dur und Moll. Deutsche Haus- und Festlieder
    (Mit Klavierbegleitung). Berlin, Martin Warneck 1906." My translation.

49 Schwarz, *Die Herkunft der Siebenbürger und Zipser Sachsen*. The result was
    that heterogeneous groups from the middle Rhine and the middle Moselle
    regions formed the bulk of these first medieval settlers.

50 Schullerus, "Weihnachtsbräuche der Siebenbürger Sachsen."

51 Sigerus, "Weihnachtsbäume in Siebenbürgen."

52 Wittstock, "Volkstümliches der Siebenbürger Sachsen," 58.

53 Schneeweis, *Die Weihnachtsbräuche der Serbokroaten.*

54 Ibid., 157.

55 Schneeweis, "Über karpathorussische Weihnachtsbräuche," 98;
Schneeweis, *Die Weihnachtsbräuche der Serbokroaten,* iv.

56 The term 'German-speaking' is used here to evade inadequate 'ethnic' or
'national' categorizations and follows the contemporary official practice
of counting the different minorities inside the Hungarian national state
according to individually expressed preferences in private language use.
Of course academics with a 'German' background in that time period
and region were at least bi- if not multi-lingual, just as most of their
'Hungarian' colleagues mastered German as the scientific *lingua franca* of
the time.

57 Seewann, "Die ungarischen Schwaben: Einige zentrale Aspekte ihrer
Geschichte"; Seewann, *Geschichte der Deutschen in Ungarn.*

58 Mollay, ed., *Schwartz Elemér emlékére.*

59 Schwartz, "Die deutschungarische Volkskundeforschung," 26.

60 'Religious' here meant proper, church-sanctioned religious practice; this
separated Schwartz and his disciples from proponents of a more '*völkisch*'
understanding of *Volksglaube* (folk belief) as a survival of original primitive
Germanic religion, that lived on in contemporary superstition and folk
custom. One such contemporary counterpart to Schwartz and his disciples
was Basch, "Deutscher Volksglaube in Ungarn."

61 On the importance of this carol in German-speaking contexts, see also the
chapter by Juliane Brauer in this volume.

62 Damó, *Stille Nacht, heilige Nacht in der Protestanischen Kirche Ungarns;*
Gagybátori Eckerdt, *Német karácsonyi dallamok a magyar templomban;*
Kiss, *Stille Nacht, heilige Nacht.* Dissertations or other academic
qualifications had to be written and published in Hungarian.

63 Komjathi-Schwartz, *Europa singt "Stille Nacht, heilige Nacht..."*

64 Despite his efforts, he could not find any Turkish, Roma ('Gypsy'), or
Serbian versions; see ibid., 7.

65 Ibid., 37–8.

66 Weber-Kellermann, "Der Luzienstuhl im deutschen und ungarischen
Volksglauben."

67 Hermann, "Der volkstümliche Kalenderglaube in Ungarn"; Richter,
"Der heilige Abend in Deutsch-Proben," 119; Basch, "Deutscher
Volksglaube in Ungarn," 38; Kretzenbacher, "Lucienbraut, Santa Lucia
und die dunkle Luz."

68 Weber-Kellermann, "Der Luzienstuhl im deutschen und ungarischen Volksglauben."
69 Weber-Kellermann, "Zur Frage der interethnischen Beziehungen in der Sprachinselvolkskunde."
70 Weber-Kellermann, *Das Weihnachtsfest.*

Bibliography

Basch, Franz. "Deutscher Volksglaube in Ungarn." *Neue Heimatblätter* 1, no. 1 (1935): 23–41.

Baskar, Bojan. "Small National Ethnologies and Supranational Empires: The Case of the Habsburg Monarchy." In *Everyday Culture in Europe: Approaches and Methodologies*, edited by Nic Craith Máiread, Kockel Ulrich, and Reinhard Johler, 65–80. Burlington, VT: Ashgate, 2008.

Bausinger, Hermann. "Das Weihnachtsfest der Volkskunde. Zwischen Mythos und Alltag." In *Politische Weihnacht in Antike und Moderne. Zur ideologischen Durchdringung des Festes der Feste*, edited by Richard Faber and Esther Gajek, 169–82. Würzburg, Germany: Königshausen u. Neumann, 1997.

Beitl, Richard. *Deutsche Volkskunde: Von Siedlung, Haus und Ackerflur, von Glaube und Volk, von Sage, Wort und Lied des deutschen Volkes.* Berlin: Deutsche Buch-Gemeinschaft, 1933.

Boette, Werner. *Religiöse Volkskunde.* Leipzig, Germany: Reclam, 1925.

Damó, Piroska. *Stille Nacht, heilige Nacht in der Protestanischen Kirche Ungarns.* Budapest: Typoskript, 1941.

Donia, Robert. "The Proximate Colony: Bosnia-Herzegovina under Austro-Hungarian Rule." In *Wechselwirkungen: The Political, Social, and Cultural Impact of the Austro-Hungarian Occupation of Bosnia-Herzegovina (1878–1918)*, edited by Clemens Ruthner, Ursula Reber, Raymond Detrez, and Diana Reynolds Cordileone, 67–82. New York: Peter Lang, 2015.

Dow, James. *German Volkskunde: A Decade of Theoretical Confrontation, Debate and Reorientation (1967–1977).* Bloomington, IN: Indiana University Press, 1986.

Effendi Ugljen, Sadik. "Etnographische Varia." *Wissenschaftliche Mitteilungen aus Bosnien und der Herzegowina* 3 (1895): 552–7.

Gagybátori Eckerdt, László. *Német karácsonyi dallamok a magyar templomban (Deutsche Weihnachtsmelodien beim ungarischen Gottesdienst).* Budapest: Egyetemi Német Nyelvészeti és Néprajzi Int., 1943.

Gajek, Esther. "Nationalsozialistische Weihnacht: Die Ideologisierung eines Familienfestes durch Volkskundler." In *Politische Weihnacht in Antike und Moderne: Zur ideologischen Durchdringung des Festes der Feste*, edited by Richard Faber and Esther Gajek, 183–216. Würzburg, Germany: Königshausen & Neumann, 1997.

Haberlandt, Arthur. "Weihnachtsbaum - Paradiesbaum – Lichterbaum." *Oberdeutsche Zeitschrift für Volkskunde* 10 (1936): 158–62.

Herfurth, Franz. "Unsere Weihnachtsbräuche." *Sächsischer Hausfreund* 72 (1911): 109–27.

Hermann, Anton. "Der volkstümliche Kalenderglaube in Ungarn." *Zeitschrift des Vereins für Volkskunde* 4 (1894): 304–23, 392–411.

Hoffmann-Krayer, Eduard, ed. *Volkskundliche Bibliographie für die Jahre 1917 bis 1937/38*. Strasbourg, Germany: Karl J. Trübner, 1919.

Hoffmann-Krayer, Eduard, and Hanns Bächtold-Stäubli, eds. *Handwörterbuch des Deutschen Aberglaubens*, vol. 10. Berlin: Walter de Gruyter, 1927.

Huth, Otto. *Der Lichterbaum: Germanischer Mythos und deutscher Volksbrauch*. Berlin-Lichterfelde, Germany: Widukind-Verlag, 1938.

Jacobeit, Wolfgang, Hannjost Lixfeld, and Olaf Bockhorn, eds. *Völkische Wissenschaft: Gestalten und Tendenzen der deutschen und österreichischen Volkskunde in der ersten Hälfte des 20. Jahrhunderts*. Cologne, Germany: Böhlau Verlag, 1994.

Johler, Reinhard. "Eine 'Ost/West'-Ethnographie. Volkskundliche Perspektiven auf Europa." *Schweizerisches Archiv für Volkskunde* 96 (2000): 187–200.

– "European Ethnology: A Chance for an Anthropological 'East-West'-Dialogue?" In *Breaking the Wall: Representing Anthropology and Anthropological Representations in Post-Communist Eastern Europe*, edited by Viroel Anastasoaie, Csilla Könczei, Enikö Magyari-Vincze, and Ovidiu Pecican, 275–86. Cluj, Romania: EFES, 2003.

Judson, Pieter. "When Is a Diaspora Not a Diaspora? Rethinking Nation-Centered Narratives about Germans in Habsburg East Central Europe." In *The Heimat Abroad: The Boundaries of Germanness*, edited by Krista O'Donnell, Renate Bridenthal, and Nancy Reagin, 219–47. Ann Arbor, MI: University of Michigan Press, 2005.

Kállay, Benjamin von. *Die Lage der Mohammedaner in Bosnien*. Charleston, France: Bibliolife, 2009.

Kamberovič, Husnija, Carl Bethke, and Jasna Turkalj, eds. *"Nijemci" u Bosni i Hercegovini i nova istraživanja i perspektive - "Die Deutschen" in Bosnien und Herzegowina und Kroatien Neue Forschungen und Perspektiven*. Sarajevo: Institut za Istoriju Sarajevo, 2015.

Kaser, Karl, Dagmar Gramshammer-Hohl, and Robert Pichler, eds. *Europa und die Grenzen im Kopf.* Wieser Enzyklopädie des europäischen Ostens 11. Klagenfurt, Austria: Wieser, 2003.

Kiss, Edith. *Stille Nacht, heilige Nacht... Egy karácsonyi ének magyar változatai [Die ungarischen Varianten des Weihnachtslieder].* Budapest: Dunántúl Pécsi Egyetemi Könyvkiadó, 1947.

Komjathi-Schwartz, Elmar. *Europa singt "Stille Nacht, heilige Nacht..."* Schlern-Schriften 230. Innsbruck, Austria: Wagner, 1963.

Korff, Gottfried. "Change of Name as a Change of Paradigm: The Renaming of Folklore Studies Departments at German Universities as an Attempt at 'Denationalisation.'" In *Folklore: Critical Concepts in Literary and Cultural Studies,* edited by Alan Dundes, 238–60. London: Routledge, 2005.

Kretzenbacher, Leopold. "Lucienbraut, Santa Lucia und die dunkle Luz." In *Zur Interethnik: Donauschwaben, Siebenbürger Sachsen und ihre Nachbarn,* edited by Ingeborg Weber-Kellermann, 226–9. Frankfurt am Main, Germany: Suhrkamp, 1978.

Kuhn, Walter. *Deutsche Sprachinsel-Forschung: Geschichte, Aufgaben, Verfahren,* vol. 2. Ostdeutsche Forschungen. Plauen, Germany: Wolff, 1934.

Mackensen, Lutz. *Volkskunde der deutschen Frühzeit.* Leipzig, Germany: Quelle & Meyer, 1937.

Meier, John, ed. *Deutsche Volkskunde.* Berlin: Walter de Gruyter, 1926.

Meyer, Arnold. *Das Weihnachtsfest: Seine Entstehung und Entwicklung.* Tübingen, Germany: J.C.B. Mohr, 1913.

Mollay, Károly, ed. *Schwartz Elemér emlékére. Elmar von Schwartz zum Gedächtnis.* Budapest: Kiada a Magyar Néprazi Társaság, 1991.

Naumann, Hans. *Grundzüge der deutschen Volkskunde.* Leipzig, Germany: Quelle & Meyer, 1929.

Penny, Glenn H., and Stefan Rinke. "Germans Abroad: Respatializing Historical Narrative." *Geschichte und Gesellschaft* 41, no. 2 (2015): 173–96.

Perry, Joe. *Christmas in Germany: A Cultural History.* Chapel Hill, NC: University of North Carolina Press, 2010.

Peßler, Wilhelm. *Handbuch der Deutschen Volkskunde.* Potsdam, Germany: Athenaion, 1934.

Richter, Stephan. "Der heilige Abend in Deutsch-Proben." *Karpatenland* 6 (1933): 111–21.

Schmoll, Friedemann. *Die Vermessung der Kultur: Der "Atlas der deutschen Volkskunde" und die Deutsche Forschungsgemeinschaft 1928–1980,* vol. 5. Studien zur Geschichte der Deutschen Forschungsgemeinschaft. Stuttgart, Germany: Franz Steiner Verlag, 2009.

Schmutzler, Emil. *Altorientalische Teppiche in Siebenbürgen.* Leipzig, Germany: Hiersemann, 1933.

Schneeweis, Edmund. *Die Weihnachtsbräuche der Serbokroaten.* Wiener Zeitschrift für Volkskunde / Ergänzungsband 15. Vienna: Verlag des Vereines für Volkskunde, 1925.

– "Über karpathorussische Weihnachtsbräuche." *Karpatenland* 8 (1935): 97–112.

Schullerus, Adolf. *Siebenbürgisch-sächsische Volkskunde im Umriß.* Wiesbaden, Germany: Quelle & Meyer, 1926.

Schullerus, Pauline. "Weihnachtsbräuche der Siebenbürger Sachsen." In *Sachs', halte Wacht!* 1 (1927): 34–5.

Schwartz, Elmar von. "Die deutschungarische Volkskundeforschung." In *Deutsche Volkskunde im ausserdeutschen Osten: Vier Vorträge,* edited by Gottlieb Brandsch, Elmar von Schwartz, Gustav Jungbauer, and Viktor Schirmunski, 26–40. Berlin: Walter de Gruyter, 1930.

Schwarz, Ernst. *Die Herkunft der Siebenbürger und Zipser Sachsen: Siebenbürger und Zipser Sachsen, Ostmitteldeutsche, Rheinländer im Spiegel der Mundarten.* Munich, Germany: Verlag des Südostdeutschen Kulturwerks, 1957.

Seewann, Gerhard. *Geschichte der Deutschen in Ungarn: Band 2, 1860 bis 2006.* Marburg, Germany: Herder Institut, 2012.

– "Die ungarischen Schwaben: Einige zentrale Aspekte ihrer Geschichte." *Jahrbuch für Europäische Ethnologie* 8 (2013): 173–98.

Sigerus, Emil. *Siebenbürgisch-sächsische Burgen und Kirchenkastelle.* Hermannstadt/Sibiu, Romania: J. Drotleff, 1900.

– "Weihnachtsbäume in Siebenbürgen." *Korrespondenzblatt des Vereins für Siebenbürgische Landeskunde* 38, no. 3 (1915): 37–8.

Spamer, Adolf. *Die Deutsche Volkskunde,* vol. 2. Berlin, 1934.

– *Weihnachten in alter und neuer Zeit.* Volksart und Brauch. Jena, Germany: Diederichs, 1937.

Sparks, Mary. "The Good Woman of Sarajevo." *History Today* 63, no. 12 (2013): 1–9.

Spieß, Karl von. *Deutsche Volkskunde als Erschließerin deutscher Kultur.* Berlin: Stubenrauch, 1934.

Strobel, Hans. *Bauernbrauch im Jahreslauf.* Leipzig, Germany: Koehler & Amelang, 1936.

Weber-Kellermann, Ingeborg. *Weihnachten der Volksgemeinschaft.* Berlin: Verlag Grenze and Ausland, 1944.

– "Der Luzienstuhl im deutschen und ungarischen Volksglauben." *Hessische*

Blätter für Volkskunde 49/50 (1958): 295–316.

– "Zur Frage der interethnischen Beziehungen in der Sprachinselvolkskunde." *Zeitschrift für Österreichische Volkskunde* 62 (1959): 19–47.

– *Das Weihnachtsfest: Eine Kultur- und Sozialgeschichte der Weihnachtszeit.* Munich, Germany: Bucher C.J., 1987.

– "Erinnern und Vergessen: Selbstbiographie und Zeitgeschichte." In *Ingeborg Weber Kellermann: Erinnern und Vergessen. Autobiographisches und weitere Materialien*, edited by Siegfried Becker and Andreas Bimmer, 15–32. Marburg, Germany: Jonas Verlag, 1998.

Weiser-Aall, Lily. *Jul, Weihnachtsgeschenke und Weihnachtsbaum: eine volkskundliche Untersuchung ihrer Geschichte.* Stuttgart, Germany: Perthes, 1923.

Wietschorke, Jens. "Historische Ethnografie: Möglichkeiten und Grenzen eines Konzepts." *Zeitschrift für Volkskunde* 106 (2010): 197–224.

Wittstock, Oscar. "Volkstümliches der Siebenbürger Sachsen." In *Beiträge zur Siedlungs- und Volkskunde der Siebenbürger Sachsen*, edited by Alfred Kirchhoff, Band 9:57–125. Forschungen zur Deutchen Landes- und Volkskunde. Stuttgart, Germany: Engelhorn, 1895.

Wolff, Larry. *Inventing Eastern Europe: The Map of Civilization on the Mind of the Enlightment.* Stanford, CA: Stanford University Press, 1994.

Wrede, Adam. *Deutsche Volkskunde auf germanischer Grundlage.* Berlin: A.W. Zickfeldt, 1936.

Zender, Matthias. *Atlas der deutschen Volkskunde: Neue Folge.* Marburg, Germany: N.G. Elwert Verlag, 1958.

Ziegler, Regine. "Weihnachten bei den Sachsen in Siebenbürgen." *Wandern und Reisen* 1 (1903): 720–2.

– "Weihnachtsfeier im siebenbürgischen Sachsendorf." *Das Land* 12 (1903): 92–3.

6

"The First 'White' Xmas": Settler Multiculturalism, Nisga'a Hospitality, and Ceremonial Sovereignty on the Pacific Northwest Coast

Pamela E. Klassen

Introduction

In this chapter, I consider Christmas festivities as a revealing lens on the practices of hospitality and hostility that shaped relationships between Indigenous peoples and settlers on the Pacific Northwest Coast. In Canada, settler colonial legitimacy – the sense that undergirds Canadians' view that they have settled and inhabited their land as part of a lawful nation-state – has long depended on multicultural celebrations and rituals that perform and enact diversity as the heart of community. At the same time, Indigenous people have engaged with Christian and Canadian holidays and ceremonies as one venue for challenging the supposed naturalness of Canada. Since the earliest days of engaging with representatives of the Crown and of Canada, Indigenous people have blended oratory, regalia, and rituals such as pipe-smoking and feasting as acts of ceremonial sovereignty both strategic and hospitable.[1] They have continued to perform their sovereignty as nations by way of some of the same celebrations designed to efface that sovereignty, such as Royal Visits, "heritage" days, and anniversaries of Canadian Confederation.[2]

Christmas celebrations may also be put to public work in the performance of ceremonial sovereignty. In Canada, Christmas has often been a quasi-Christian venue for the display of settler multicultural diversity, as a time to renew family and cultural traditions of home decoration, cuisine, and social gatherings. On the Northwest Coast, the long tradition of Indigenous adaptations of Christmas rituals to traditions of winter feasting shows that Christmas is a site of ritual, commensality, and memory also put to use by Indigenous peoples.[3] In this chapter, I focus on a particular case of a 1913 "backwoods Christmas" gathering in what came to be called northwestern British Columbia, which brought together a peculiar mix of settler multiculturalism and Indigenous ceremonial sovereignty. Gathering together in the Nass River valley, the long-time Nisga'a inhabitants, a missionary family hailing from England, and recently arrived settlers who came from across Canada and Europe enacted and embedded their claims to the land.

In December 1913, this group of people gathered on land that the Nisga'a considered to be their unceded territory and that the settlers considered, some rather tentatively, to be their new homes. Having lived there since the 1880s, Church of England missionary James McCullagh knew that he was on Nisga'a land. He had watched the decades-old Nisga'a protest against colonial settlement and knew well the frequent Nisga'a petitions to kings, queens, and officials of land commissions to recognize their territorial rights. When he titled his account of the 1913 Christmas gathering as the "first 'White' Xmas" in the Nass Valley, McCullagh boldly racialized the snowy holiday in a way that both obscured and underscored these years of Nisga'a resistance. Recording the events of the Christmas festivities in a "Souvenir Booklet" printed on his proof press (a small tool for producing a pre-publication draft), he claimed the land as white space through a Christian holiday celebration practised by settlers and Nisga'a alike.[4]

McCullagh's first "White" Christmas is an example of what historian Jean O'Brien has called "firsting and lasting," a process by which settlers declared their pioneering "firsts" as a way to erase Indigenous jurisdiction over the land.[5] Marking places that settlers touched down, such as when naming the "First Methodist Church" in a town or the "first white man" to build a homestead, firsting declares that white presence on the land is the seed of progress and innovation. Often paired with firsting, "lasting" seals a narrative of progressive whiteness, by declaring the disappearance or extinction of Indigenous people as the "last" of their kind. Both firsting and lasting have remained pervasive tools of what Aileen Moreton-Robinson has called the "white possessive," meaning the sense, engrained in colonial narratives and laws of entitlement, that colonial occupation of Indigenous territory is justified by whiteness itself.[6]

Firsting and lasting are also key placeholders for colonial public memory, announcing the newness of Euro-American settlement with sites of memory that erase or ignore much deeper pasts. Though the Souvenir Booklet was likely never widely distributed and may have never made it past the proofs stage of the publication process, it remains a complicated site of memory for the ways that it included voices of the Nisga'a participants, such as Chief Andrew Mercer. Participating in the performance of Christmas through song, speech, and feasting, the Nisga'a challenged the white possessive even as they welcomed the settlers to celebrate the holiday in their Council Hall.

Before sketching the path of my argument, I offer two caveats about how this chapter fits into a book focused on multiculturalism and public memory. "Multiculturalism" was not a term in use in early-twentieth-century Canada, and it had yet to be embedded in Canadian law. The skits and dances of the 1913 Christmas gathering, however, presaged multiculturalism's underlying ideology of celebrating bonds forged across cultural and ethnic difference while warily acknowledging or unwittingly revealing the persisting inequity and colonial dominance that such difference entailed.[7] The public memory enacted during this Nass Valley Christmas also needs to be qualified, as most of the settlers had no memories whatsoever of the land on which they lived. Only a few years earlier, in 1907, had the "city" of Prince Rupert – a muddy collection of shacks, boardwalks, and hastily built wood-frame buildings – been founded, with the hope that its future status as a railroad terminus would make it into a leading port city providing access to Asian markets.

The settlers arriving in the Nass Valley in 1913 were there because they hoped that their fortunes would be tied to the growth of the city, which would soon be linked with the rest of the country by the Grand Trunk Pacific Railway, completed in 1914. Following the colonial infrastructure of railroads and telegraph wires, the Nass Valley settlers hoped they would be the farmers who helped to feed the cities of the empire. In contrast to these settler narratives of the city of the future, the Nisga'a told a story rooted in having lived in the Nass River Valley "from time immemorial." They embedded their public memory and their dreams for the future in the land and waters of their territory. The main livelihood of the Nisga'a came from the food they caught in the Nass River, which flows west to join the Pacific Ocean near Prince Rupert, just south of what is now called Alaska.

Missionaries first arrived in the region in the 1850s. When James McCullagh arrived on the Nass River in 1883 some Nisga'a slowly grew to welcome him and to join – and build – the church and mission house, while others remained strongly opposed to his arrival.[8] By the early twentieth century, McCullagh and his fellow Anglican missionaries were encouraging settlers from eastern Canada, Great Britain, and Europe to move to the Nass Valley. The Nisga'a, for their part, openly opposed "Whitemen" settling their lands, arguing that they had never surrendered their land to the government, and had never agreed to the concept of "reserves."[9]

The 1913 Christmas festivities in the Nass Valley are an example of the plasticity of Christmas in the hands of its participants. The Souvenir Booklet printed by McCullagh under the auspices of what he called the "Nass Valley Agricultural Association" gives a detailed account of three days of Christmas festivities based in the Council Hall of the Nisga'a, at Aiyansh. As a document of religion and public memory, the Souvenir Booklet is a fascinating materialization of Christmas performances, which McCullagh hoped could achieve many "moral and social" goals in the midst of cultural and religious difference. While the Souvenir Booklet perpetuates racialized stereotypes and multicultural classifications that grouped people within templates of national or religious characteristics and behaviours, it also preserves strong Nisga'a critiques of white settlement on their land. As a form of public memory embedded in a ritualized, seasonal narrative of a young woman who gave birth to a baby, Christmas provided a supple story for all the participants in the Nass River celebrations and allowed for Nisga'a offers of hospitality and claims of sovereignty in the face of settler arrival.

Tacking back and forth between stories and speeches in the Souvenir Booklet and a longer history of Christmases past among the Nisga'a, I trace how the first "White" Xmas exemplifies the "coordinates of Christmas" spelled out in our introduction: 1) the multicultural awkwardness of Christmas as a supposedly universal but specifically Christian act of public memory that seeks to liturgically remind people of the theologies of incarnation and redemption, by which God forgives human sins through the birth of Jesus; 2) the hope that Christmas festivities promote harmony and help to overcome cultural differences through shared food, song, and gift-giving shaped by the seasonal habitus of Christmas; and 3) the usefulness of Christmas for the performance of public memory in a way that facilitates larger claims about nations and conflicts between them, and that shapes the meaning of the past and the future.

Christmas, Christianity, and the Potlatch

Christmas had long troubled missionaries and colonial officials up and down the Northwest Coast. After the arrival of missionaries to their territories, many Indigenous peoples adapted Christmas, the Christian version of wintertime feasts and gift-giving, to their own traditions of seasonal feasting, which missionaries and colonial officials came to know as the potlatch. For many Northwest Coast Indigenous nations, the feasting system was a form of public witness of political authority, territorial claims, and kinship ties, as well as an opportunity for economic redistribution.[10] Large gatherings in which hosts gave gifts to their guests to thank them for witnessing storytelling and speeches that marked public memory, political legitimacy, and spiritual obligation, feasts were demonized by missionaries, and eventually outlawed by the colonial government.[11] The long history of anxiety on the part of missionaries and colonial officials about Christmas as a screen for "heathen" ritual informs James McCullagh's loquacious enthusiasm for the first "White" Xmas of 1913.

Since the mid-nineteenth century, missionaries along the Northwest Coast had received year-round assistance from the colonial government in their attempts to convert Indigenous peoples. The Dominion of Canada, founded in 1867, expanded to include British Columbia as a province in 1871. Unlike most territory to the east, in British Columbia the vast majority of Indigenous peoples, including the Nisga'a, did not enter into treaties with the Crown, in part because the provincial government thought treaties to be superfluous, contending that they could simply claim the land as theirs without such negotiation.[12] Despite Northwest Coast nations' continued insistence on their sovereignty, in 1876 the Dominion government promulgated the Indian Act, a set of colonial laws that designated a diversity of Indigenous peoples as "Indians" and as wards of the state. And then in 1884, Canadian lawmakers, at the insistence of many missionaries, amended the Indian Act to outlaw the potlatch:

> Every Indian or other person who engages in or assists in celebrating the Indian festival known as the Potlatch or in the Indian dance known as the Tamanawas is guilty of a misdemeanor, and shall be

liable to imprisonment for the term of not more than six nor less than two months in any gaol or other place of confinement; and any Indian or other person who encourages, either directly or indirectly an Indian or Indians to get up such a festival or dance, or to celebrate the same, or who shall assist in the celebration of same is guilty of a like offense, and shall be liable to the same punishment.[13]

. In 1895, a further amendment replaced the term "potlatch" with the more generic language of "an Indian festival, dance, or other ceremony of which the giving away or paying or giving back of money, goods, or articles of any sort forms a part." Both versions of the law sought to outlaw the feasting system as a political and spiritual practice.[14]

While some Indigenous Christians supported the anti-Potlatch law, the feasting system persisted among coastal Indigenous nations as the socially attuned exchange of goods to remember and acknowledge ancestors, to claim clan names and territories, and to redistribute resources.[15] To avoid the threat of jail or fines, Indigenous people often held them in parallel with Christmas celebrations. In 1916, Elizabeth Soal, Anglican missionary in the Gitxsan territory of Hazelton, BC, just east of Aiyansh, lamented the tenacity of the potlatch: "Should a person of importance die, say in spring or summer, a small feast is held at the time, but at the following Christmas season, the great time for feasting, the next-of-kin, if he wishes to be well thought of, will impoverish himself and tribe by purchasing great stores of biscuits, candies, apples, sugar, blankets, and money, and then ostentatiously distribute same to all invited guests."[16] Indigenous organizers made strategic use of Christian symbols and rituals to continue their own practices of sovereignty through ceremony.

In their arguments against the potlatch ban, Indigenous leaders also used Christmas as a lever. As historian Tina Loo has phrased it, Indigenous people in British Columbia were adept at cultural comparison: "They also argued that the potlatch was the same as Christmas; both were social and spiritual ceremonies that linked the present with the past and marked that link with gift-giving. So why was one illegal and the other not?"[17] Along the Northwest Coast, Kwakwakawakw, Ts'msyen, Nisga'a, and other Indigenous feast participants demonstrated a willingness to engage with religious difference in both a participatory and a comparative way in order to achieve their own ceremonial sovereignty.

Spiritual Whiteness on the Nass River

James McCullagh had his own memories of winter feasting in both Christian and Nisga'a ritual styles. He had long tried to drive the Nisga'a feasting system out of the valley, and had been joined by some Nisga'a Christians in the effort.[18] Nevertheless, the feasting system continued as a vital part of Nisga'a communal political life that undergirded the Indian Land Movement.[19] The Nisga'a knew that their ongoing territorial conflict with provincial and federal governments would only intensify with the imminent completion of the Grand Trunk Pacific Railway and the waves of white settlers that would follow. The Church of England missionaries in the region also knew that the railroad, as the conduit of colonial settlement, would bring about a shift from what they called "Indian work," focused on converting Indigenous people to Christianity, to "White work," directed at settlers.[20] The newly arrived settlers, a few of whom had met serious resistance from the Nisga'a when they first tried to stake claims to the land, had been drawn to the rocky northern land in the hopes of establishing farms or businesses that would benefit from the railroad. In the midst of all this contestation over land and place, the missionary seized on the Christmas celebration as a moment of hospitality by which he hoped to train the settlers into Christian community, in part with the help of the Nisga'a as hosts.

The Nass River Christmas of 1913 was multicultural on two interrelated planes: first, it celebrated the ethnic diversity of the settlers, and second, it translated such diversity into a unified whiteness in distinction to the Nisga'a, who were collapsed into the larger category of "Indians." On the first plane of ethnic diversity, the souvenir booklet propagated ethnic stereotypes of Germans, Irish, and English, emphasizing how they could all get along when brought together through the presumed harmony of Christmas. On the second plane of marking whiteness, Christmas bound together the linguistically and nationally diverse settlers in a kind of spiritual whiteness which sought to legitimate their settlement on Indigenous land as a form of progress. Similar to other early-twentieth-century attempts to shore up the "spiritual fitness" of settlers through drawing on Indigenous or pseudo-Indigenous lore, the souvenir booklet depicted rituals, skits, and songs that were meant to bind the settlers as multicultural – and white – through performances of both Christian liturgies and "Indian" heritage.[21] But at the same time, setting the booklet's account of Nisga'a

hospitality within a longer history of Nisga'a claims to sovereignty under-
cuts any harmonious narratives of settlement implied by such performances
of whiteness.

In 1907, when settler Joshua Priestley first claimed land next to the
Nisga'a reserve, his arrival and his claim of ownership were quickly disputed
by Nisga'a chiefs in letters and in face-to-face meetings – including one
letter they delivered to him on Christmas Eve of that year.[22] Recounting
these communications to the provincial police, Priestley said: "They claimed
40 miles up and 40 miles down the river and (I believe) 40 miles each
side, in which they were resolved to have NO white people as settlers, and,
if these demands were not granted, they, and all Indians in the Province,
and perhaps the Dominion, aided by Japanese – from whom they were
descended – would rise and slay all the white people till not one of them
was left, and they intimated that if I further proceeded with my land I
should be one of the first to go."[23] The racial turn in Priestley's testimony
brought in yet another racialized group in the region, the Japanese, who
worked in large numbers in canneries at the mouth of the Nass.

Chief Andrew Mercer's testimony in 1908 to the same group of police
did not take on the threatening tone of Priestley's claim, though he did
acknowledge the Nisga'a desire to have no white settlers in the region:

> [W]e have discarded the map of the reserves drawn up by the Indian
> Department. We want more land, and we do not see that there is
> much room around us for settlers in view of what we require for
> ourselves. We have not the slightest wish to oppose in any way the
> laws and government of the country if we are satisfied with regard to
> the land. We know that there would be no prosperity for us in the
> land apart from the Whiteman, and we are willing for them to have
> what they want after our claims are considered and satisfied.[24]

As his speech at the 1913 Christmas celebrations will demonstrate, Andrew
Mercer's mix of candour and accommodation in this claim to Nisga'a
sovereignty matched the tone of his other letters and speeches.[25]

The conflict was still brewing in the spring of 1910, when Nisga'a printers
used the mission printing press to print an "Indian Protest against white
settlers coming into the Aiyansh Valley, Nass River, British Columbia."[26] In
September of 1910, a fire in the mission house destroyed the printing press.
Not long after, a Nisga'a revival of feasting and traditional rituals began,

perhaps due to an illness that had swept through the community.[27] The feasting continued as Christmas approached, leading James McCullagh to despair that he was losing his "flock" of Nisga'a converts. In a characteristic blend of sacrificial self-pity and sarcastic pique, McCullagh questioned the viability of his mission: "I doubted whether it was right of me to keep on burdening the Christian Church with a mission among a people who, after twenty-seven years' work among them, could rise not higher than the glorification of a dead man and desire no other pleasure than that to be extracted from a keg of fermented berry juice."[28] Referring not to Christian traditions of glorifying the crucified Jesus or of drinking Communion wine, McCullagh was instead alluding to Nisga'a attendance at a settlement feast for a man in their community who had died.

McCullagh's letters detail how he spent many nights in the week before the Christmas of 1910 in a lonely vigil in the church, praying for the return of his congregants. When they did come back in ones and twos, he forced these Nisga'a men and women to repent to him privately in confession, and then publicly in the church. He then went even further in his punishments by denying Christmas altogether. He refused to let the choir decorate the church as usual: "Instead, I had the purple hangings put out, and the Church was in mourning on Christmas Day."[29] In Aiyansh that year, Christmas looked like Lent, as the church was adorned not for the birth of the Christ Child but for the death of Jesus the man.

By 1912, Nisga'a men and women had rebuilt the burnt mission house, this time making it large enough to accommodate many visitors. By 1913, the settlers who would end up celebrating the first "White" Christmas had arrived at their makeshift farms. To gather for the winter festivities, many settlers travelled by horse and sleigh to Aiyansh, staying over in the mission house and in other homes – including those of the Nisga'a.[30] On Christmas Day, 1913, fifty-one newly arrived white settlers and a peace officer gathered for Christmas festivities in the Council Hall, generously provided by the Nisga'a for the occasion. The next day, the Nisga'a joined them for Boxing Day festivities. Over the course of three days, the settlers and the Nisga'a exchanged stories, dances, food, and Christmas cheer; the two groups both claimed the land as their own through speeches, performances, and gestures of Christmas hospitality. The Nisga'a came from their villages of Aiyansh and Gitlaxdamiks. The settlers had arrived in the valley from a variety of places, including Quebec, Denmark, Ireland, England, Newfoundland (which was then separate from Canada), and Germany. As we will see, the

Christmas celebrations were neither strictly white, nor entirely organized by the missionary. But in the aftermath of the celebrations, McCullagh put his mark on the proceedings by printing the "First 'White' Xmas."

McCullagh had a wider tradition of missionary Christmas texts from which to find inspiration. In 1905, one of McCullagh's colleagues and friends, the Reverend Henry Elliott Fox, wrote a preface for a collection of stories, written by missionaries for an audience of British children, entitled *Christmas Time in Many a Clime*. Fox was the honorary secretary of the Church Missionary Society of the Church of England, making him one of McCullagh's bosses and frequent correspondents, as well as the leader of a vast network of CMS missionaries across the world. Each chapter in *Christmas Time in Many a Clime* tells a similar story: children and adults who had not converted to Christianity were bereft of faith and love, and Christmas offered the perfect celebration to remedy their loss. Especially lamenting the children who were without the Christian God, the missionaries tell how carols and liturgies of Christmas, along with gifts of dolls, toys, and oranges given out beside the Christmas tree, were powerful vehicles to attract such children to the Christian gospel, particularly if they had already attended missionary schools.[31]

McCullagh's colleague in the Canadian mission field, E.W. Greenshield, a CMS missionary among the Inuit of the Arctic island of Blacklead, in what is now Nunavut, phrased the aftermath of Christmas this way in his contribution to Fox's volume:

The children go back once more to the cold snow houses, and to their hard, rough life, but they carry something with them to brighten their lives, and as from time to time they look upon this prize, whatever it may be, they will think of that happy "Kooveanaktovik," [time of rejoicing] and they will remember the friends and "fellow-believers" in Britain who love them and care for them, and help to give them, as it were, a little sunlight in their long dark winter. Above all, it helps them to remember Christmas, and with Christmas the great and joyous fact which we all love to remember at that blessed season that "Jesus Christ came into the world to save sinners."[32]

With chapters describing missionary Christmases in Kashmir, Uganda, Japan, and even Bethlehem, the site of the Nativity itself, the book had textbook precision in its messaging: Jesus is the light of the world, and by Christmas feasts and trinkets children will know and remember him.

McCullagh's Christmas publication was also written with remembrance at the fore, but had a more adult and more local focus. Notably, it also included both settler expectations and Nisga'a enactment of ceremonial sovereignty. The text begins with a map of the settlers' plots of land and documentation of their formation of the "Nass Valley Agricultural Association" on 26 December 1913, with Rev. James B. McCullagh elected as honorary president. But it also includes a speech from Nisga'a leader Andrew Mercer, who reflected not only on the pleasures of Christmas, but also on the injustices of colonialism. Throughout, the booklet demonstrates considerable anxieties on the part of the missionary about just how to inculcate the proper seasonal habitus in order to evoke what he considered to be the real living meaning of Christmas in those gathered around the tree. For example, McCullagh had hoped to give a speech after Christmas dinner explicating the true importance of Christmas but lamented that he was "crowded out" (or perhaps shut up) by other events. So he wrote this meaning out in a letter after the fact to the settlers, insisting on the importance of shared "actions": "A community is very rightly termed a 'body'; therefore the action of inherent members must be determined by, and limited to the good of the whole body."[33] With the heavy editorial and printing hand of the missionary in play, the souvenir booklet is a portrait at once unreliable and revealing of how Christmas brought out whiteness and what McCullagh called "Indian"-ness on the Nass River.

The souvenir booklet focused on 25 and 26 December, giving detailed accounts of the days' events. McCullagh prefaced the booklet with his hope that social "cohesion" would flow in the wake of the Christmas celebrations:

> We have been happy in each other, very much so, and we feel that this the first 'White' Xmas in the valley has struck such a note of harmonious cohesion among ourselves, and also of considerate friendship towards the Indians, as to make it a worthy model for other Christmases yet to come ... This booklet is compiled and printed at Aiyansh by the Missionary as a souvenir of this happy time. Instead of forgetting, we shall live it all over again, and remember with gladness the backwoods Christmas we had together in Nineteen-Hundred-and-Thirteen.[34]

In McCullagh's account, Christmas Day began with Holy Communion in the Church at 8:00 am, followed by breakfast, and an 11:30 a.m. Divine Service, which was delivered "in English, because of White parishioners present, and the Sermon was especially preached for them."[35] While Nisga'a men, women, and children attended and some sang in the choir at the church services, it seems that they were not present at Christmas dinner. Mr Currie, the telegraph operator, organized the dinner of cured roast beef and plum pudding, with decorations provided by the unnamed wife of a German settler, Mr Herrman.

The dinner commenced at 2:30, with local foods that would be the envy of adherents of today's local food movement: "Over thirty guests, great and small, sat down to dinner … nearly everything on the table was locally raised and home-cured. This made our dinner interesting as well as appetising; for, as Simple-Lifers, we want to know all the possibilities of local production and home curing."[36] At 7:00 p.m., gifts were distributed around the Christmas tree, much to the delight of children and adults, and "[t]hus we brought our 'White' Xmas to a close."[37] Consistently framing the whiteness of Christmas with his pun-driven quotation marks, McCullagh accentuated his delight at the newness of white settlers on the Nass while, perhaps unknowingly, signalling the anxiety and discomfort that this settlement brought to all participants.

McCullagh, an inveterate poet, also included in the booklet an "echo" of his Christmas Day sermon, which he had transformed into rhyming couplets. The sermon was a curious mix of biblical references and popularized theories of evolution and genetics – a "religio-racial" blend of spiritual whiteness.[38] McCullagh counselled settlers to start their new lives by forgetting their past mistakes: "God says He will not remember: He forgives; you may forget." At the same time, he warned them to get things right this time, turning to evolutionary metaphors for the "divine life" to insist that the seeds of their new settlement were of utmost importance for the future:

But we know that in the Future lies the Promise of our race,
And the spirit that is in man there will find a spirit place.
These are days of life-selection: what we choose and what we sow
We shall reap, and gather into our own spirits as we grow.
If we live and labour only for this body and this life,

We assimilate corruption, gendered of this mundane strife.
But if we, with heart discerning, woo the Spirit's breath divine,
We shall gather *life eternal*, and attain to God's *design*.[39]

The future-promised race to which McCullagh referred was a multicultural blend of spiritual whiteness. He noted cultural differences by portraying the settlers via stereotypes of their national origins, but ultimately McCullagh saw the Danish, German, Québécois, Irish, and English settlers all as white men. To the eyes of the Nisga'a, they looked white as well, as shown by their 1910 protest flyer, printed on the mission press, "against white settlers coming in to the Aiyansh valley."[40]

Judging from McCullagh's reflections in the souvenir book, the new settlers were not convinced they needed a missionary, and nor were they imbued with the proper colonial spirit. He cautioned that harmonious life in the Nass Valley depended on a Christian-inflected Golden Rule and law-abiding neighbourliness: "Every man is a social unit: and every social unit has a specific moral quality of its own: and this moral quality is determined by the spirit of intention. There are two spirits of intention, – 1: That which dominates the mind by selfish considerations; and, 2., that which rules according to right."[41] McCullagh's fears that the settlers did not understand the moral and spiritual requirements of colonial settlement underlay much of his prose, including his worries about the mixing of settlers and Nisga'a at the Boxing Day banquet and the dance over the next two evenings, at which alcohol was likely served.

The Boxing Day Banquet and Concert was also held in the Council Hall, and the Nisga'a joined in for this night of feasting and entertainment, which this time was not interlaced with Christian ritual. The program featured lively performances, including several appearances by the Aiyansh Brass Band, a regionally well-known group of Nisga'a men, and a dance troupe of "Indian maidens" performing a "Berry Song" written in the Nisga'a language by McCullagh. Melita Priestley, McCullagh's then twenty-eight-year-old daughter from his first marriage, and wife of Arthur Priestley, the son of Joshua, the first settler to the region, performed another song, "There's Nobody Just Like You." Melita also appeared on the very first pages of McCullagh's souvenir booklet in his dedication: "For Melita, 1st copy."

Other settler contributions took the form of both stereotype and racialized appropriation. Herbert Snowden sang "An Irish Song" entitled

"How Paddy Crossed the Ocean," while S.C. Gordon sang "The Shannon Over." Gordon also delivered a song in blackface, entitled "The Whistling Coon," which was itself a performance of whiteness via racist imitations of blackness, performances that were common to other missionary Christmas celebrations.[42] Comic routines and an "Essay on Man, illustrated by L. Jesson," a Danish settler, rounded out the entertainment portion of the program.[43] Tacking between clichés and symbols of cultural specificity and human universality, the settlers' contributions to the evening's program performed the construction of whiteness through multicultural diversity in the Nass Valley.

Two Christmas Speeches

These accounts of the settler-hosted Christmas Day and Boxing Day banquets are strongly dominated by the voice of McCullagh, who liberally sprinkled his own poetic and epigrammatic reflections throughout the text. The only other voices that have any prominence in the booklet come via two speeches, the first by Andrew Mercer, the Nisga'a chief who was a leading Anglican and land claims activist in Aiyansh. The second is from a German settler, "Dr. Justus Schmidel, M.D." Mercer's speech is noted as translated by McCullagh, the second is not.

Justus Schmidel was a German immigrant who had travelled throughout North America, recording his adventures in *Ein Harte Schule: Erlebnisse in Amerika* (*A Difficult School: Experiences in America*). Schmidel's "Epilogue" to the Christmas booklet highly praised the work of McCullagh, and noted the struggles and failings of the settlers:

Far away from father, mother, relatives and friends, a sad Christmas it would have been indeed without the kindness shown to us. Mr. McCullagh, in your Christmas sermon you told us to forget our mistakes, to forget the past ... But however much we may forget the past we can never forget the kindness you have so often shown us during the past. A short time ago there were quite a few amongst us rough pioneers in this equally rough country, who were, as the saying goes, "poor friends of the Church," and equally poor friends of the representative of the Church – the preacher! This feeling of antipathy you have overcome, Mr. McCullagh; and this is a great victory you have won – a credit to you. What words could not do, your unselfish kind deeds have accomplished. You have most of us brought nearer [to] Church.[44]

Insisting that "[t]he body will perish, but the memory of our good deeds is immortal!" Schmidel assured McCullagh that his name would always be remembered by "Whites and Indians," and would live on forever in the "pioneer history" of the Nass River.

It is difficult to know if Schmidel's echoing of McCullagh's themes of forgetting the past and joining the Church were entirely his own flourishes, or were added by McCullagh at the printing press. In his own book from the 1920s, Schmidel wrote in German, so a comparison between the texts is not possible. His colourful turns of phrase – "the lonely denizens of the forest"; the "valley of 'Eternal Bloom'" – are certainly reminiscent of McCullagh's prose. Clearly, however, using Christmas to remember the goodness in others and to celebrate community was key to his rhetorical aims.

Delivering a resolution on behalf of all the settlers, Schmidel closed his speech by offering "our heartfelt thanks for the pleasure, kindness and hospitality shown to us on this our first Christmas in Aiyansh. The numerous little considerations shown, the way in which you have put yourselves out in order that we might have an enjoyable Yuletide, makes us feel very happy." Overflowing with gratitude for McCullagh, and with barely a mention of the Nisga'a, Schmidel wished that in the future, McCullagh and his family would "live to enjoy many more Christmases among us."

Schmidel's wish for his own future Christmases in the valley was not to come true. Whether or not he actually delivered the words as written in the booklet, Schmidel did not live much longer in the Nass Valley. Despite being a doctor and serving as vice-president of the Agricultural Association, and despite being a white man, Schmidel was deported as an enemy alien in the middle of the First World War. He maintained a fondness for Canadian immigration, however, even working in Germany as a booster for the Canadian National Railway company during the 1920s, and leading trips to Canada to find prairie settlements for German farmers.[45] The war cleared out most of the settlers from the Nass Valley, as most of the men did not return after serving overseas, and eventually, even Arthur and Melita Priestley left Aiyansh in 1930.[46]

Andrew Mercer's speech at the Boxing Day banquet also expressed a vision for what would lead to harmonious relations along the Nass. According to McCullagh, Mercer spoke in the Nisga'a language, and began with an historic appeal to affection and friendship:

> For the first time in the history of the Indian people the Whiteman has admitted us within the bounds of a common social friendship with himself. At this season of the year it is very appropriate to emphasise this feature of a common friendship. The pleasure afforded us by the presence here to-night of all the White settlers is very real. We are glad to see them, and to sit down to table with them. We have no hostile feelings against the Settlers, and we believe they have none against us. It is true there are questions at issue between ourselves and the government of the country: we have grievances, and our feelings in regard to them are more or less bitter; but we have learned to distinguish between things that differ, and the Settler is not responsible for any injustice done to us. Therefore we desire that a very real friendship should subsist between ourselves and the Settlers now resident in the valley. This cannot be done on a one-sided disposition of heart: it must be mutual to exist at all.

Mercer's references to Nisga'a grievances about land are well documented in other writings by him, many of which are in English.[47]

By contrast to his strongly worded resistance to colonial rule during the conflict with Joshua Priestley in 1907–08, however, Mercer's Christmas speech in 1913 included an unusually denigrating approach to his own heritage. Perhaps influenced by McCullagh's Christmas sermon, or perhaps brought in line with the sermon by McCullagh's translation and editing, Mercer's speech acknowledged that it was difficult for the Nisga'a to accommodate the future-focused approach of the settler culture. On the one hand, he insisted that whites needed to understand differences between themselves and the Indians, while on the other he accused his people of backwardness in a critical voice that did not match many of his other writings:

> We have to fight behind as well as before – to contend with the magnetic influence of the past as well as strive after the attraction

of the future. To have a future before us is a new thing to the
Indian mind. To hold on to the past, to repeat it, to live looking
back at it, is an attitude of mind opposed to the new life to which
you have introduced us. Our thoughts and view-points are not the
same as yours. When we try to think and act like you the Indian
mind trips us up, and makes us appear ridiculous. One day we are
down, the next day we are up; and we mean to keep on getting up
again and again until finally we shall stay up … And if we do not
all at once produce exactly the same pattern of civilization that you
produce you will give us credit at least for doing our best amid the
entanglements that beset our path.[48]

For Mercer, the white focus on newness – on firsting and lasting, on innovation at all costs – was a view that privileged a particularly colonial version
of civilization. The approach to public memory embedded in Nisga'a
traditions, such as feasting, was both valued and troubled by Mercer.
     First framing a Nisga'a orientation to the magnetic past by a progress
narrative of spiritual whiteness, Mercer then sounded a stronger note more
in keeping with some of his other extant writing:

We are not aliens! We are here in our own native land – the land
where our fathers were born, lived and died. If you, in developing
the country, deprive us of our original means of subsistence, so
that of necessity we are compelled to sell our labour as you do for a
living, it is manifestly unfair that any discrimination should be made
against us. On the contrary, there is by right a certain consideration
due to us from you, which should be given without asking.[49]

Concluding with a gesture of hospitality, Mercer invited all the settlers
to a Nisga'a hosted dinner and concert the next night, promising that
"[s]everal items on the programme will deal with the Indian life of the past
which we trust you will find interesting."[50] McCullagh recorded Mercer's
invitation, but did not include an account in the booklet of the Nisga'a-run
celebrations. Andrew Mercer's frank assessment of the potential dangers
of the settlers' effects on Nisga'a territory and economy made clear the
dangers of progress narratives, including those celebrating the gifts of
Christmas. His simultaneous hospitality embodied a Nisga'a version of
futurity rooted in ancestral pasts.[51]

Conclusions

As a dogged effort that sought to create a newly shared seasonal habitus in a context of colonial settlement, James McCullagh's souvenir booklet offers an excellent example of the ways that Christmas can incite and create distinctions of spiritual and material, home and away, and cultural specificity and universal humanity. Christmas may also incite distinctions of race. Read against the longer history of Christmases past on the Nass River, McCullagh's souvenir booklet was a determined attempt to re-make and re-member a Christmas that grounded white settlers as a Christian community on Nisga'a land. The ceremonial sovereignty articulated by Andrew Mercer in his speech and hospitality, however, was equally determined.

A printing press in the Nass Valley also preserved a later account of Christmas, this time directly from the perspective of the Nisga'a. A 1922 issue of *Trail Cruiser*, a Nisga'a edited and printed publication, suggests that Christmas became a very Nisga'a affair in the year after McCullagh's death in 1921. The Gitlaxdamiks City Council sent out greetings thanking people for the pleasant Christmas Holiday and the friendship shown to them and hoping that all would "meet and enjoy many Happy New Years together in the future."[52] The Nisga'a Church Council, chaired by Andrew Mercer, established prizes for the best decorated houses, which was a "hot contest." A New Year's Eve Watch Night service was added, with Nisga'a layman Charles Morven leading the services, and young men lighting fireworks during a procession throughout the town. The next day, 2 January, the chiefs gave speeches and prizes were awarded. Though these speeches are not extant, based on the organizational efforts of the Indian Land Committee in the Nass Valley at that time, messages of ceremonial sovereignty were undoubtedly prominent.

Attuned to the power and plasticity of Christmas as a time of seasonal memory and communal relationship-building materialized through gift-giving, the Nisga'a of the Nass River approached Christmas as a time to look back at the past, while voicing their expectations of the future. For the Nisga'a, that would eventually mean a new treaty negotiated with Canada in 2000, after decades of attempts by the government, especially through the Indian Act and residential schools, to dismantle Nisga'a governance and ceremony, and to destroy Nisga'a family ties and language fluency. Christmas remains an important and popular celebration in the Nass

Valley, as well as among Nisga'a who have moved to urban centres. As Sherry Small, a Nisga'a woman living in Vancouver, told a reporter in 2006, Nisga'a people continue to bring together Nisga'a and Christian stories in the celebration: "We gleaned the edicts of life from Txeemsin: the sharing, the caring. Like Jesus, he taught that the more you help others the more nourished you become. Christmas allows us to stop in our tracks and remember their teachings."[53] As a time of remembrance often documented through print and pictures, Christmas is a particularly rich site for reflecting on how the intersection of religion and public memory is profoundly and unpredictably shaped by discourses of race and nationalism. In the early-twentieth-century Nass Valley, Christmas offered an opportunity for an Anglican missionary to mark the spiritual whiteness of multicultural settlers at the same time that a Nisga'a leader proclaimed the ceremonial sovereignty of his nation.

Notes

1 For a broader discussion of how Indigenous sovereignty takes forms both symbolic and ritualized, see Borrows, *Canada's Indigenous Constitution* and "Wampum at Niagara."

2 Radforth, "Performance, Politics, and Representation"; Mason, "The Banff Indian Days Tourism Festivals"; Bohaker and Iacovetta, "Making Aboriginal People 'Immigrants Too'"; Furniss, *The Burden of History*; Rutherdale and Miller, "'It's Our Country.'"

3 Loo, "Dan Cranmer's Potlatch."

4 McCullagh, "Souvenir Booklet."

5 O'Brien, *Firsting and Lasting*.

6 Moreton-Robinson, *The White Possessive*.

7 See, for example, Wise and Velayutham, eds., *Everyday Multiculturalism*; Chazan et al., eds., *Home and Native Land*.

8 May, "Feasting on the AAM of Heaven."

9 Carter, "Alfred Carter to F. Hussey, Nisga'a/Priestley Land Dispute." I discuss McCullagh's role in the "Indian Land Question" in more detail in Klassen, *The Story of Radio Mind*.

10 Halpin and Seguin Anderson, *Potlatch at Gitsegukla*; Bracken, *The Potlatch Papers*.

11 Cole and Chaikin, *An Iron Hand upon the People*; Loo, "Dan Cranmer's Potlatch."

12 Harris, *Making Native Space.*

13 Harring, *White Man's Law,* 268.

14 Ibid., 268.

15 Cole and Chaikin, *An Iron Hand upon the People*; Halpin and Seguin Anderson, *Potlatch at Gitsegukla*; Robertson, *Standing up with Ga'axsta'las.*

16 Soal, "Hazelton."

17 Loo, "Dan Cranmer's Potlatch," 159.

18 May, "Feasting on the AAM of Heaven."

19 Cole and Chaikin, *An Iron Hand upon the People,* 46–7.

20 I discuss this shift to "White work" in more detail in Klassen, *The Story of Radio Mind.*

21 See, for example, McCallum, "'The Fundamental Things,'" and Deloria, *Playing Indian.*

22 From Carter: "In regard to Mr. Priestly, I am sorry to say that he is a man devoid of tack, and one that does not understand the ways of Indians, or the conditions of the country, and to all appearances, in my opinion, never will." Carter, "Alfred Carter to F. Hussey, Nisga'a/Priestley Land Dispute."

23 Priestley, "J. Priestly to Hussey Re against Land Claims."

24 Andrew Mercer, quoted in Carter, "Alfred Carter to F. Hussey, Nisga'a/Priestley Land Dispute."

25 On the complicated mix of Indigenous resistance to and use of colonial law, see Foster, "Letting Go the Bone."

26 Flyaway et al., "Indian Protest." I discuss this protest in more detail in Klassen, *The Story of Radio Mind.*

27 May, "Feasting on the AAM of Heaven."

28 Moeran, *McCullagh of Aiyansh,* 183.

29 Ibid., 185.

30 Eleanor McCullagh, quoted in Moeran, 193. Eleanor was James's second wife, and was the mother of two small children at the time of the Christmas festivities.

31 For further discussion of this text, see Knor, "Christmas in the Diaspora."

32 Fox, *Christmas Time in Many a Clime,* 32.

33 McCullagh, "Souvenir Booklet," 5.

34 Ibid., 3.

35 Ibid., 10.

36 Ibid., 10.

37 Ibid., 10.

38 Weisenfeld, *New World A-Coming.*

39 McCullagh, "Souvenir Booklet," 12. Italics in original.

40 Flyaway et al., "Indian Protest." Printed at Aiyansh. For more discussion of this pamphlet see Klassen, *The Story of Radio Mind.*

41 McCullagh, "Souvenir Booklet," 7. This is a section called "Blazing the trail." Later on, he repeated this view in poetic verse:
    "And if Man be part of Nature, What the aim of his desire.
    Is it not that he, being spirit, unto Spirit *must* aspire?
    It is then in spirit region Man must seek his destined goal..."

42 "The Whistling Coon" was a song popularized and recorded by African-American singer George Johnson, who was the first African-American recording artist. The song, with what would now be considered highly racist lyrics, was popular throughout North America and Britain, where it was often sung in blackface performances. Brooks and Spottswood, *Lost Sounds*; Pickering, "Eugene Stratton." See also Johnson, "'I'm Sorry Now We Were So Very Severe.'"

43 I am unsure if this is a popularized version of Alexander Pope's 18th-century poem, or something original to Jesson.

44 McCullagh, "Souvenir Booklet," 24.

45 Marchildon, *Immigration and Settlement, 1870–1939*, 419.

46 Priestly, "Arthur F. Priestly Interview."

47 For example, Andrew Mercer in Mercer, "Indians' View of Land Question."

48 McCullagh, "Souvenir Booklet," 16–17. Mercer's section is called "The Indian Speech."

49 Mercer in McCullagh, "Souvenir Booklet," 17.

50 McCullagh, "Souvenir Booklet," 17.

51 On Indigenous futurity, see Däwes and Hauke, *Native American Survivance*; Nixon, "Visual Cultures"; Recollet, "Gesturing Indigenous Futurities."

52 *Trail Cruiser*, January 1923.

53 Small, quoted in Todd, "Like Most Aboriginals, Nisga'a Fuse Christmas Traditions."

Bibliography

Bohaker, Heidi, and Franca Iacovetta. "Making Aboriginal People 'Immigrants Too': A Comparison of Citizenship Programs for Newcomers and Indigenous Peoples in Postwar Canada, 1940s–1960s." *Canadian Historical Review* 90, no. 3 (2009): 427–62.

Borrows, John. "Wampum at Niagara: The Royal Proclamation, Canadian Legal History, and Self-Government." In *Aboriginal and Treaty Rights in Canada: Essays on Law, Equality, and Respect for Difference*, edited by Michael Asch, 155–72. Vancouver, BC: University of British Columbia Press, 1997.

– *Canada's Indigenous Constitution*. Toronto: University of Toronto Press, 2010.

Bracken, Christopher. *The Potlatch Papers: A Colonial Case History*. Chicago, IL: University of Chicago Press, 1997.

Brooks, Tim, and Richard Keith Spottswood. *Lost Sounds: Blacks and the Birth of the Recording Industry, 1890–1919*. Champaign, IL: University of Illinois Press, 2004.

Carter, Alfred. "Alfred Carter to F. Hussey, Nisga'a/Priestley Land Dispute." 13 May 1908. GR 0429 Box 15 File 03 2119/08 B.C. Attorney General Correspondence inward, 1908. Royal British Columbia Museum and Archives.

Carter, Sarah. "'Daughters of British Blood' or 'Hordes of Men of Alien Race': The Homesteads-for-Women Campaign in Western Canada." *Great Plains Quarterly* 29, no. 3 (2009): 267–86.

Chazan, May, Lisa Helps, Anna Stanley, and Sonali Thakkar, eds. *Home and Native Land: Unsettling Multiculturalism in Canada*. Toronto: Between the Lines, 2011.

Cole, Douglas, and Ira Chaikin. *An Iron Hand upon the People: The Law against the Potlatch on the Northwest Coast*. Vancouver, BC: Douglas & McIntyre, 1990.

Däwes, Birgit, and Alexandra Hauke. *Native American Survivance, Memory, and Futurity: The Gerald Vizenor Continuum*. New York: Routledge, 2016.

Deloria, Philip Joseph. *Playing Indian*. New Haven, CT: Yale University Press, 1998.

Flyaway, J.K., J.R. Badweather, S.A. Zeedawit, A.M. Nahneigh, J. Nakmauz, Amos G. Neesgwaksaw, Samuel Weeshakes, and Johnny O'Yea. "Indian Protest Against White Settlers Coming in to the Aiyansh Valley, Naas River, British Columbia." 17 May 1910. Image GR-0429, 2561/10, courtesy of the Royal British Columbia Museum and Archives.

Foster, Hamar. "Letting Go the Bone: The Idea of Indian Title in British Columbia, 1849–1927." In *Essays in the History of Canadian Law*, edited by John McLaren, Hamar Foster, and David H. Flaherty, 28–86. Toronto: University of Toronto Press, 1995.

Fox, H.E. *Christmas Time in Many a Clime*. First edition. London: Church Missionary Society, 1905.

Furniss, Elizabeth. *The Burden of History: Colonialism and the Frontier Myth in a Rural Canadian Community*. Vancouver, BC: University of British Columbia Press, 1999.

Halpin, Marjorie, and Margaret Seguin Anderson. *Potlatch at Gitsegukla: William Beynon's 1945 Field Notebooks*. Vancouver, BC: University of British Columbia Press, 2011.

Harring, Sidney. *White Man's Law: Native People in Nineteenth-Century Canadian Jurisprudence*. Toronto: University of Toronto Press, 1998.

Harris, Cole. *Making Native Space: Colonialism, Resistance, and Reserves in British Columbia*. Vancouver, BC: University of British Columbia Press, 2002.

Johnson, Val Marie. "'I'm Sorry Now We Were So Very Severe': 1930s Colonizing Care Relations between White Anglican Women Staff and Inuvialuit, Inuinnait, and Iñupiat People in an 'Eskimo Residential School.'" Toronto, ON: Paper presented at the University College Senior Common Room, University of Toronto, October 2017.

Klassen, Pamela. *The Story of Radio Mind: A Missionary's Journey on Indigenous Land*. Chicago, IL: University of Chicago Press, 2018.

Knor, Sarah. "Christmas in the Diaspora: Dislocating Symbols in Kipling, Cary and Dabydeen." In *Symbolism 14: Special Focus – Symbols of Diaspora*, edited by Rüdiger Ahrens and Klaus Stierstorfer, 111–29. Berlin: Walter de Gruyter, 2015.

Loo, Tina. "Dan Cranmer's Potlatch: Law as Coercion, Symbol, and Rhetoric in British Columbia, 1884–1951." *Canadian Historical Review* 73, no. 2 (1992): 125–65.

Marchildon, Gregory. *Immigration and Settlement, 1870–1939*. Regina: University of Regina Press, 2009.

Mason, Courtney. "The Banff Indian Days Tourism Festivals." *Annals of Tourism Research* 53 (2015): 77–95.

May, Nicholas. "Feasting on the AAM of Heaven: The Christianization of the Nisga'a, 1860–1920." Toronto: PhD dissertation, University of Toronto, 2013.

McCallum, Mary Jane. "'The Fundamental Things': Camp Fire Girls and Authenticity, 1910–20." *Canadian Journal of History* 40, no. 1 (2005): 45–66.

McCullagh, James Benjamin. "Souvenir Booklet: Nass Valley Agricultural Association." Aiyansh Press, 1913. NWP 970.7 M133. Royal British Columbia Museum and Archives.

Mercer, Andrew. "Indians' View of Land Question." *The Evening Empire*, 11 January 1911.

Moeran, Joseph William Wright. *McCullagh of Aiyansh*. London: Marshall Brothers, 1923.

Moreton-Robinson, Aileen. *The White Possessive*. Minneapolis: University of Minnesota Press, 2015.

Nixon, Lindsay. "Visual Cultures of Indigenous Futurisms." *GUTS: Canadian Feminist Magazine* (20 May 2016). http://gutsmagazine.ca/visual-cultures/.

O'Brien, Jean. *Firsting and Lasting: Writing Indians out of Existence in New England*. Minneapolis: University of Minnesota Press, 2010.

Pickering, Michael. "Eugene Stratton and Early Ragtime in Britain." *Black Music Research Journal* 20, no. 2 (2000): 151–80.

Priestley, Joshua. "J. Priestly to Hussey Re against Land Claims." 13 May 1908. GR 0429 Box 15 File 03 2119/08 B.C. Attorney General Correspondence inward, 1908. Royal British Columbia Museum and Archives.

Priestly, Arthur F. "Arthur F. Priestly Interview." Interview by Imbert Orchard. Audio recording, 2 February 1966. T1229:0001-2. Royal British Columbia Museum and Archives.

Radforth, Ian. "Performance, Politics, and Representation: Aboriginal People and the 1860 Royal Tour of Canada." *The Canadian Historical Review* 84, no. 1 (2003): 1–32.

Recollet, Karyn. "Gesturing Indigenous Futurities through the Remix." *Dance Research Journal* 48, no. 1 (2016): 91–105.

Robertson, Leslie. *Standing Up with Ga'axsta'las: Jane Constance Cook and the Politics of Memory, Church, and Custom*. Vancouver, BC: University of British Columbia Press, 2012.

Rutherdale, Myra, and Jim Miller. "'It's Our Country': First Nations' Participation in the Indian Pavilion at Expo 67." *Journal of the Canadian Historical Association* 17, no. 2 (2006): 148–73.

Soal, [Elizabeth]. "Hazelton." *North British Columbia News*, July 1916, 5th edition.

Todd, Douglas. "Like Most Aboriginals, Nisga'a Fuse Christmas Traditions." *Vancouver Sun*, 21 December 2006. http://vancouversun.com/news/staff-blogs/like-most-aboriginals-nisgaa-fuse-christmas-traditions.

Trail Cruiser, January 1923. Archives of the Provincial Synod of British Columbia and Yukon.

Weisenfeld, Judith. *New World A-Coming: Black Religion and Racial Identity during the Great Migration*. New York: NYU Press, 2017.

Wise, Amanda, and Selvaraj Velayutham, eds. *Everyday Multiculturalism*. New York: Palgrave Macmillan, 2009.

7

Oy Tannenbaum, Oy Tannenbaum! The Role of a Christmas Tree in a Jewish Museum

Yaniv Feller

Introduction

The ubiquitous Christmas scene of a decorated fir tree in the living room surrounded by gifts is so iconic that it has travelled to climates without evergreens and homes without Christians. Christmas is a fest of scholarly interest precisely because of its many iconic and ironic juxtapositions, including that of "Jesus and Father Christmas," who "are opposed in ways to make a structuralist's mouth water."[1] There are also the broader themes of secularization and religion, private and public, local traditions and globalization, family and society, intimacy and alienation in the modern world, and also, as many of the chapters in this volume show, the break-down of these dichotomies.[2] My interest is in what the Christmas tree, not just the icon or idea of the Christmas tree, but a very specific plastic tree placed at a strategic point in the Jewish Museum Berlin (hereafter JMB), can tell us about the construction of history and the work of the museum.

Christmas tree, Jewish Museum, Berlin. These do not seem to fit together. Why would a Christmas tree be in a museum at all, and a Jewish museum in particular? Why Berlin? What is the Christmas tree doing there? An examination of this tree, I contend, offers insights into the larger narrative told by the JMB. Its placement in the museum, however, already signifies the collapse of the very story it was meant to illustrate. What at first appears as a story of German-Jewish acculturation and assimilation emerges upon a closer look as the breakdown of this linear narrative. Furthermore, when this historiography and its breakdown are understood, the Christmas tree at the JMB invites reflection about the museum as a space in which public memory is produced through objects, things, and storytelling.

The Museum

The Jewish Museum Berlin is a national institution in Germany and one of the most important Jewish museums in Europe. The story the JMB tells to the German public and to hundreds of thousands of tourists a year is therefore a prism to contemporary German society. First, there is the historical aspect. The JMB is important because the history of Jews in Germany is considered central for the understanding not only of Jewish life in Europe, but also of the Holocaust. Although the JMB is not a Holocaust museum, the Holocaust plays an important role there and is the reason many visitors come to this museum.

Second, the Jewish Museum is in Berlin, reunified Germany's capital city. It signifies and is an agent in Germany's coming to terms with its past. In other words, it is as much about "the Germans" and their needs for a usable past as it is about "the Jews." This process is also evident in the museum's institutional organization. Unlike Jewish museums in North America, it is not a community museum but a federal institution that receives its budget from the German government.[3] Michael Steinberg notes that the JMB's role in German society results in uneasy tension that ends up re-ascribing national separateness. The museum, he writes, places "the history of the Jews on a field separate from the history of other Germans. Here the museological quandary duplicates the historiographical one: giving the Jews 'their' history adopts a functionally nationalist paradigm for the organization of historical patterns and groups which may do violence to the subject positions of precisely those whom the gesture seeks to redress."[4]

Finally, there is the building itself. Designed by Daniel Libeskind, originally as an addition to the Berlin-Museum, it is a monumental and intentionally disorientating structure, alluding to German-Jewish historical experience itself. Putting aside the debate about Libeskind's architectural choices, the building is considered an architectonic milestone and attracts many visitors who might not have been interested in Jewish history otherwise.[5] In order to get to the permanent exhibition, one needs to go through an underground passage, where the visitor is confronted with three axes: the axis of exile, the axis of the Holocaust, and the axis of continuity. It is after visiting the other axes, with their disorientating effect and focus on traumatic experience, that the visitor usually goes up the stairs to the "axis of continuity," which is the permanent exhibition space proper. It is there that she will later find the Christmas tree. But before moving to the tree of the permanent exhibition, it is worth taking a short detour into a territory of controversy – the idea of Chrismukkah.

Excursus: An (Un)happy Chrismukkah

The notion of "Chrismukkah," a compound holiday combining Christmas and Hanukkah, became a popular term in North America at least since its appearance in an episode of the successful television show *The O.C.* in 2003. In the German context it was not as common. The Jewish Museum Berlin's exhibition *Weihnukka: Geschichten von Weihnachten und Chanukka* (October 2005–January 2006) (*Chrismukkah: Stories of Christmas and Hanukkah*) caused considerable uproar. Maybe it was the provocative title that led Stephan Kramer, the general secretary of the *Zentralrat der Juden in Deutschland* at the time, to claim that the exhibition does not present a picture of a living Judaism, but of one that is thoroughly assimilated. The Orthodox rabbi Yitshak Ehrenberg noted that one of the core messages of Hanukkah is that Jews should protect their cultural and religious tradition. This exhibition, he protested, goes against this central message. The exhibition, it was further argued, is a "feel good" for non-Jewish Germans, who can consume a lovely and easy-to-digest version of a mixed holiday, disregarding in the process both the tragic past and what is seen by some as an uncertain future. On the other hand, one can argue – as does Cilly Kugelmann, the program director at the JMB at the time – that the fact that the exhibition provoked an intra-Jewish discussion is yet another sign of its success.[6]

These critiques focused on the idea of a shared holiday, rather than the exhibition itself, in which the two holidays were mostly presented separately, with only one room dealing with their fusion in the North American context. Cary Nathenson argued nonetheless that the exhibition attempted to create a "universal" Jewish identity that is presumably free from time and space but is in fact Americanized. The exhibition, he complained, is a concession to the German non-Jewish public; it presents a harmonious picture of assimilation where none is to be found. "Ultimately," he writes, "the *Weihnukka* exhibition, and the Jewish Museum itself, can be read as shorthand for the desire for a global identity, an identity that supplants the traditional and conflict-laden conceptions of diaspora and its 'insider-outsider' dichotomy. It is a fantasy of universal appeal, potentially satisfying desires of Jews and non-Jews (as evidenced additionally by the claim in one journalist's report on the exhibit that some Turkish-German families also now have Christmas trees at home)."[7]

Nathenson's critique reflects the tone and message of critiques of the JMB more broadly, namely that it has a "preference for generalizing the Jews out of their own identity" instead of emphasizing their particularity, especially as it is exemplified in religious terms.[8] But Nathenson goes even further in his search for "authentic" Jewish life unperturbed by "syncretism." Some of his most snarky comments are reserved for Russian Jews emigrating to Germany, who "might not even be Jewish, according to the standards of the very same official German-Jewish community."[9] Such claims, however, see "identity" as a stable, perfect, and unchanging one-to-one fit without different and contesting aspects. Nathenson ignores the theoretical insights that warn us against this type of forced inscribing of identity and claims for authenticity. Instead, one could argue, a more productive route is to focus on the contesting, simultaneously present, and multifaceted definitions of the "I" and "we."[10]

The Bourgeois Tree

The Jewish Museum Berlin had a Christmas tree long before the *Weihnukka* exhibition. In fact, a Christmas tree was placed there from the opening of the permanent exhibition in 2001. Given the debate surrounding the Chrismukkah exhibition, it might come as a surprise that the Christmas tree in the permanent exhibition did not provoke the same kind of response. Although it is difficult to reason from absence, there are at least three plausible complementary explanations for this phenomenon. First, unlike the temporary exhibition, which had touched upon contemporary Jewish life and practice, the Christmas tree at the permanent exhibition is located as part of a historical exhibition; firmly rooted in the period 1850–1933, it can be categorized as "historical," as a relic of a phenomenon past, as opposed to being relevant for the present. Another possible reason is that Chrismukkah can be considered an art of "syncretism," an unholy mixture of things that should be kept apart. By contrast, the Christmas tree in the permanent exhibition is an unapologetic Christmas tree, and not a variation on the Hanukkah-bush. Finally, the fact that Chrismukkah is much more a North American phenomenon than a European one might have created anxiety not only of a Jewish-Christian syncretism but also of a German-American one, even though as mentioned this was hardly the focus of the 2005 exhibition.[11] In sum, unlike the Chrismukkah exhibition, the permanent exhibition's Christmas tree could be perceived as a historical object that does more than reflect contemporary anxieties.

The visitor enters the part of the exhibition containing the Christmas tree after having experienced the Jewish emancipation and Enlightenment, followed by a thematic presentation, somewhat disjointed from the chronological discussion, of the Jewish life cycle, from circumcision, marriage, and death to kosher food. It is after this section that the visitor reaches a segment dedicated to family life (*Familienleben*). The description of family life is done in several ways, including an impressive collection of portraits and family scenes (mostly from the late nineteenth and early twentieth centuries), family photos, and a section on and for children. There is a certain feeling of openness and calmness when approaching the Christmas tree.

That the tree and its surroundings should provide a welcoming feeling is a curatorial decision made evident by a text that describes this section as *Die gute Stube* (The Parlour). Unlike Libeskind's use of exposed concrete, the floor here has a warm wooden colour and decorative panels recalling family life. These further evoke a feeling of homeliness (*Heimlichkeit*) that is conveyed in this setting of a bourgeoisie living room.[12] The idea of a museal representation of a home setting has a long tradition. In the context of Jewish museums, this mode of presentation has been popularized following Isidor Kaufmann's "Sabbath Room" in the Jewish Museum in Vienna (1899). This room, remarkable in the context of Jewish museums at the time, was a three-dimensional experience of the home during Sabbath, with silver candlesticks, challahs, and everything else needed. It was not only a representation of a Jewish ceremony at home; it also conveyed the ideas of Sabbath and of home itself as a warm, stable, and harmonious place. The "Sabbath Room" addressed Jews and non-Jews alike, hoping to dispel false antisemitic perceptions that the latter might have regarding Jewish rituals.[13] This basic idea has been mimicked numerous times in other Jewish museums. A century after Kaufmann, the JMB still used a similar mode of presentation in the form of a Sabbath table as part of its life cycle segment. At the same time, by playing on this mode of homely setting and inserting the Christmas tree into the *gute Stube*, one could argue that

Figure 7.1   The Christmas tree at the Jewish Museum Berlin.

the result of the curation is a question about what homeliness meant for Jews in Germany in the nineteenth century.

Other objects in the *gute Stube* besides the Christmas tree include a glass cabinet containing various decorative items such as a porcelain candelabra, beautiful coffee silverware, a large oil portrait of the then high-society family Plesch, and another painting on the other wall. Across from the tree stands a concert grand piano. The place is inviting for a group to sit, quite a rarity in Libeskind's building. Near the tree there is a glass vitrine with Hanukkah menorahs.[14] The tree dominates the setting – as it would in a typical living room – for several reasons. First, it is more colourful than the other objects in the room. Second, it is not displayed inside a glass vitrine and is therefore more inviting. Finally, the tree functions as one large object as opposed to several small ones. In short, the tree overshadows, quite literally, the menorahs and other objects and captures the centre of attention.

The museum as a site of public memory places Christmas firmly within the domestic sphere. The Christmas tree stands in the family segment because it was considered a familial event for many German families around that time.[15] In fact, the emergence of the German-Jewish bourgeois family can be dated to about the same time as the emergence within broader German culture of the Christmas tree as a place of gathering and gift-giving.[16] The intersection between Jews and the Christmas tree occurs at this point, because the tree is a symbol of acculturation and the transformation of bourgeois society. In this process, it is important to note, Jews were not passive actors, entering into a fully formed society. Rather, they were active agents in the shaping of this modern society, both within the Jewish community, e.g. through the changing of religious customs, and outside of it, by entering certain professions that can be seen as catalysts of this type of society.[17] Just like in the bourgeois culture in general, so in Christmas: Jews were not only mimicking their neighbours; they might have been also actively propagating the Christmas tree. An early-nineteenth-century police report in Vienna notes that Fanny Arnstein, a Jewish *salonnière* originally from Berlin, had a big, decorated tree in her living room. This was done, writes the report, "according to a Berlin custom." This implies that the Christmas tree was not an integral part of the Viennese traditions of the time.[18] Thus, the first person to import this custom to Vienna might have been a Jew.

Figure 7.2   Schlemiel caricature hanging on the Christmas tree at the Jewish Museum Berlin.

The Christmas tree in the JMB is presented as part of the "Family Life" segment that deals with the construction of the family in the nineteenth century. Jewish families often celebrated Christmas in conjunction with Hanukkah, as a national holiday and not a religious one, according to the explanation attached to the Christmas tree in the Jewish Museum. The way the tree is located in the exhibition, however, suggests a broader context. The Christmas tree continues the story of the Enlightenment told earlier. It is a narrative, perhaps hidden but triumphal nonetheless, that leads from the German-Jewish philosopher Moses Mendelssohn to a happy family life and a merry Christmas, which is followed by Jewish choices in modern German society, Jewish religious reform, and then Jewish successes in financial, artistic, and scientific enterprises.[19]

Many of the visitors to the Jewish Museum Berlin take it for granted that the Christmas tree is placed in the domestic context. German guided school groups do not ask "Why is there a Christmas tree in a Jewish Museum?" but rather "Why is it here at this time of the year?" It makes no sense for some to have a Christmas tree in April or June, but the fact that it is placed in a Jewish museum poses no cognitive dissonance for them. Israeli and Jewish tourists, by contrast, are often puzzled by the presence of the tree. In both cases, the effect is one of alienation – the tree does not seem to belong: neither in a museum nor at most times of the year.

It is when we look at the tree more closely that the reading of the museum as conveying a unidirectional, triumphal history is disturbed. I want to highlight two items related to the tree: one of the decorations on the tree and the portrait beneath it. Alongside more traditional decorations, at least one catches the eye: it is from the magazine *Schlemiel*, which, in 1904, published a biting caricature titled "Darwinist."

It shows the transformation of a Hannukah menorah into a decorated Christmas tree. The caption reads: "How the Hanukkah-lights [menorah] of the goatskin merchant Cohn in Pinne developed into the Christ-tree of the councilor of commerce Conrad in Tiergartenstraße (Berlin W.)." The same effect is achieved by the curatorial text that accompanies the Christmas tree. Although the text explains the parallels between Christmas and Hanukkah and states that Jews celebrated Christmas "as a German rather than a religious festival," it also explains the *Schlemiel* caricature, thus drawing the visitor's attention to it in case it was missed. This Christmas tree's decoration incorporates an intra-Jewish debate about the need for celebrating Christmas.

Another object that immediately catches the visitor's attention is the Christmas present under this particular tree – a portrait of Theodor Herzl, widely regarded as the founding father of Zionism. "What is Herzl doing beneath a Christmas tree?" I heard some Israeli visitors wondering among themselves in Hebrew. Isn't Zionism supposed to reject the assimilationist ideology, as exemplified by the *Schlemiel* caricature? This portrait can be read as an example of how Zionism was in disjunction with the prevailing German-Jewish bourgeois culture, yet could still be integrated, or at least tolerated to a certain extent.

Herzl's portrait beneath the Christmas tree is based on a story told by Gershom Scholem, the German-Jewish scholar of Jewish mysticism, who was a Zionist from an early age. In his autobiography *From Berlin to Jerusalem*, he tells the following story, which can be heard in the audio-guide, as well as read on a text attached as a Christmas decoration: "Christmas was celebrated in our family from the time of my grandparents ... It was said that this was a German national holiday, which we celebrated not as Jews but as Germans ... Of course, that made an impression on me as a child, and in 1911, when I had just begun to learn Hebrew, I took part for the last time. There was a picture of Herzl under the Christmas-tree, in a black frame. My mother said, 'Since you're so interested in Zionism, we chose this picture for you.' From then on, I left the house at Christmas."[20] Scholem instead went to his uncle to celebrate Hanukkah. The gift exposes a generational and cultural shift: Scholem's mother treated his Zionism as a hobby. For Scholem, a young Zionist trying to assert his Jewish identity, the placement of Herzl under the Christmas tree was sacrilegious; it was exactly the opposite of what he was searching for.

The placement of Herzl's portrait under the tree at the museum occasions a Jewish critique of Christmas celebration in a similar way to the *Schlemiel* caricature.[21] Yet this perspective provides just one layer of meaning. The curatorial voice here is by no means an adoption of the Zionist position. Indeed, the decision to put a Christmas tree in the exhibition already implies a rejection of a simple Zionist narrative against assimilation. One can take the implication of the Herzl portrait a step further by thinking about the role that the Christmas tree played for Herzl himself. Rabbi Moritz Güdemann noted after a visit to the Herzls on 24 December 1895, "I was admitted to the big front room and found there – one can imagine my surprise – a big Christ-tree! Shortly after came Herzl accompanied by Oppenheim, who was also an editor of *Neue Freie Presse*. The conversation – in the presence of the Christ-tree – was slow, and I excused myself shortly." Herzl had his own account of that day. He had just lit the Christmas tree with his children when Güdemann came, and "seemed disgruntled because of the Christian custom. Well, I don't let myself be pressured by anyone! Well, as far as I am concerned it should be called the Hanukkah-tree – or the Winter Solstice?"[22] This story is told in the *Weihnukka* exhibition catalogue but not in the permanent exhibition, which is a missed opportunity to have yet another additional layer of interpretation through the important reminder that the father of Zionism had no problem placing a Christmas tree in his living room.

The Christmas tree and *gute Stube* are quite popular among visitors. It is due to their own appearances (warm colours, etc.), but maybe there is another reason at play as well: it is because visitors recognize something familiar while still grasping that their recognition is only partial. It is always at the same time misrecognition. In this, the Christmas tree reflects the museum itself. According to Gottfried Korff, the museum, by presenting things past, is a place of constant interplay between the familiar and the foreign.[23] Through its presence in the exhibition and its decorations, the Christmas tree invites a process of alienation for all visitors: those who come with a preconception that the Christmas tree has no role in Jewish life are confronted by it in a Jewish museum. Those who take the Christmas tree for a cultural given, on the other hand, are confronted by the critiques of it, by both Scholem's story and the *Schlemiel* caricature.

The alienation provoked by the Christmas tree at the JMB serves as a moment of learning in the museum. Without being schoolbook didactic, the Christmas tree conveys important insights to the visitors about the way Jews celebrated Christmas, and rejected it. This is achieved through the moment of shock or confusion created by the presence of the Christmas tree. This "a-ha!" moment, the metaphorical lightbulb, was considered by Walter Benjamin to be the great achievement of a good exhibition.[24] The Christmas tree functions as a moment of learning – about Jews and their relation to Christmas, about acculturation, and about the meaning of Christmas as a bourgeois celebration – while facilitating a process of unlearning. By encountering a Christmas tree in a Jewish museum, the visitor is confronted with her own conceptions of Judaism, Jewish life, and Christmas, and they all prove to be problematic. The contrasting interpretations of the same moment in the exhibition allows the visitor to gain an insight into the complexities of German-Jewish history, as well as to her own preconceived notions of it.

The Christmas Tree as a Thing

When looked in relation to its immediate context, the JMB Christmas tree further complicates a triumphal historiography of assimilation. The tree as a place of gathering and homeliness is surrounded, as we have seen, by objects that reinforce this feeling of homeliness: family portrait, piano, household objects, and so on. The tree undoes the one-dimensional picture of Jews celebrating Christmas; similarly, so does its placement among historical objects challenge any presumed harmony of German-Jewish life.

The Christmas tree at the JMB is a "thing" and not an object, but in a different, one is tempted to say more mundane, way than is commonly understood in philosophical terms and in the study of material culture.[25] For Kant, the thing-in-itself (*Ding an sich*) is a central notion delineating the fact that all our relations to the phenomenal realm are mediated through our categories, such as space and time. This means that the thing-in-itself cannot be sensually experienced.[26] Derrida, for his part, in a not-so-hidden dialogue with Kant, argued for the irreductability of the thing into an object: "I owe to the thing an absolute respect which no general law would mediate: the law of the thing is singularity and difference as well. An infinite debt ties me to it, a duty without funds or foundation. I shall never acquit myself of it. Thus the thing is not an object; it cannot become one."[27] The seeming inaccessibility of the things, not because they are not available in the phenomenal realm but precisely because they are real and therefore resist theorizing, is central to what Bill Brown terms "thing theory."[28] These complex philosophical reflections receive a very different, almost opposite, interpretation in museum praxis. As a quip among museum workers goes, objects have inventory numbers; things do not. Objects are what museums collect, archive, and reposit for the next generations; they are the bread and butter of museums' work.[29] Things, by contrast, are considered mostly decorative. They do not have value for the museum in and of themselves. It sounds as if the meaning ascribed by the museum to the "thing" is the opposite of that used in "thing theory," but I argue that they may lead to similar theoretical results.

The Christmas tree at the JMB is a thing in a museal sense, a decorative item that was bought for the purpose of presentation. Its historical significance is meagre; it is an early-twenty-first-century item that serves the dramaturgy of the museum. The Christmas tree is no more than a means of illustration. Any other Christmas tree would do. If it is of any historical worth, it is only through its presence in the museum for so many years, and even that is questionable. The objects in the *gute Stube* surrounding the tree are objects in the more precise museal sense: they are historical items bought by or donated to the museum for preservation and presentation. As such, they reflect the difficult history of German Jewry. The fact that they are in the museum, as opposed to the homes in which they were used, already calls into question any attempt to idealize a picture of Jewish integration into German society in the long nineteenth century. It is with regard to the other objects in the space that the tree's homeliness becomes uncanny; the *Heimlichkeit* becomes *unheimlich*.

This can be exemplified by every historical object surrounding the tree but is most evident with regard to the piano that stands across from it. As the text accompanying the piano explains, it was donated to the museum in 2004 by Tessa Uys. Uys is the daughter of pianist Helga Bassel, who owned this piano in Berlin in 1930. After the Nazis rose to power, Helga, a gifted musician, was expelled from the Reich's Music Chamber. She emigrated to South Africa in 1936, taking the piano with her. There, she never mentioned her Jewish past. It was only after her death that her daughter discovered the fact of their Jewishness. This story, along with a photo of Helga Bassel playing the piano in Berlin, forces the visitor to rethink the calmness and warmth communicated by the space around the Christmas tree.

The history of the piano qua historical object, when contrasted with the Christmas tree, exposes the tension inherent to the museum as a shaper of public memory. It reminds us that underneath the cultural atmosphere of the museum lurks barbarism and violence that resulted in death and expulsion.[30] Both the object and the museum in which it is placed are situated not only within a picture of German-Jewish harmonious family life, but also within a history of violent destruction of the very same family fabric.

The Museum Unwrapped

The images evoked by Christmas are of family gathering around the Christmas tree, the unwrapping of gifts, lights that shine in the dark nights, and of course, a happy, fat, red-cheeked, white-bearded Santa. Happiness is not only a desired condition in Christmas; it is expected and demanded. Maybe this is where the Christmas anxiety comes from: the feeling that one is not as happy as one should be.[31] This is also the reason why the Grinch, a grumpy figure that deviates from the choir of happiness, is so memorable: he breaks the illusion of unity in joy.[32]

The Christmas tree allows us to unwrap the layers of meaning at work at the Jewish Museum Berlin. Upon a cursory glance, it tells the story of Christmas as many would like to imagine it, Christmas as signifier of family and happiness: a German-Jewish family behaves like their non-Jewish compatriots in the celebration of an explicitly Christian holiday, albeit in a bourgeois fashion. This merry Christmas receives a tinge of bitter irony the closer one approaches the tree, whose decorations include a Jewish caricature of assimilation and whose sole associated gift is a portrait of Theodor Herzl. The double alienation achieved by the tree assures that both the acceptance of the celebratory narrative of integration and its Zionist critique cannot be unequivocally asserted.

It is mere decoration, the Christmas tree at the Jewish Museum Berlin. Yet precisely because it is a dramaturgical tool, "empty" of historical content in and of itself, it sheds light on the dark history of the objects surrounding it. The Christmas tree allows us to gain insights not only on how German Jews treated Christmas, but also on how the museum itself functions. In this regard, the Christmas tree is perhaps more like Easter's empty grave than Christmas's manger – it is the empty centre, the thing, that leads us to understand the story the museum tells its visitors.

Notes

Most of the work on this chapter was done during my tenure (2015–17) as an exhibition curator for the upcoming new permanent exhibition at the Jewish Museum Berlin. I thank my colleagues there, Inka Bertz, Maren Krüger, and Tanja Petersen, for many conversations about various aspects of this chapter. Special thanks to Cilly Kugelmann and Michal Friedlander for encouraging me to think about the multiple layers of exhibitions. All opinions and interpretations expressed here are mine and do not represent the Jewish Museum Berlin.

1 Doniger, "Hang Santa," 17.
2 For other attempts to conceptualize Christmas, see Miller, ed., *Unwrapping Christmas*, and Miller, *Weihnachten: Das globale Fest*.
3 On the debates prior to the opening of the museum, see Lackmann, *Jewrassic Park*.
4 Steinberg, *Judaism Musical and Unmusical*, 180.
5 Schneider and Libeskind, *Between the Lines*; Wolf, ed., *Daniel Libeskind and the Contemporary Jewish Museum*; Young, *At Memory's Edge*, 152–83.
6 Kauschke, "Der Rest vom Fest."
7 Nathenson, "Chrismukkah as Happy Ending?" 66. It should be noted, however, that to Americanize is not necessarily to universalize as Nathenson's argument might imply. What gives the Jewish discussions in North America their vitality, and humour, is precisely the tension of being a Jew in a society that celebrates Christmas, a tension that is not harmonized nor resolved, but rather lived. An example on the lighter side of the spectrum might illustrate the point. In Larry David's *Curb Your Enthusiasm*, the episode "Mary, Joseph, and Larry" centres on the Christmas celebration of a mixed couple, Larry and his non-Jewish wife Cheryl. Larry refuses initially to have a Christmas tree in the living room, explaining: "I'm a Jew, to have a tree in the house, it's bad luck. You know, my guy [pointing upwards] might not, may think I'm switching or something, you know, he might not understand." He later explains to his friend Jeff that having a Christmas tree for the first time is "unsettling." A huge tree is nonetheless placed in his house, and Christmas carols are sung late at night, much to Larry's dismay. The entire comic premise of the episode, with all its Christmas-related misfortunes that befall Larry, is predicated on this disharmony, on the "unsettling" feeling, and not on the giving up of Jewish identity. See David, "Mary, Joseph, and Larry."

On the way Turkish-German families celebrate Christmas, see Sophie
Reimers's article in this volume.

8   Rothstein, "The Problem with Jewish Museums," 59.

9   Nathenson, "Chrismukkah as Happy Ending?" 59.

10 A classic example is Bhabha, *The Location of Culture*, especially 277.

11 Most writing on Chrismukkah as a multicultural celebration, and the
    problems it raises, is done in the North American context. See for
    example Plaut, *A Kosher Christmas*, and Mehta, "Chrismukkah: Millennial
    Multiculturalism."

12 The *Stube* has different regional connotations. Whereas in East Germany it
    simply refers to the living room, in older households in West Germany it
    refers to a very specific type of living room, one that maintains the feeling
    of bourgeoisie almost to a degree of holiness. Children are rarely allowed
    to enter this type of *gute Stube*, and only if they behave well. I thank Julia
    Carls for a helpful discussion on this subject.

13 The fame of Kaufmann's "Sabbath Room" was partly the result of its
    presentation at the Dresden Hygiene Exhibition in 1911. See Purin, "Isidor
    Kaufmann's Little World," 129–45; cf. Berger, *The Jewish Museum*, 166–70.

14 The constellation around the tree, as well as its decorations, have changed
    throughout the years. The glass vitrine containing the Hanukkah
    menorahs was an upgrade from the 2001 original and was created to be the
    same size as the tree, reflecting feedback the museum received about the
    prominence of Christmas. Throughout the article, I am referring to the
    latest iteration, as present in the photo, which was presented until 2017
    when the permanent exhibition closed.

15 On the development of Christmas as a family celebration, see Weber-
    Kellermann, *Das Weihnachtsfest*, and Eberspächer, "Lichtglanz und
    Kinderglück."

16 Richarz, "Der jüdische Weihnachtsbaum."

17 Lässig, *Jüdische Wege ins Bürgertum*; van Rahden, *Jews and Other Germans*;
    Jensen, *Gebildete Doppelgänger*; Baader, *Gender, Judaism, and Bourgeois
    Culture in Germany*.

18 Richarz, "Der jüdische Weihnachtsbaum," 282.

19 Shortly after this segment there is an attempt to problematize this
    harmonious picture. After taking the stairs down to the first floor, the
    visitor encounters the segment "German and Jew at the Same Time,"
    which discusses the various ways in which Jews tried to integrate into

German society. The options there include conversion and baptism, expressions of patriotism, but also communism and Zionism. Because of the way visitors walk in this space, they are much more likely to encounter Zionism and baptism rather than the other alternatives.

20 Quoted from the English audio-guide text. For the original German, see Scholem, *Von Berlin nach Jerusalem*, 41–2.

21 The portrait under the tree is probably not the one Scholem received for Christmas in 1911, because this portrait was made by Hermann Struck and more likely dates to the 1920s.

22 Both quoted in Richarz, "Der jüdische Weihnachtsbaum," 285; cf. Richarz, "Weihnukka," 96.

23 Korff, "Fremde (der, die, das) und das Museum (1997)," 146.

24 Benjamin, "Bekränzter Eingang," 559; cf. Korff, "Omnibusprinzip und Schaufensterqualität," 733–5.

25 For a brief theoretical summary of the thing (*Ding*) in the museum, see Thiemeyer, "Die Sprache der Dinge." The German offers further complications which the English is spared. There is not just the distinction between a thing and an object but also between different things or objects, using the words "Gegenstand" (standing opposed), "Objekt," and "Ding." At least at the JMB, it is more common to use the distinction between "Deko" and "Objekt."

26 This is a central distinction in Kant's philosophy and it is developed in many places throughout the first critique. See, for example, Kant, *Critique of Pure Reason*, xxvi–xxvii.

27 Derrida, *Signéponge-Signsponge*, 14.

28 Brown, "Thing Theory." See also the subsequent works, among others: Brown, *Things*; Brown, *Other Things*. David Morgan summarizes this theoretical position well, writing that "things resist the epistemic spell of objecthood." Morgan, "Thing," 256.

29 Gottfried Korff does not use the distinction object/thing but he has the former in mind when he talks about collecting and presenting "museum things" (*Museumsdinge*). See Korff, "Zur Eigenart der Museumsdinge (1992)," 140–5.

30 Benjamin, "Über den Begriff der Geschichte," 696.

31 Doniger, "Hang Santa," 18.

32 On the Grinch see Isaac Weiner's chapter in this volume.

Bibliography

Baader, Benjamin Maria. *Gender, Judaism, and Bourgeois Culture in Germany, 1800–1870*. Bloomington, IN: Indiana University Press, 2006.

Benjamin, Walter. "Über den Begriff der Geschichte." In *Gesammelte Schriften*, 1st ed., edited by Theodor Adorno, Gershom Scholem, Rolf Tiedemann, and Hermann Schweppenhäuser, 693–704. Frankfurt am Main, Germany: Suhrkamp, 1972.

– "Bekränzter Eingang: Zur Ausstellung 'Gesunde Nerven' im Gesundheitshaus Kreuzberg." In *Gesammelte Schriften*, 4th ed., edited by Theodor Adorno, Gershom Scholem, Rolf Tiedemann, and Hermann Schweppenhäuser, 557–61. Frankfurt am Main, Germany: Suhrkamp, 1980.

Berger, Natalia. *The Jewish Museum: History and Memory, Identity and Art from Vienna to the Bezalel National Museum, Jerusalem*. Leiden, Netherlands: Brill, 2017.

Bhabha, Homi. *The Location of Culture*. London: Routledge, 1994.

Brown, Bill. "Thing Theory." *Critical Inquiry* 28, no. 1 (2001): 1–22.

– *Things*. Chicago, IL: Chicago University Press, 2004.

– *Other Things*. Chicago, IL: University of Chicago Press, 2016.

David, Larry. "Mary, Joseph, and Larry." *Curb Your Enthusiasm*. HBO, 10 November 2002.

Derrida, Jacques. *Signéponge-Signsponge*. Translated by Richard Rand. New York: Columbia University Press, 1984.

Doniger, Wendy. "Hang Santa: Review of Daniel Miller's Unwrapping Christmas." *London Review of Books* 15, no. 24 (1993).

Eberspächer, Martina. "Lichtglanz und Kinderglück: Zur Entwicklung der Familienweihnacht." In *Weihnachtszeit: Feste zwischen Advent und Neujahr in Süddeutschland und Österreich, 1840–1940*, edited by Nina Gockerell, 11–17. Munich, Germany: Prestel, 2000.

Jensen, Uffa. *Gebildete Doppelgänger: Bürgerliche Juden und Protestanten im 19. Jahrhundert*. Göttingen, Germany: Vandenhoeck & Ruprecht, 2005.

Kant, Immanuel. *Critique of Pure Reason*. Translated by Paul Guyer and Allen W. Wood. Cambridge: Cambridge University Press, 2003.

Kauschke, Detlef. "Der Rest vom Fest: Die Ausstellung 'Weihnukka' löst heftige Debatten aus." *Jüdische Allgemeine Zeitung*, 12 January 2006. http://www.juedische-allgemeine.de/article/view/id/5047.

Korff, Gottfried. "Omnibusprinzip und Schaufensterqualität: Module und

Motive der Dynamisierung des Musealen im 20. Jahrhundert." In *Geschichte und Emanzipation: Festschrift für Reinhard Rürup*, edited by Michael Grüttner, Rüdiger Hachtmann, and Heinz-Gerhard Haupt, 728–54. Frankfurt, Germany: Campus, 1999.

– "Fremde (der, die, das) und das Museum (1997)." In *Museumsdinge: deponieren – exponieren*, 146–54. Cologne, Germany: Böhlau Verlag, 2002.

– "Zur Eigenart der Museumsdinge (1992)." In *Museumsdinge: deponieren - exponieren*, 140–5. Cologne, Germany: Böhlau Verlag, 2002.

Lackmann, Thomas. *Jewrassic Park: Wie baut man (k)ein Jüdisches Museum in Berlin*. Berlin: Philo, 2000.

Lässig, Simone. *Jüdische Wege ins Bürgertum: Kulturelles Kapital und sozialer Aufstieg im 19. Jahrhundert*. Göttingen, Germany: Vandenhoek & Ruprecht, 2004.

Mehta, Samira. "Chrismukkah: Millennial Multiculturalism." *Religion and American Culture: A Journal of Interpretation* 25, no. 1 (2015): 82–109.

Miller, Daniel, ed. *Unwrapping Christmas*. Oxford, UK: Clarendon Press, 1993.

– *Weihnachten: Das globale Fest*. Translated by Frank Jakubzik. Frankfurt am Main, Germany: Suhrkamp Verlag, 2011.

Morgan, David. "Thing." In *Key Terms in Material Religion*, edited by S. Brent Plate, 253–9. London: Bloomsbury Publishing, 2015.

Nathenson, Cary. "Chrismukkah as Happy Ending? The Weihnukka Exhibition at the Jewish Museum Berlin as German-Jewish Integration Fantasy." *Journal of Jewish Identities* 6, no. 1 (2013): 57–69.

Plaut, Joshua Ali. *A Kosher Christmas: 'Tis the Season to Be Jewish*. New Brunswick, NJ: Rutgers University Press, 2012.

Purin, Bernard. "Isidor Kaufmann's Little World: The 'Sabbath Room' in the Jewish Museum of Vienna." In *Rabbiner, Bocher, Talmudschüler: Bilder Des Wiener Malers, Isidor Kaufmann, 1853–1921*, edited by Tobias G. Natter, 129–45. Vienna: Jüdisches Museum der Stadt Wien, 1995.

Rahden, Till van. *Jews and Other Germans: Civil Society, Religious Diversity, and Urban Politics in Breslau, 1860–1925*. Translated by Marcus Brainard. Madison: University of Wisconsin Press, 2008.

Richarz, Monika. "Der jüdische Weihnachtsbaum: Familie und Säkularisierung im deutschen Judentum des 19. Jahrhunderts." In *Geschichte und Emanzipation: Festschrift für Reinhard Rürup*, edited by Michael Grüttner, Rüdiger Hachtmann, and Heinz-Gerhard Haupt, 275–89. Frankfurt, Germany: Campus, 1999.

– "Weihnukka: Das Weihnachtsfest im jüdischen Bürgertum." In *Weihnukka: Geschichten von Weihnachten und Chanukka*, edited by Cilly Kugelmann, 86–99. Berlin: Nicolai Verlag, 2005.

Rothstein, Edward. "The Problem with Jewish Museums." *Mosaic*, February 2016. https://mosaicmagazine.com/essay/2016/02/the-problem-with-jewish-museums/.

Schneider, Bernhard, and Daniel Libeskind. *Between the Lines: Extension to the Berlin Museum with the Jewish Museum.* New York: Prestel, 1999.

Scholem, Gershom. *Von Berlin nach Jerusalem: Jugenderinnerungen.* Frankfurt am Main, Germany: Suhrkamp, 1977.

Steinberg, Michael. *Judaism Musical and Unmusical.* Chicago, IL: Chicago University Press, 2007.

Thiemeyer, Thomas. "Die Sprache der Dinge: Museumobjekte zwischen Zeichen und Erscheinung." *Museen für Geschichte.* Deutsches Historisches Museum (2011).

Weber-Kellermann, Ingeborg. *Das Weihnachtsfest: Eine Kultur- und Sozialgeschichte der Weihnachtszeit.* Munich, Germany: Bucher C.J., 1987.

Wolf, Connie, ed. *Daniel Libeskind and the Contemporary Jewish Museum: New Jewish Architecture from Berlin to San Francisco.* New York: Rizzoli, 2008.

Young, James Edward. *At Memory's Edge: After-Images of the Holocaust in Contemporary Art and Architecture.* New Haven, CT: Yale University Press, 2000.

8

"What Exactly Do You
Celebrate at Christmas?":
Different Perceptions of Christmas among
German-Turkish Families in Berlin

Sophie Reimers

Introduction

It was during the second winter of my research among an immigrant family made up of three generations in the neighbourhood of Neukölln in the city of Berlin that Maral, one of my interlocutors, asked me a simple question: "What exactly do you celebrate at Christmas?" At this point I had participated in the family's daily life for almost two years and had gotten to know all of them, especially Maral, quite well.[1] Still, her question turned our conversation in an unexpected direction. The family had come to Berlin from rural Turkey in the 1970s and had lived there ever since, so her inquiry led to a moment of hesitation on my part. I was simply not sure how to classify her question; did she not know the origins of the holiday – the story of Jesus being born in a barn in Bethlehem – or was she just unsure about the details? Or did she want to hear my personal reasons for celebrating Christmas?

At the time, Maral and I had been interacting closely with each other for a while. Up until she posed her startling question, I had almost always experienced our exchanges as being shaped by mutual understanding. This one small question, however, seemed to widen the gap between us. If Maral indeed did not know the story of Christmas, it could have merely been a sign of how secularized Christmas practices had become. But it might have also been the consequence of her limited interaction with members of the kind of bourgeois milieu that shapes the Christmas habitus. I was astonished that the story of Christmas – so natural to me thanks to having heard it regularly for over thirty years, from early childhood onward – could have passed Maral by, leaving her unfamiliar with a central element of the holiday.

When I returned to this ethnographic vignette during the process of data analysis sometime later, it seemed to me that my confusion also indicated how Christmas was connected to a wider array of questions involving issues of belonging and integration. Thus, further investigating the different meanings of Christmas in the context of immigration appeared promising. I will return to the above vignette after first sharing some thoughts and observations about Christmas in a multicultural and especially in a religiously diverse context. To begin, I will set out the approach that I follow in this chapter and provide some relevant background information on the field of Christmas research.

In the following pages I share ideas, questions, and problems linked to Christmas in urban spaces shaped by immigration, and also relate to certain tactics, as mentioned by Pamela Klassen and Monique Scheer in their introduction to this volume, that are applied in the family I worked with to find a way to involve or avoid Christmas. My essay is framed by broad questions about Christmas in relation to daily life in a multicultural city, the formation of traditions and power relations, and the claiming of space for alternative rituals. These questions are explored through a focus on the specific empirical example of a Muslim Turkish-German family and the different meanings Christmas takes on in this context.[2] In order to gain insight into the stories of an immigrant family in Berlin, it is necessary to take turns that will lead us briefly away from Christmas, as is inevitable when writing about a family that does not celebrate it. Needless to say, the ways in which Christmas is thought of and (not) put into practice in this particular family are not representative of the (imagined) Turkish community in Germany. Rather, thinking about these questions is an attempt to develop ideas about the diverse connections and various layers that form at the intersection of Christmas and multiculturalism. In addition to my research data I include several articles, a film sequence, and various other discursive materials that enrich my understanding and highlight different aspects of the meanings that Christmas can take on in an immigrant family. While this sample of material is designed to reveal the connotations Christmas can have in different constellations, I do not claim to deliver an overview. Rather, I am making an attempt to sketch out how Christmas is negotiated in a multicultural context and asking whether these negotiations reflect current ideas about how multicultural communities are structured. Lastly, while my fieldwork led me to focus on families, this does not imply that other perspectives and experiences outside the heteronormative family sphere are less relevant to the topic.

A Short History of Turkish-German Immigration

Today the Imrens, the family who opened their home to me for my research, live in Neukölln, Berlin, a culturally heterogeneous neighbourhood. Before highlighting the historical background of their immigration to Germany, it is necessary to briefly introduce the three generations for a better understanding of the family structure. My ethnographic fieldwork and interviews focus on twenty-one family members that can be allocated to three generations: the first generation are the two retired grandparents (Ferda and Can), the second generation their four children (Feza, Maral, Elif, and Fatih) and the children's spouses (all from Turkish families and, with one exception, born in Turkey), and the third generation are Ferda and Can's eleven grandchildren, who were all born between 1981 and 2007 and raised in Berlin. After the end of my ethnographic inquiry, in 2015 grandchildren Meryem and Melek both got married and in 2016 each of them had a child, initiating the fourth generation.

Can Imren first came to Berlin in 1968 when the German government was recruiting so-called "guest workers"; he planned to work for a limited period of time, send money home, and then return to Turkey. The German Federal Republic's recruitment of guest workers in Turkey began over fifty years ago in 1961 and was carried out through a contract between the Turkish and German governments. The recruitment motivated over 900,000 people to immigrate to Germany within a twelve-year period.[3] As the term "guest worker" indicates, the German government planned for the workers to eventually return to their homelands, but for the majority, this return was never realized for two main reasons.[4] First, family members who had initially stayed behind followed the workers to Germany; second, children were born. Thus, for many, the return to Turkey was repeatedly delayed. There are now nearly three million people of Turkish descent living in Germany, representing the country's main immigrant group. The majority identify themselves as Muslim.[5]

Immigration changed not only German society, a fact that was not acknowledged in public discourse for a long time, but also, ultimately,

1st generation

Can	∞	Ferda
*1941 in Turkey	(1960)	*1943 in Turkey

2nd generation

Children of Can and Ferda	Feza	Maral	Elif	Fatih
	*1962 in Turkey	*1965 in Turkey	*1966 in Turkey	*1968 in Turkey
Spouses	Ali	Muhammet	Cenk	Fatma
	*1958 in Turkey	*1964 in Turkey	*1967 in Turkey	*1978 in Germany

3rd generation

	Osman	Melek	Oktay	Muhammet
	*1982 in Germany	*1987 in Germany	*2007 in Germany	*1997 in Germany
	Meryem	Nuriye		Aynur
	*1989 in Germany	*1990 in Germany		*1999 in Germany
		Gülay		Özlem
		*1992 in Germany		*2000 in Germany
		Cengiz		Emre
		*1999 in Germany		*2003 in Germany

Table 8.1   Three generations of the Imren family with dates of birth.

the immigrants themselves.[6] For the Imren family, one of the unfamiliar practices in their new life-world was Christmas. When Can and Ferda had been living and working in Berlin for several years, their four children left their Turkish village to join them. Maral was one of the children. At first she was overwhelmed by the strange city – its sounds, smells, and lights. She recounts that during these first years when they were living in Wedding, a traditional workers' district of Berlin, the owner of the neighbouring kiosk offered the children little presents and sweets around Christmastime. This small incident is all she remembers when talking about her childhood experiences of Christmas. Sure, her parents were invited to Christmas parties at work, and her younger siblings also joined in on Christmas celebrations at school, but it was not an important element of their family life. Maral's memory of receiving candy hints at the ambivalence that Christmas customs engender. For newcomers Christmas initially appears to be a strange ritual; participating in the celebration indicates belonging, while forgoing it marks one as an outsider. On the other hand,

"Christmas spirit" includes ideas of sharing, of crossing boundaries, and of inviting neighbours that parallel many Muslim immigrants' own traditional celebrations (for instance, the Sugar Feast). Viewed critically, the inclusive gestures associated with Christmas could also be seen as missionary and paternalistic.

For the Imrens, celebrating Christmas did not seem to be an option since the family identifies as Muslim. Especially during their first years in Germany this perspective seemed to be a sufficient response to the ritual; the more rooted in Berlin the family became, however, the more they altered their response. Since first coming to Germany the family has undergone changes: it has grown, and the third and now fourth generation feel at home in Berlin. All of the family's generations identify as Muslim, but a closer look makes it obvious that even within this one family the label of "Muslim" does not imply homogeneity. Beliefs and religious practices vary between individuals; for some, religious rituals such as praying or religious symbols such as headscarves are part of everyday life. For others, being religious is a rather abstract concept that is only relevant on special occasions. While Muslim holidays such as Ramadan, *Şeker Bayramı* (the Sugar Feast), and *Kurban Bayramı* (the Sacrifice Feast) are celebrated, Christmas is not (yet) an integral part of the family's rituals.

First Encounters with Christmas

When thinking about Christmas and the ways in which Turkish immigrants relate to this ritual, it is helpful to consider what it is like to arrive in a new social life-world. Most of the men and women who came planned to return after several years of work, so spouses and children were often left with grandparents or other relatives in Turkey. This was also the case for the Imrens in the 1970s; Ferda and Can and their children were separated for six years until the decision was made to reunite the family in Berlin. Temporary separations such as these were not the exception (and are still common in many different contexts of immigration worldwide), but even without this separation, the process of immigration caused and still causes families to transform in various ways.[7] For the Imrens, the process of separating and reuniting altered how the family functioned; when the children rejoined their parents in Germany, things did not automatically go back to how they were in Turkey. Individual shifts in status within the family had occurred, and it was no longer self-evident that they should live together as a single unit. Against the backdrop of these destabilizing shifts and transformations, Christmas, a ritual that the family had not yet learned and whose specific habitus they lacked, represented yet another unknown sphere.

Kathrin Audehm describes the function of rituals for families (among other groups) as confirming and reinforcing cohesion. For Audehm, rituals function as a way to make integration and solidarity visible and to highlight relevant values and traditions from both the family's history and its social milieu.[8] She demonstrates that an important condition for the functioning of ritual interactions is their rather monotonous repetition. While Christmas works along these lines for many families in Germany, it was unable to perform a similar function for the Imren family. Having been apart from each other for several years, the Imrens had to renew their memories of family rituals and rebuild their traditions. Simple rituals such as family dinners or outdoor picnics on the weekend helped to initiate new ties and create moments of being together as a family. Understanding Christmas in this multicultural setting can be linked to acknowledging the situation of newly arrived families whose experience is marked by fragility and a sense that the future is yet undetermined.

The ambivalence of Christmas rituals in the context of Turkish-German immigration is pointedly depicted in the film *Almanya*,[9] a 2011 comedy directed by Yasemin Şamdereli. The movie tells the story of a family of three generations moving from eastern Turkey to Germany. It follows their initial sense of alienation, their struggles with intergenerational conflicts, and their gradual transition to feeling at home in Germany. The scene that shows their first "German Christmas" is a comic hyperbole that high-lights two important and intertwined aspects of the holiday – its links to nationality and the concept of Christmas as a celebration for children. The scene is introduced by a narrator who tells us that the family has been living in Germany for quite some time and that the three children have adapted to "German culture." Accordingly the children act as the family's Christmas experts; they rigorously examine their mother's attempt to mimic the Christmas ritual of placing presents under the Christmas tree. Being unpractised, she mixes up the ritual sequence ("First you put the presents under the tree, and then you ring the bell," her son corrects her)[10] and does not wrap the presents, which leads to disappointed children and general irritation. What is playfully implied here is that Christmas, presented as one of the typical rituals of German culture, provides the family with a chance to begin to establish the sense that they belong to the German nation. The children, who have been socialized in Germany, want to participate in the ritual; this causes their parents to struggle to maintain their authority on unknown terrain. The sequence also represents Christmas's appeal to children (one part of the scene shows the kids staring at toys in a festively decorated store window). All in all, the scene offers a glimpse of the intergenerational conflicts that can be triggered by the mélange of interests wrapped up in Christmas celebrations. Not coincidentally, the scene ends with the parents discussing whether their children, who appear strange to them in their enthusiasm for Christmas, have become too German. They ask themselves if they should send the children to Turkey for holidays in order to reinforce their cultural roots.

Maintaining their "own" traditions in order to preserve ties with the family's history also was and still is one of the objectives in the Imren family. In this sense, not celebrating Christmas might also be regarded as a defensive act on the part of the Imrens that is intended to prevent the children from assimilating into the culture of the German majority and drifting away from their roots. The ambiguities of the parental role in this context can only be understood by taking into account the all-encompassing changes that it undergoes with immigration. As Suarez-Orozco and Suarez-Orozco illustrate, in the new culture immigrant parents cannot always provide the "map of experience" that is required to guide the children. Instead the typical relation is reversed – children give explanations to the parents.[11] This reversal is also portrayed in the Christmas scene in the above-mentioned film, and in this case it leads to the parents' attempt to reinforce their children's relationship with the Turkish village.

The short scene also indicates how Christmas produces multiple experiences, only some of which line up with the idealized image of Christmas celebrations. Trying to belong by attempting to blend into typical Christmas scenes leads to irritation and confusion. Instead of successfully producing a feeling of belonging, the attempt to mimic a Christmas celebration depicted in the film rather bluntly reveals distances and differences. The assumption that underlies the interaction between the children and their parents is that there is a right way to celebrate Christmas and that the celebrations of German families, who shape this tradition, should serve as a template. The movie certainly overdraws the contrast between the celebrations of German and of immigrant families using certain clichés, but constructing the immigrant other against an allegedly homogenous majority is a common discursive practice. This construction can lead us to overlook the reality that Christmas traditions are not as stable or unchanging as is often thought.

The image of Christmas as one of the highlights of family life, a day of familial harmony shaped by old traditions and stable rituals and wreathed in candlelight and the scent of cookies and fir trees, is nothing more than a popular narrative presented in literature and in the media – at least that's what Doris Foitzik states in her exploration of Christmas as a German *Erinnerungsort* (memorial space).[12] The Christmas celebration is not only a newer invention than is often thought (in fact, it emerged in the nineteenth century), it has also undergone constant transformations and was often the subject of ideological struggles. Being closely linked to the bourgeois family, the ritual was also touched by changes in this sphere. Foitzik describes how, even when patriarchal structures were still functioning, families were overwhelmed by the task of dedicating themselves to their children's happiness in a way that was laid out by a predefined ideology. Her historical perspective on Christmas helps to counter the image of a homogenous and stable tradition. With this history in mind, it is not surprising that today Christmas is the subject of debates over who shapes public spaces and who determines which rituals and traditions are relevant in a multicultural society.[13]

The ideal that Christmas creates an "island of feeling"[14] might still be meandering through modern society, but the diversification of families and lifestyles has eroded the idea of one homogenous Christmas. In this sense, the imperfection of the first Christmas of the immigrant family depicted in the film might not be an exception, but rather a typical experience of this family ritual. When we approach the diverse ways in which holidays are celebrated or not celebrated, different connections manifest and we discover that there are no clear-cut lines as to how to incorporate Christmas and other traditions into family life.

Transforming Christmas Rituals

Transformations shape the experience of immigrants. The Imren family's story allows us to trace how biographies are in constant flow, paralleled by changing attitudes, positions, practices, and traditions.[15] Like many other experiences, Christmas was new and unknown territory for the Imrens during their first years in Berlin. As they enlarged their network, opportunities to get to know Christmas and to participate in the seasonal habitus increased. New marriages and a growing family can also mean the addition of new traditions. Maral celebrated Christmas for the first time after she got married; she was invited to attend the celebration of her sister-in-law Elke's family. Learning more about the tradition of Christmas from her new German relatives did not automatically make Maral feel more integrated into her husband's family or move her to adopt Christmas as her own. One quite prosaic factor that can lead to the decision not to celebrate Christmas is that workers receive extra salary for working during the holidays. Due to their growing family, this is an opportunity that Maral's husband currently seizes. In this sense socio-economic factors might also influence Christmas practices, especially among low-income groups.

Even if a family does not adopt the tradition of celebrating Christmas, they still absorb elements from the field of Christmas rituals. Christmas symbols are included in a globalized array of secularized consumption goods – even if Muslim families do not celebrate Christmas, many of them still participate in the seasonal consumption that is an essential part of the holiday.[16] In a conversation about Christmas, Maral and her daughter Melek described to me how they enjoy the festive change of scenery in the city around December. Melek experiences a special atmosphere; she enjoys the lights and decorations and feels overwhelmed by the excitement produced as part of the build-up to Christmas. Shopping streets are crowded, people seem busy, and certain music and pathos are more common than during the rest of the year. As a resident of an urban area, she perceives a shift in its public spaces; even though the religious aspect of the celebration is not part of her frame of reference, the atmosphere is part of her experience. Christmas percolates through public life and therefore influences private life as well. Immigrants' supposed sense of being distanced from Christmas does not translate to an overall stance towards the cultural ritual. Almost unnoticed, certain aspects of it become part of everyday life and are integrated into and shape personal experience.

Children are often the driving force behind the inclusion of certain elements of Christmas traditions in family life, an inclusion that reflects a desire to try something new. Today Christmas as a social ritual is inseparable from childhood; most Christmas traditions in Germany are child-focused, so this group is especially drawn to the celebration, or at least to specific components of it. It was Maral's youngest son Cengiz who first expressed the wish to put up a tree in the family's apartment. The decorated tree as the most significant symbol of (German) Christmas has obviously not lost its appeal despite being rejected as a symbol of conservative family life during the student movement in the 1960s and 70s. The symbol of the tree is still omnipresent, and we encounter it in most shopping malls, in films, and on products, and, as Yaniv Feller's chapter shows, even in Jewish museums. The image of several generations gathered together to celebrate is one aspect of Christmas that the Imren family can relate to as it communicates values such as family cohesion and solidarity. Although this should not be taken as a generalization, socialization in rural areas of Turkey often emphasizes the collective.[17] This orientation towards the collective is not static; it is balanced with individualistic objectives. Being closely connected to family, however, remains of great importance among all three generations of the Imren family. The conservative image of family promoted within the context of Christmas is compatible with family ideals expressed by my interlocutors. Thus this image is another aspect of Christmas that attracts them, one that goes beyond the mere appeal of Christmas aesthetics and goods.

With their first tree, one prominent Christmas symbol entered the family's apartment. Other Christmas-related wishes that the children of the third generation expressed to their parents, however, were not fulfilled. Each time the children challenged their family's decision not to participate in Christmas, they were, as Maral recounted to me, placated by the explanation that Christmas was not "their" celebration and that they had other holidays instead – holidays that also included family dinners, decoration, festive clothing, and presents. Christmas, categorized as a Christian holiday, was not perceived by the family as part of an adaptable cultural repertoire. This perception does not automatically lead to conflict, but the fact that Muslim holidays in Germany do not have the same collective dynamic as in mainly Muslim countries is not without significance.[18]

While the Imren family seems to have taken a relatively clear position regarding the Christmas question, there are multiple ways in which parents mediate between their goals and their children's demands. It could be assumed that their position towards Christmas is shaped by their religious identification and that more secular individuals are more open to this ritual. My fieldwork indicates that this pattern is too simple, but only with further research could this question be answered in any meaningful way. On the surface, various strategies for integrating Christmas do not seem to be indicators of religious (or national) affiliations. In this sense Melek, who works as a kindergarten teacher, experiences the ambivalent ways in which multiple Muslim families respond to the holiday – from strict avoidance of all religiously associated rituals to general participation. While Maral and the other second-generation parents of the Imren family allowed their children to participate in festive activities of different sorts and only claims that reached further into the private sphere were denied, other families perceive this kind of participation as a conflict. At work, Maral's daughter Melek encounters some families who avoid celebrations that are classified as non-Muslim and accordingly keep their children at home during Halloween, the lantern parade on St Martins Day, St Nicholas, Christmas, and Easter. They also refuse to have their children participate in baking Christmas cookies during Advent or celebrating Carnival in February. The avoidance of Christmas traditions is, however, a rather uncommon way to handle the situation; many Muslim families take a completely different route.

It is children who as the defining audience for Christmas rituals shape how this tradition is integrated. Parents can be torn between the wish to let the children participate and a wish to transmit traditions that are important to the family. Celebrations such as Christmas might be perceived as an overwhelming influence on children, one that parents have to control if they don't want their children to prioritize the traditions of the cultural majority. Most families do not adopt this either-or perspective; rather, compromises, mixing, and testing are the modes in which traditions develop among diverse families. Constant change and negotiation underlie these traditions, and it is not least of all the intense urge to consume created by products targeted at children that pushes families to experiment with Christmas rituals.

Immigrants integrate Christmas in various ways and contribute to a process of transformation of this cultural ritual with its pieced-together character that is defined by different elements extracted from their old contexts and put together in a new one.[19] Some parts of Christmas – such as the tree or the presents – are involved in this process of reassembling and develop into new kinds of traditions. One new style of celebrating combines Christmas and New Year's by taking an element of Christmas, the presents, and transferring it to the context of New Year's such that children receive "New Year gifts" on 31 December. In this sense, Muslim families in multicultural Berlin are mediating between their children's interests and their own ideals of family traditions by reinventing the holiday. This development can be also observed in Istanbul, where it has become more and more common to put up Christmas trees around New Year's, a development that can be interpreted as an expression of the globalization and at the same time secularization of Christmas. Both Istanbul and Berlin can be understood as transnationalized cultural spaces.[20] Whatever the details of these adaptations and transformations are, Christmas as a cultural practice is as hybrid as the urban settings and their inhabitants that produce these altered ritual forms.

Christmas as a Subject of Negotiation

Simply describing Christmas practices in a multicultural space such as Neukölln, Berlin, as hybrid rituals that represent the diversity of this space's inhabitants does not sufficiently account for the dynamics that take place within and around Muslim immigrant families as they confront Christmas. We must also explore questions of inclusion and exclusion. Among my research participants, forms of exclusion are increasingly tackled by the third generation. The urban environment of Berlin is their life-world, although on a smaller scale it is the family that shapes their experiences. In the Imren family, the parents of the second generation try to provide a cultural context and transmit knowledge from a culture that is seen as Turkish or, to be more specific, as belonging to the Black Sea area.[21] Although they are growing up in a German city, it is natural to the third generation to be surrounded by the Turkish language at home, to celebrate Muslim holidays, and to eat Turkish food or dance traditionally (specifically a form of dance called the circle dance) at weddings or circumcision parties. In kindergarten or later at school the socialization context is enlarged and new rituals and perspectives are learned.

Problems arise when negative stereotypes about their cultural background dominate interactions in contexts where there is little room for alternative representations. In the third generation, experiences of discrimination and segregation are described as crucial biographical events that require processing and positioning among available categories. Adolescents need to carve a path between the values, perspectives, and judgments that structure their family life and the ones that emerge in other contexts such as at school or within their peer group. While the first two generations accepted the cultural stereotypes that were attributed to them to a certain degree and saw marginalization as a somewhat legitimate dynamic (as they themselves identified as outsiders), the third generation claims to be equal and desires to be recognized as a whole with their multi-layered belongings. The biographies of members of this generation show that their sense of equality is threatened when individuals with a so-called "*Migrationshintergrund*" (immigrant background) are constantly marked as different and not belonging. This experience can provoke different reactions: in the case of my interview partners it initiates a search for possible modes of identity and belonging that provide recognition and security.[22] Islam, or more specific ideas, practices, and symbols linked to Islam, serves as a framework for this quest. However, identifying as a Muslim is not an unambiguous affiliation when living in a culture that is dominated by negative images of Islam. Often, a Muslim other is constructed in public discourses in order to solidify the identity and confirm the homogeneity of a certain in-group such as a society or nation.[23]

When adolescents experience segregation or sense that their self-made identity as Turkish-Germans is not accepted, they draw more heavily on the resources provided by what they see as their own Turkish Muslim cultural roots. Within this context, they sometimes view Christmas as a symbol of the German Christian majority's culture, and as such as a ritual that is not equally accessible to everyone. Making the choice to accept their parents' decision to prioritize what are seen as their own traditions can also signify solidarity not only with their parents but also with the minority group with which they are associated.

Kindergartens and schools have already been mentioned as important spheres of cultural socialization in Germany, specifically since they commonly teach traditions such as Christmas. For the children of the Imren family, it was kindergarten that introduced them to several rituals connected to Christmas. In preschool education it is very common to plan the educational program for November onwards in anticipation of St Nicholas, Advent, and Christmas. It is only recently that schools have begun to question whether this type of programming does not adequately reflect the religious diversity in Germany and to discuss the possibility of integrating other traditions, which a few schools have already done. This rather reluctant turn towards the celebration of more diverse traditions in schools illustrates Germany's hesitant position towards immigration and the related societal transformations. To develop a new concept of how to meet the requirements of a society shaped by immigration is a task that still requires attention, especially since, as Rommelspacher points out, the alleged neutrality (hence secularity) of the public sphere is a myth.

The German public sphere is distinctly influenced by Christian churches, which are involved in the creation of educational policy, broadcasting, and ethical questions concerning abortion. In this sense the demand that religion should be kept within the private sphere is actually directed to non-Christian confessional groups.[24]

Transmitting the traditions of the cultural majority while leaving out alternatives has been the modus operandi of the educational system up till now. While early education, specifically kindergarten, does not follow a strict curriculum, it is nonetheless guided by *Bildungspläne* (educational compasses) developed by the *Ministerien der Bundesländer* (state ministries) in order to define specific educative objectives. The educational program in elementary school is also influenced by political guidelines, although how these guidelines are implemented varies widely depending on the institution and its educators. Ultimately it is the *Kita* (kindergarten) that decides how to change certain traditions (such as Christmas rituals and others) or integrate new ones and how to proceed in the face of conflicting parental ideas and wishes. One example of how Christmas is involved in diverse educational contexts is presented on the website of the DIK (German Islam Conference).[25] Under the category "Religious Celebrations in School" is a 2008 article by Canan Topçu entitled "Muslim Kids Participate in Celebrating Christmas."[26] In the article we learn about Hafsa, a five-year-old girl from a Muslim family who attends a Catholic kindergarten in Frankfurt am Main and participated in the kindergarten's 2008 Nativity play. The author notes that while he usually would not have reported on a kindergarten Nativity play, the participation of a girl with a Muslim background made this particular play worth noting. Thus the article can be analyzed on two levels: first, the story presented in the article is an example of how a Muslim family deals with the celebration of Christmas in kindergarten. Second, the article itself functions as a primary document that reflects the author's representative way of thinking about the dynamics between Muslim families and Christmas celebrations.

In a quotation in the following section, Hafsa's mother Saime explains that she made a conscious decision to enrol her daughter in a Catholic kindergarten; she wants her daughter to directly experience the religious culture of the Christian country in which they are living. She does not see these experiences as creating a conflict for her Muslim daughter; rather, she sees her daughter's Christian kindergarten education as an expansion of her horizons. Although the teachers at Hafsa's Catholic kindergarten are willing to include alternatives to Christian rituals in their curriculum, it is not commonly done here. They lack the knowledge to teach children about non-Christian traditions and are thus dependent on parents to get involved and provide their expertise, which parents have not yet done. Hafsa's mother Saime does not perceive the *Kita*'s focus on Christian religious repertoire as a problem, because as she explains, for her, Muslim celebrations belong first and foremost to the family sphere. It is in the home that her daughter is introduced to Muslim religious values and traditions. Saime's statements show us that different interests are negotiated in the creation of a curriculum and that much of the power to choose one approach over another lies with the parents. Indeed, it is Saime, not one of the kindergarten teachers, who offers to occasionally tell the children stories about Muslim celebrations such as Ramadan and the Sugar and Sacrifice Feasts as these days approach. Since the teachers lack the knowledge to do so, Saime steps into the role of expert and takes over the presentation of information about non-Christian rituals.

Over all, Topçu's article is an interesting example of the typical ideas that crop up when Christmas is placed against the backdrop of Muslim immigration. First, it emphasizes that being Muslim is somehow irreconcilable with celebrating Christmas. The assumption that there wouldn't be anything noteworthy about the Nativity play if it weren't for the one child with a Muslim background constructs these circumstances as strikingly unusual. We do not learn anything about the other children and can only make assumptions about them. Approached from this angle, they appear as the homogenous norm from which Hafsa deviates. This tendency can also be observed in other contexts whenever Christmas and Muslims or the group of Turkish-Germans are addressed.

The question of whether and how Christmas is celebrated seems to be frequently posed to Germans with a non-Christian background. Accordingly, different actors who are seen as representatives of this "community" deal with the question and provide answers. For example, the German-Turkish portal "Ay-Yildiz" ("Half-moon-Star"), which is an online venue for Turks in Germany, approaches the issue by describing a diverse range of practices, from integrating Christmas as a recurring family tradition to not celebrating it at all. The question inspires great interest, but the answer is neither short nor coherent and involves the issue of representation. This question is also addressed in a book by Aiman Mazyek, a media consultant and chairman of the Central Council of Muslims in

Germany, released in 2016 and titled "What Do Muslims Do at Christmas?
Islamic Belief and Daily Life in Germany."[27] There is only a small section
on Christmas as the book tries to cover various fields, from human rights
and gender equality to paradise and mosque building. Mazyek describes
his reason for choosing the title in the introduction:

> The title of this book was developed knowing that speechlessness
> is often due to a fear of the unknown. Islam is often a synonym
> for this unknown. 'What do Muslims do at Christmas?' Below I
> will answer this question very concretely but on a personal level.
> In general my title is supposed to express much more than the
> simple question implies: We as humans are much more alike than
> we perceive – when we are among family, when we celebrate, when
> we join together in fellowship around common table, or enter
> into wedlock. Christmas, Chanukka, Ramadan – these words have
> always connoted the idea of an encounter, something that we are
> often missing today.[28]

Mazyek links the question about Christmas to a fear of the unknown and
a perspective that stresses differences rather than connections. He concedes
that he is replying to the question by describing his own practice, since
decisions about whether and how to celebrate are made at the individual
level, leading to a wide range of practices.

Since Mayzek aims at reconciliation and enabling understanding, he
highlights connections and emphasizes openness towards the rituals of
Christian culture. In an interview he reported that he has created the
tradition of giving an "oriental pastry" to his neighbours as a present during
Christmastime and that the practice of offering each other congratulations
on the occasion of important religious holidays has established itself within
his social network.[29] As the chairman of the Central Council of Muslims
in Germany, Aiman Mazyek plays the role of a representative in the public
sphere; thus, we must consider the symbolic character of his remarks.
His words imply that enhancing the public's knowledge about Islam can
mitigate reservations and insecurities. Specifically, he argues, it must be
taught that the differences between migrant communities and the majority
are less significant than the similarities.

Mazyek's approach to answering typical questions about Christmas in
the Muslim community is not at all – or perhaps only cautiously – critical

of these types of inquiries. He accepts the questions as legitimate and answers in a way that is intended to smooth over presumed underlying conflicts. The dynamic between inquirer and respondent that emerges in Mazyek's book mirrors other aspects of the dynamic between Muslims and immigrants and the so-called German majority. Questions such as "How do Muslims celebrate Christmas?" or "What do you as a Turk do on Christmas?" are easy to come up with, and it is precisely this ease that explains why these questions are problematic: they have a tendency to oversimplify and homogenize, constructing the immigrant/Muslim other as different. Although it appears to be an interesting and legitimate question, especially because it cannot be assumed that every group performs the ritual of Christmas in the same way, inquiring about how different groups of people celebrate tends to push the diverse forms of celebration within the immigrant community itself into the background.

This dynamic can be clarified by returning to Topçu's article and once again examining the example of Christmas practices in kindergarten. In the article the author goes on to describe another *Kita* that also only celebrates Christmas and other Christian holidays, leaving out alternative religious holidays. The kindergarten teacher Ümit Gündüz comes from a Turkish-German family herself, and she perceives it as a normal part of her work to teach the kids Christian rituals. Although many boys and girls from Muslim families attend the institution, the *Kita* does not plan to integrate other celebrations. The multiple questions that regularly come up around Muslim holidays are, however, informally answered during morning circles. This indicates how diversity among the educational staff could eventually initiate changes, since the group would have a broader knowledge of diverse cultural traditions to share with the children.

When questioned about the participation of Muslim families in Christmas celebrations, Gündüz replies that "there are only a few hardliners who ignore our invitation." With this remark, we return to the crucial implications of Christmas inquiries. In this case the term "hardliner" describes a person who refrains entirely from participating in Christmas celebrations, while generally it is often applied in political or ideological contexts. It communicates the judgment that the decision not to participate in Christmas celebrations is a rather extreme and marginal one. It would be interesting to learn whether the teachers opened up a conversation with the concerned parents and how the issue was resolved. A further hypothetical question could be whether the members of a family without a Muslim background would also be judged to be hardliners for not celebrating Christmas.

Even though most families seem to find a feasible arrangement, the sole reign of Christmas and other Christian holidays is being questioned more and more. This is also the case in the aforementioned kindergartens in Frankfurt. Irrespective of whether or not they are public or Christian institutions, according to Topçu hardly any kindergartens in Frankfurt celebrate Muslim holidays. The head of one institution recalls how the composition of the classrooms has changed over the years as more and more children from immigrant families arrive. Today, 90 percent of the children in this particular institution in Frankfurt have a so-called immigration background and more than half of them are from Muslim families. Over the years, the staff has grown more and more uncomfortable celebrating Christmas, to the point that they renamed the festivities "end of year celebration." The change didn't last, however; the name reverted to Christmas and all of the children's parents, without exception, joined in the celebrations.

This episode can be seen as typical of the kind of ambiguity and unease that surrounds Christmas. Up until now, no consistent guidelines or codes designed to help meet the requirements of diverse groups in public contexts such as kindergartens or schools have emerged. Especially in settings where the majority come from immigrant families, however, this lack might be challenged. On the website of the DIK (German Islam Conference), Canan Topçu's article is supplemented with a link to the official guidelines for addressing religious questions in school contexts developed by the DIK.[30] In it, it is stated that religious plurality is a reality in Germany to which schools are adapting. This is said to lead to uncertainties that should be tackled by reviewing the legal situation concerning religious freedom and the state's obligation to educate. The guidelines convey a certain caution when it comes to religious practices that are connected to Islam and outlines both their compatibilities and incompatibilities with the educational mandate. It is not immediately evident how to transfer the legal perspective provided in the guidelines to the setting of Christmas in kindergarten described in Topçu's article. The guidelines can be interpreted as an attempt to show how arrangements can be found that satisfy the majority without changing the basic constellation of public spaces.

Opening up conversations about adapting or adding new Christmas traditions in the context of increasingly diverse spaces can lead to confrontations that are about more than religious holidays. This dynamic is visible in the public commentary on a decision passed by the district office in Kreuzberg, Berlin, in 2013. The municipality announced that they would no longer allow Ramadan or Christmas celebrations in public spaces. The district was struggling to process an overwhelming number of applications to hold public celebrations for various holidays and decided, on the grounds of equal treatment, to no longer allow religious festivities of any kind in public spaces. Eventually, the Ramadan celebration was renamed "*Sommerfest*" (summer party) and took place anyway.

In an interview with the city councilman responsible for deciding to no longer allow public religious celebrations, a reporter questioned the decision by pointing out that other large celebrations were still allowed in the public spaces of the district (specifically, the "Carnival of Cultures," the "Beer festival," and the "gay-lesbian festivals"). The article presents the politician's answer, that these celebrations have a long tradition in the district, as ridiculous: "I had to laugh: Christmas and Ramadan have even longer traditions."[31] Other articles commenting on the handling of religious festivities in the district convey a serious concern over the ban. Among anti-Islamic activists, the ban on religious celebrations in public spaces is interpreted as a further step towards Islamization and marginalization of Christian culture despite the fact that the change concerned all religious groups. The immediate classification of the decision as anti-Christian is extreme and represents one end of a whole spectrum of different positions. Nevertheless, it is clear that the handling of religious celebrations in a multicultural context is a highly sensitive field that triggers ideological debates. The complex of Christmas rituals still functions as an important force for cohesion despite its diffusion into different realms and the heterogeneous ways in which it is practised. Christmas provides the opportunity to imagine everyone – people throughout Germany, or even throughout the Christian world – sharing in rituals that have a long history. Christmas is seen as a celebration that connects people. There are not many social events in Germany that create a comparable dynamic or foster such a strong sense of simultaneity. Even if they are disrupted or dissolve into different social areas, even if their performance does not quite match up to the bourgeois ideal of Christmas, Christmas rituals still compel us to perform them.

Another social sphere that also creates the dynamic of a shared ritual is soccer games during the European or World Championship. In the context of these soccer rituals, the issues of multicultural societies are negotiated. Beneath exchanges on the growing diversity of the national soccer players run questions about which team Turkish-Germans will support; here, rooting for the German team is classified as a sign of belonging and integration. In 2009, the German Islam Conference published a brochure that presents the outcome of three years of dialogue. The cover shows a picture of six young people standing at a window holding the German national flag. It is an image of cultural and religious diversity: two blonde women, two dark-haired men, a dark-haired woman, and one woman with a headscarf form the group of friends smiling into the camera. In his dissertation on the DIK, Fabian Engler describes this image as an expressive celebration of national community.[32] Since flags in Germany are most commonly displayed during soccer games, the image could be linked to the context of the 2006 World Cup. This World Cup introduced the new practice of celebrating the national team in public spaces using not only flags, but also various other items in colours corresponding to the flag.

Is there a link between the ritual of Christmas and the ritual of soccer in the context of cultural diversity? In both cases, the question of participation is not just a private, individual decision; rather, it is negotiated in the public sphere. The decision to participate or not to participate is interpreted as a marker of one's stance towards the so-called cultural majority and thus of one's openness to integration as demonstrated through the acceptance of existing traditions and perspectives. Being perceived as an immigrant or Muslim Other has implications for the discursive connotations attached to the act of refraining from celebrating Christmas or waving a German flag for the soccer team. A highly significant difference between Germans who are not thought to have an immigrant or Muslim background and those who are is how their decision to participate in specific rituals is evaluated as a marker of national or cultural belonging.

The decision not to incorporate the tradition of Christmas into the family should be seen as an ambiguous one. It could be understood as part of a complex process of identity formation in which a certain cultural repertoire is transmitted, re-evaluated, and reshaped. Some fragments of the repertoire are left out or altered while others maintain their significance. During childhood and adolescence, the experience of realizing that one's family has its own traditions and religious holidays that differ from those of the majority might stabilize identity or, on the contrary, destabilize it, depending on the environment. These kinds of experiences open up an interior space that can be filled with a diverse range of feelings – for instance, a sense of regret at not belonging, or a sense of solidarity with an alternative group (or both simultaneously). In the case of the Imren family, Maral's children as well as other members of the third generation have accepted their family's decisions and seem to understand their parents' attempt to pass on cultural traditions associated with Turkey rather than fully adapting to local rituals. Nevertheless, these decisions might be renegotiated among following generations experiencing a Christmassy Berlin.

Final Remarks

In this chapter I attempted to uncover the underlying issues surrounding the Christmas ritual in settings shaped by immigration. This increasingly secularized holiday is adapted in different contexts in various ways and appears as hybrid as the actors of its globalized environment. An analysis of contemporary Christmas does not necessarily stand in contrast to the history of the tradition, despite how this history is constructed in conservative contexts. Christmas traditions are not as old, stable, or homogenous as those who see this custom as endangered present them. It is Christmas's focus on children in particular that leads to its continued celebration. The fear of spoiling children's joyful experiences also motivates Muslim immigrants to compromise on their own religious beliefs and find a way to claim certain parts of the tradition for their families. These newly claimed elements of Christmas are placed into a new context and filled with alternative meanings.

The analysis of Christmas-related negotiations highlights distinct approaches to the holiday that represent different ideas about how a multicultural community can and should function.[33] The educational sector's attempts to deal with religious plurality represent a rather conservative model of multiculturalism, because they do not aim to give Christian traditions and traditions from other religions equal status. In the case of public celebrations in Kreuzberg it is a liberal multiculturalism that underlies the decision to ban all religious festivities from public spaces.[34] The uncertainties surrounding these institutions and decisions indicate that an overarching consensus on how to deal with cultural and religious diversity has not yet been reached. The disguising of religious celebrations through their renaming represents the constant renegotiation of traditions. The lines in these negotiations are blurred; people's decisions do not neatly correspond with distinct ethnic or religious affiliations. Accordingly, the problem of representation is yet another source of debate, especially when certain actors claim to speak for "the Muslims," "the immigrants," or "the Christians." Questions about whether and how to celebrate Christmas might appear benign at first glance, but they are connected to the issues of belonging and othering.

In conclusion, I would like to return to the ethnographic vignette with which I began. Maral's question about Christmas and my surprise and initial impulse to perceive it as an indication that we were more different than I thought possibly reveals my own connections to the bourgeois culture that shapes the normative ideal of Christmas. The Imrens, in fact, have not had extensive contact with a bourgeois milieu because the places where they have lived, Neukölln and Wedding, are shaped to a much greater degree by their working-class populations than by bourgeois culture. Consequently, for Maral Christmas does not evoke the same ideas and pictures as it does for me, a realization that is likely to apply to most individuals.

In fact, there are similarities between Maral's and my approaches to unfamiliar rituals, which I realized when the family invited me to a celebration of the Sacrifice Feast. The celebration was organized by the Culture and Educational Association, which the family visits regularly. The street was closed off for the occasion and the whole neighbourhood was invited. Families were dressed festively, children were shyly singing Turkish songs on a small stage, mothers handed out tea, and food was served. The experience of familial togetherness seemed just as important as individuals' enjoyment of the festival. Before the public celebration, the whole family was invited to their grandparents' house for a big family meal. Towards the end of the evening I realized I could have asked Maral the same question – "What do you actually celebrate at the Sacrifice Feast?" I forgot to ask, but I still enjoyed the celebration.

Notes

1 From 2011 to 2013, I participated in daily family life and conducted interviews as part of my PhD research on immigration, biographies, and education. All names have been anonymized. See Reimers, "Migration, Bildung und Familie."

2 The term "Turkish-German" is used here because the family members chose this hyphenated label to describe themselves.

3 Bozkurt, *Conceptualising "Home,"* 32–3.

4 In 1999 William Safran pointed out that "53% of the Turks were hoping to return to Turkey within the next few years and only 5% were planning to remain in Germany permanently." According to Safran, the *Rückkehrmythos* (myth of return) was also fuelled by German elites who were reluctant to reevaluate Germany's status towards immigration. Safran, "Diasporas in Modern Societies," 367.

5 81% of the portion of the German population that originally came from Turkey is classified as Muslim. Haug, "Muslimisches Leben in Deutschland."

6 Safran relates the lack of openness towards immigration to the structuring of German society, which traditionally defined citizenship on the basis of descent, ignoring the duration of residence in the country. See Safran, "Diasporas in Modern Societies," 367.

7 Extended separation from parents is a globally common phenomenon that has not yet been researched extensively. Hajji, "Abschied auf ungewisse Zeit"; Phoenix, "Transforming Transnational Biographical Memories." The issue was captured artistically in 2016 when Hakan Savas Mican put on a theatre performance at the Ballhaus Naunynstraße in Kreuzberg, Berlin. He presented (auto)biographical accounts of the experience of separation in the context of immigration. Titled "On My Way Home," the piece told stories of disruption as well as of reconciliation. According to these accounts, separation was often experienced as a radical cut during childhood. Mican, *On My Way Home.*

8 Audehm et al., "Rituale," 432.

9 *Almanya* is the Turkish word for Germany.

10 My translation.

11 Suarez-Orozco and Suarez-Orozco, *Children of Immigration,* 90.

12 Foitzik, "Weihnachten," 155.

13 According to Foitzik, the paradox of Christmas is that despite being a Christian celebration of peacefulness, it was more often used for the purpose of war propaganda than as a serious plea for peace during the last hundred years.

14 Original in German: "*Insel des Gefühls*"; see Foitzik, "Weihnachten," 157.

15 Naturally, this fluidity is not restricted to the social realities of immigrants; nevertheless, hybridity is often regarded as particularly relevant for ethnic others, while the majority appears pure and unchanged. See Erel, "Paradigmen kultureller Differenz und Hybridität."

16 Rüdiger Vossen traces the Christmas tradition of gift-giving, which is related to the commercial dimension of Christmas, through history. He writes that until the nineteenth century, servants were entitled to receive gifts (shoes, clothing, or natural produce) for Christmas. As material wealth increased, this tradition increasingly focused on "good and courteous" children. See Vossen, *Weihnachtsbräuche in aller Welt*, 2019–20. John Storey regards the commercial dimension of Christmas as significant. Referring to English Christmas, he argues that Christmas has been shaped by its commercial dimension from the beginning. Storey, "The Invention of the English Christmas," 20.

17 Schiffauer, *Die Migranten aus Subay*, 34.

18 This is also addressed in another article on "Muslim Christmas" in the weekly newspaper *Die Zeit*, which quotes a Turkish-German vendor who complains that there is no special atmosphere in Germany during Muslim holidays such as Ramadan. Pazakaya, "Muslimische Weihnachten."

19 This notion of culture as a processual object of negotiation, translation, and transformation relates to the concept of hybridity that in cultural studies is especially linked to Homi Bhabha. Bhabha emphasizes the translational element of culture, specifically the need to translate cultural forms and to understand them in different contexts under different circumstances. Bhabha, *The Location of Culture*, 172.

20 Faist, "Developing Transnational Social Spaces."

21 The family stems from the Black Sea region; their link to this region is reconfirmed in different contexts through the use of, for instance, the language of Pontos Greek, specific music at celebrations, or specific traditional dances.

22 The concept of identity here is understood as Stuart Hall proposes it: as a construct that is neither enclosed nor essential. It is "a matter of 'becoming' as well as 'being'" and cannot be fixed. Hall, "Cultural Identity and Diaspora," 225. Cultural identifications change in different contexts; they do not form a stable core, although they transform within the boundaries of certain restrictions.

23 Gert Pickel identifies both a specific defensiveness and a prevalence of stereotypes towards Muslims not only in Germany but also in the whole of Europe. Debates on integration in Germany essentially focus on Muslims who are presented as adversaries to "modern, enlightened values." Pickel, "Religiöse Pluralisierung als Bedrohungsszenario?" 48.

24 Rommelspacher, *Anerkennung und Ausgrenzung*, 182.

25 The German Islam Conference is a governmental initiative that is
    supposed to create a dialogue between representatives of the state and
    the main actors of Islamic organizations in Germany. German Islam
    Conference, "Gemeinsame Werte als Grundlage des Zusammenlebens."

26 Topçu, "Muslimische Kinder feiern Weihnachten mit."

27 Mazyek, *Was machen Muslime an Weihnachten?* My translation of title.

28 Ibid., 11. My translation.

29 "Weihnachten: Auch Muslime feiern das Fest."

30 Topçu, "Muslimische Kinder feiern Weihnachten mit."

31 Schupelius, "Kreuzberg: Weihnachts- und Ramadan-Verbot."

32 Fabian Engler analyzes the DIK (German Islam Conference) in his
    dissertation "Islam and Germany: The Disputed Mutual in the German
    Islam Conference," which dissects the multiple dimensions of interaction
    between representatives of the German State and of Islamic congregations
    as well as so-called secular Muslims.

33 Rommelspacher, *Anerkennung und Ausgrenzung*, 180.

34 Rommelspacher also describes a third approach called critical
    multiculturalism. This approach is not represented in my empirical
    examples, but might be helpful for questions about whether and how
    to integrate the celebration of diverse religious holidays into public life.
    From this perspective, the significance of cultural and ethnic affiliations
    is questioned and their diversity and fluidity is recognized. Thus, it
    would not suffice to insist on the right to official holidays for all religious
    communities, as a liberal multiculturalism would urge. As a critical
    perspective, it would also question the validity of officially celebrating the
    holidays of the majority, so that everyone could decide whether or not to
    work on those days. Ibid., 186.

Bibliography

Audehm, Kathrin, Christoph Wulf, and Jörg Zirfas. "Rituale." In *Handbuch Familie*, edited by Jutta Ecarius, 424–40. Wiesbaden, Germany: vs Verlag für Sozialwissenschaften, 2007.

Bhabha, Homi. *The Location of Culture*. London: Routledge, 1994.

Bozkurt, Esin. *Conceptualising "Home": The Question of Belonging among Turkish Families in Germany*. Frankfurt, Germany: Campus Verlag, 2009.

Erel, Umut. "Paradigmen kultureller Differenz und Hybridität." In *Jenseits des Paradigmas Kultureller Differenz*, edited by Martin Sökefeld, 35–52. Bielefeld, Germany: Transcript, 2004.

Faist, Thomas. "Developing Transnational Social Spaces: The Turkish German Example." In *Migration and Transnational Social Spaces*, edited by Ludger Pries, 36–72. London: Routledge, 1998.

Foitzik, Doris. "Weihnachten." In *Deutsche Erinneringsorte*, edited by Etienne François and Hagen Schulze, 154–68. Munich, Germany: C.H. Beck, 2001.

German Islam Conference. "Gemeinsame Werte als Grundlage des Zusammenlebens." Federal Ministry of the Interior, 2015.

Hajji, Rahim. "Abschied auf ungewisse Zeit: Viele Gastarbeiter mussten Kinder zurücklassen - zu deren Schaden." WZB *Mitteilungen*, no. 124 (2009): 36–9.

Hall, Stuart. "Cultural Identity and Diaspora." In *Migration, Diasporas and Transnationalism*, edited by Steven Vertovec and Robin Cohen, 299–314. Cheltenham/Northampton, UK: Edward Elgar Publishing, 1999.

Haug, Sonja. "Muslimisches Leben in Deutschland." Edited by German Islam Conference. Berlin: Federal Ministry of the Interior, 2009.

Mazyek, Aiman. *Was machen Muslime an Weihnachten?: Islamischer Glaube und Alltag in Deutschland*. Munich, Germany: Bertelsmann Verlag, 2016.

Mican, Hakan Savas. *On My Way Home*. Theatre, 2016. http://www. ballhausnaunynstrasse.de/stueck/on_my_way_home.

Pazakaya, Utku. "Muslimische Weihnachten." *Die Zeit*, 20 December 2000. http://www.zeit.de/2000/52/Muslimische_Weihnachten.

Phoenix, Ann. "Transforming Transnational Biographical Memories: Adult Accounts of 'Non-Normative' Serial Migrant Childhoods." In *Ethnicity, Belonging and Biography*, edited by Gabriele Rosenthal and Artur Bogner, 267–84. Berlin: LIT Verlag, 2009.

Pickel, Gert. "Religiöse Pluralisierung als Bedrohungsszenario?" In *Religionen Dialog Gesellschaft*, edited by Katajun Amirpur and Wolfgang Weiße, 19–56. Münster, Germany: Waxmann, 2015.

Reimers, Sophie. "Migration, Bildung und Familie: Ethnografische Annäherung an den Alltag dreier Generationen zwischen türkischem Dorf und Neuköllner Kiez." Bielefeld, Germany: Transcript Verlag, 2018.

Rommelspacher, Birgit. *Anerkennung und Ausgrenzung: Deutschland als multikulturelle Gesellschaft*. Frankfurt, Germany: Campus Verlag, 2002.

Safran, William. "Diasporas in Modern Societies: Myths of Homeland and Return." In *Migration, Diasporas and Transnationalism*, edited by Steven Vertovec and Robin Cohen, 364–79. Cheltenham/Northampton, UK: Edward Elgar Publishing, 1999.

Şamdereli, Yasemin, dir. *Almanya*. 2011.

Schiffauer, Werner. *Die Migranten aus Subay: Türken in Deutschland, eine Ethnographie*. Stuttgart, Germany: Klett-Cotta, 1991.

Schupelius, Gunnar. "Kreuzberg: Weihnachts- und Ramadan-Verbot." *Berliner Zeitung*, 30 August 2013. http://www.bz-berlin.de/artikel-archiv/kreuzberg-weihnachts-und-ramadan-verbot.

Storey, John. "The Invention of the English Christmas." In *Christmas, Ideology and Popular Culture*, edited by Sheila Whiteley, 17–31. Edinburgh: Edinburgh University Press, 2008.

Suarez-Orozco, Carola, and Marcelo Suarez-Orozco. *Children of Immigration*. Cambridge, MA: Harvard University Press, 2002.

Topçu, Canan. "Muslimische Kinder feiern Weihnachten mit." *German Islam Conference (DIK)*, 23 December 2013. http://www.deutsche-islam-konferenz.de/DIK/DE/Magazin/IslamBildung/ReligioeseFeste/feste-node.html.

Vossen, Rüdiger. *Weihnachtsbräuche in aller Welt: Von Martini bis Lichtmess*. Hamburg, Germany: Ellert & Richter Verlag, 2012.

"Weihnachten: Auch Muslime feiern das Fest." *Berlin Hauptstadtportal*, n.d. https://www.berlin.de/special/familien/2867532-2864562-weihnachten-auch-muslime-feiern-das-fest.

9

A Christmas Crisis:
Lessons from a Canadian Public
School's Seasonal Skirmish

Helen Mo

Introduction

Canadian multiculturalism – like so many unicorns – is of recent vintage and grounded to no small degree in myth. Born in 1971 from the shrewd statecraft of Pierre Trudeau and established on a settler-colonial creation story of biculturalism[1] and immigration dreams, Canada's half-century of multicultural formation has occurred in tandem with globalization and de-industrialization, as well as social and technological revolutions that have transformed both personal and public life. In 2015, Canada elected Justin Trudeau, the son of Pierre, as prime minister, just as it was ramping up its cultural apparatus for the sesquicentennial celebrations of 2017. The country's purported tolerance, diversity, and progressivism were increasingly vaunted in international news publications and online memes alike.

On a 2016 cover featuring the Statue of Liberty crowned by a maple leaf, *The Economist* proclaimed: "Liberty moves north."[2] On Facebook, memes ostensibly depicting life in Canada alternate between the folksy and the smug: scenes of weather and wildlife characterize the former, and smug representations of Canadian progressivism (e.g. a split image juxtaposing an act of police brutality in the United States with a water-gun-wielding officer in Toronto's Pride Parade) characterize the latter. In research and policy arenas, scholars extol, critique, or try to explain the narrative of Canadian multicultural success.[3] As Cas Mudde affirms, Canada's relative success with immigration in an era of rising xenophobia in other Western democracies makes it a "multiculturalist unicorn" – a shining, solitary example of liberal multicultural success.[4]

Going by the most hopeful reports, one could almost believe that Canada has truly achieved the harmonious diversity long promised by stock photography. Wise and Veluyatham point out in the introduction to *Everyday Multiculturalism*, however, that the field of multicultural studies overemphasizes the management and assessment of diversity: for the most part, its subject is multiculturalism writ large and viewed through the technocrat's apparatus of quantifiables, census categories, and mid-range generalizations.[5] Perhaps in deference to the sheer scale of a national project, scholarly investigations of Canadian multiculturalism largely elide how individuals negotiate more local and intimate impacts of population change and the corresponding shifts in cultural norms and narratives. Such negotiations are necessarily mired in particularity and ambiguity; they are hard to count and translate poorly for international comparisons. Nevertheless, Wise and Veluyatham argue that a thorough understanding of any multicultural context requires close scrutiny of everyday negotiations of cultural difference in super-diverse spaces. Only by looking also for points of potential fracture and moments when multicultural policies are tested, they suggest, can we see how macro-political discourses filter down to shape social relations and identity. In the same volume, Giovanni Semi, Enzo Colombo, Ilenya Camozzi, and Annalisa Frizina similarly warn that top-down accounts of multiculturalism are often highly normative, reifying and essentializing groups in the pursuit of clarity and coherence.[6] Simpler stories are not always better stories.

How will the multicultural national project hold up in an era of increasing translocality, porous publics, and a more austere and precarious social contract? In what spaces and under what conditions do its daily propagations and contestations take place? As a complement to work in the fields of race, immigration, and policy, which illuminate Canadian multiculturalism from the top down, I here present something of a different vantage point: an insider's play-by-play of events that were in effect a ground-level negotiation of multicultural realities in the context of local, national, and global processes and conditions. At the time when these events unfolded, they seemed quite extraordinary. In hindsight, however, this story's elements are not unique. Variants of its themes, inciting forces, and narrative trajectories animate everything ranging from public-relations tempests in other multicultural contexts worldwide to the rise of far-right populists in Western democracies. Now more than ever, scholars have urgent reason to examine specific instantiations of multicultural discord, as the limitations of polling data, technocratic projections, and the enlightened self-interest that underpins so much political and economic theory have become more pronounced. The resurgence of open xenophobia in Western politics demonstrates that non-quantifiable elements of human experience – the narratives of aspiration, resentment, and loss; the dynamic interplay of race, class, and gender; and the power of cultural alignment with or against particular institutions – are not details to be brushed aside, but the very elements that constitute a given public and its possibilities.

A Christmas Crisis

In the early 2010s, I was a high school English teacher in a mid-sized Canadian city when the staff and students of the school where I taught became embroiled in a very sudden, very public crisis that escalated over mere hours. The crisis played out as much online as on school property and subsided within days for all save a few individuals. Its ethnographic value, however, really struck me at the time, begging analysis even as my colleagues and I were immersed in the immediacy of managing adolescent emotions and on-the-fly public relations. Years afterward, this "Christmas Crisis" (as I came to think of it) lingered in my peripheral vision, colouring my perceptions of the complex, occasionally volatile intersection of ethnicity, religion, class, and belonging in Canadian public schools, Canadian public life, and by extension the public life of diverse societies more generally. Between my own involvement, the involvement of my students, and the limits of memory, this extended anecdote can be neither perfect nor impartial. Its value should lie in the reflections that follow. Still, following Marshall McLuhan's oft-quoted line about the medium being the message, this imperfect account and its unreliable narrator are perhaps appropriate; this is nothing if not a story of imperfect accounts, unreliable narrators, and the necessity of critical hindsight.[7]

That a controversy over Christmas should erupt in a socio-economically and culturally diverse Canadian high school is not surprising. Not only are such public schools incubators of personal identity and cultural formation, they bring people with different beliefs, habits, and social imaginaries into close proximity at an age when they are especially attuned to questions of meaning and morality. Adolescents are still negotiating their alliances

with each other and with broader social units, establishing their understandings of the world, and experimenting with roles. So necessary are
these behaviours that their manifestations have become archetypal. Teen
zealots, rebels without a cause, and résumé-building "A" students largely
direct their energies into well-worn channels. Their affect and passions
are real, if not original.

Meanwhile, Christmas holds a unique place in the Western cultural
canon. Its long period of festivities overshadows the rest of the festive
calendar. Even leaving aside the religious celebration, it is the focal point of
innumerable tropes that combine the sentimental and the sacred (e.g. "home
for the holidays," "Christmas spirit," "Christmas miracles," etc.). Finally, its
very plasticity and ability to engulf other traditions, stories, and characters
make it an ideal backdrop for representations of nationhood. Every year,
in the lead-up to the winter holidays, the "War on Christmas" narrative
resurfaces in Canada, the US, the UK, and Australia – all Western, historically Christianized, and multicultural countries that have colonially-shaped
histories of immigration and thus also of controversies over integration or
accommodation. In what Geoffrey Brahm Levey describes as its own "new
and highly spirited tradition," Christmas has become a perennial site for
cultural battles over "ethno-religious hierarchy, minority inclusion, and
national identity" in multicultural societies.[8] What follows is a small-scale
exemplar of this much broader phenomenon – a very local skirmish with
global themes and implications.

Context: Windsor

My partner and I moved to Windsor, Ontario, a year after the 2008 global
economic crash. We drove through the city's core in our aged Honda
Civic, taking in the "For Sale" and "For Rent" signs posted up and down
every residential and commercial block. A die-hard auto-industry town in
an age of increasingly offshored factories, Windsor's fate was closely tied
to America's struggling Big Three automakers and had the then-highest
unemployment rate in Canada. Whole plazas of small businesses folded,
and many families attempted to rent out basements to keep up with their
mortgages. The city sits at the southernmost tip of the province, near the
southernmost point in Canada. For those visiting from about anywhere
else in the country, it is literally the end of the road. It is the last stop on
the east-west highway spanning Canada's most populous region before you

cross the river into Detroit – that American rust-belt city whose rise and decline took place on a much grander scale than Windsor's, and whose cultural impact is often more palpable in Windsor than that of other Canadian cities. In Windsor, the weather is humid and mild, people speak Fahrenheit rather than Celsius, and America is *north*.

Historically a working-class Franco-Ontarian area, successive waves of immigration from Southern Europe, Eastern Europe, the Balkans, Asia, and the Middle East have driven Windsor's growth since the mid-twentieth century. While some newcomers do struggle, living in substandard housing in the poorer north and west ends of the city, upwardly mobile first-, second-, and third-generation immigrants increasingly live out in newer or more spacious suburbs along with the majority of Windsor's middle class. Each successive wave of migration brings new businesses, foodways, and institutions to the urban landscape, and the legacies of cohorts of immigrants are visible in the community halls and places of worship distributed throughout the city. Local festivals, galas, and high-school proms regularly take place at ethnic-community venues such as the Caboto Club or the Serbian Centre. The city's "pull" factors include its many close-knit clans and community networks, the low cost of living, plucky local businesses, family-friendly neighbourhoods, and the presence of both a university and a community college. During my time there, its resident malcontents (many students among them) also told me in blunt terms that Windsor was, in their eyes, a "shithole" – a place with nothing to do, a jobs desert with little beyond the precarious service or manufacturing sectors, a backwater of narrow dreams and even narrower-minded people, a place polluted by immigrants or thick with racists. For these critics, these were less "push" factors than "pull" factors of a different sort; combined with the binding weight of inertia, familiarity, and family ties, they exerted a gravitational pull almost impossible to overcome. In this sense, Windsor is every hometown that both nurtures and eats its young.

One ladder out, for those who wanted it, was having access to translocal networks. For young people, a cousin in Toronto or a holiday visit to family "out West" often afforded a glimmer of cultural capital. A surprising proportion of my students had never left the country despite living literally minutes from the United States by bridge or tunnel, and a few had never left the city. This immobility, however, had a strong ethno-cultural dimension in that even first- or second-generation immigrants almost invariably had access to translocal and transnational ethnic or ethno-religious networks and cultural spaces. By contrast, many poor or working-class whites, whose families had been in the region for generations, were more likely to be confined to older and shabbier areas near the city centre (and near Carson Collegiate,[9] where I taught), with some rarely leaving their neighbourhoods, much less the country.

Carson Collegiate had a storied history of academic excellence and the sort of spirited performances associated with American movies – pep rallies, football games, and students sporting face-paint in school colours. Sometime after 2000, however, a nearby technical high school closed and its less academically oriented student base streamed into Carson. As the story went, this was the end of Carson's golden era. By 2009, only about half its student body was on the university track, and half was on the community college track. Students in the latter group were disproportionately poor and disproportionately white. In theory, the university stream provided an academically rigorous environment for students disposed to abstract thinking, and the college stream a more hands-on, practical curriculum for students who wished to continue in the trades or go straight into the workplace. In practice, the university-level classes contained more docile students, more students from middle-class homes, and more students whose immigrant parents were hell-bent on their offspring achieving the good life by way of higher education. College-level classes contained not only students of more concrete talents but many who were too troubled or disruptive to get by in the university-stream setting, or who lacked a parent who could or would persuade school teachers and administrators to see past a shy personality, learning disability, or rough patch. In all my years at Carson, I only taught a total of three university-stream classes. Unless otherwise specified, the students described here were from the college stream.

The Story Unfolds

It began in second period on a Thursday, with snatches of whispered conversation among a few Grade 12 students, at a volume just low enough to catch my attention. I walked by casually, teacher-ears perked. The speaker was a sweet-natured boy, small for his age. He was saying, in his quiet way: "I just don't think it's right when people come to this country and want to change our ways."

There were a few hushed qualifications from his audience, some furtive glances over shoulders. The murmured conversation continued.

I took note but – because I was eavesdropping on what was clearly a surreptitious conversation – said nothing. The remainder of the period proceeded uneventfully.

A class of Grade 11 students came next. Another cluster of kids was having a hushed conversation; again, references to culture caught my attention. They were saying something about Christmas. Their discussion seemed within the bounds of classroom chatter, and nobody was insulting someone else or openly cussing. Still, my radar for anything involving ethnicity, culture, religion had been sensitive since leaving my childhood home in Toronto's hyper-diverse "ethnoburbs."[10] Having grown up in a place that occasionally felt like its own polyglot post-metropolitan country, I had spent my adult life thus far crossing into less diverse social and professional spaces with the air of an expatriate, ready to play ambassador and explainer at a moment's notice. In Carson, I was one of a handful of visible-minority teachers. With minimal protest, I had also become the school's representative for an arcane school-board equity initiative and coordinator of the annual Multicultural Assembly. In short, for me the project of a multicultural Canada was arguably both personal and professional – more so than it would perhaps be for most teachers.

I drifted by their desks and crouched down silently, signalling that I wanted to listen in. In roundabout fashion, they eventually explained what troubled them. Something about immigrants changing Canadian ways, about Canadian customs under threat. One girl said, very soberly: "My cousin said that in Toronto, they don't even have Christmas anymore. She said they've banned Christmas." The others nodded grimly, seeming to find this plausible. I processed this – what she believed, what she had left unsaid, how she felt about it. The mood of the group was tense, plaintive. When they fell silent, I explained as gently as I could that what she had been told was untrue. Sensing that this was about more than Christmas in Canada's largest city, and that "Toronto" was here used to denote a space full of racialized Others, I made it personal: I told them about growing up in Toronto public schools, where almost every first- and second-generation kid like myself wished their friends a merry Christmas and gladly indulged in candy-cane excess. The girl looked uncertain. I wondered if our good rapport made my account plausible enough to outweigh reports of Christmas being extinguished.

As the period drew to a close, I stood among students who were clustered by the classroom door, waiting for the bell to ring. A boy ("Scott") drifted up to the blackboard next to the exit and grabbed a piece of chalk as a few of his friends loitered nearby. With an oddly theatrical flourish, he scrawled "Merry Christmas." Turning back toward his friends, who were only halfway paying attention, he declared: "There. I don't even care if I get suspended."

Something clicked and the teacher-lights went off in my head. There was an unmistakable tone of defiance in his voice and body language. He was clearly signalling that this was a subversive act and wanted his peers to know that he was unafraid of the consequences. As anyone who has recently been in a school environment knows, teachers and students share that suspension of disbelief where they can be in close proximity while each party remains seemingly unheard and unseen by the other until either party signals otherwise. Aware that his defiance wasn't directed at me even if he intended for me to witness it, I tuned in and moved slightly closer to engage.

"Merry Christmas to you, too, Scott," I said lightly. "Why would you be suspended for wishing someone a merry Christmas?"

Glances went around and Scott seemed slightly abashed. Between him and others nearby, the story came out in pieces. Our vice-principal, Mr P, was apparently suspending students for saying "Merry Christmas." Scott's friends chimed in about the unfairness of the situation. Mr P was suspending *Christian* students for saying "Merry Christmas," they claimed. My first instinct was to laugh at the implausibility of what they described, but I checked myself. Clearly, it was plausible to them. "Mr P's an Arab, you know," Scott muttered to a friend, his voice low.

And there it was. I did not yet have the full story but it unscrolled before me anyway, like the plot of a movie whose genre I knew well. Who *hasn't* seen the one about the foreigners who hate Christmas? We were entering a "teachable moment," that lucid space in which teachers' perception of time slows and everything – eye contact, word choice, pauses for emphasis – glimmers with heightened significance. I began carefully. The school would not ban, and certainly *had* not banned Christmas, I assured them. We had the "Children's Christmas Party," a charitable event that was a long-time feature of the Carson calendar, coming up, didn't we? I acknowledged their confusion about which seasonal greetings were permissible to say, but emphasized the centrality of respect and goodwill. I also acknowledged what they thought was happening and promised to find out what was going on. Looking at their conflicted expressions, I added, on an impulse: "You know that Mr P is a church-going Christian, right?"

To this day, I feel deeply ambivalent about this disclosure and cannot recall it without a twinge of guilt. In the climate of Canada's relatively private, don't-ask-don't-tell attitude about religion, it felt a little like stating that someone was heterosexual: it would neither surprise nor embarrass anyone, but it was rarely anyone else's business. More importantly, the statement implied the alternative might be problematic. Mr P's affiliation may have been open knowledge, but *these* students had not known. I knew that they did not know, but felt strongly in that moment that they needed to know. I knew that it would have the effect of fixing a crucial misapprehension in these students' minds, and it also bothered me that I knew. But my intuition proved correct, for as soon as the words were out of my mouth, a complex reaction worked itself out on Scott's face.

"Mr P's a Christian?" Scott turned to stare at a friend who normally wore her cool veneer like armour, but who now was also visibly stunned. "I … I had no idea."

Looking at Scott in that moment, and replaying the moment in my head for days afterward, the word "crestfallen" kept coming to mind. He was surprised, yes, and sheepish, but what lingered with me was the disappointment. On some level, his show of defiance had felt good – and my disclosure had deflated, however non-confrontationally, what must have amounted to a heroic arc. The big, bad Muslim – Mr P, whose job it was to discipline these kids – had appeared the perfect villain, a presumed immigrant imposing his un-Canadian ways and vindictively penalizing those who dared take pride in their country and its traditions. But subtract the detail of Mr P's purported Muslimness, and evidently the whole persecution narrative fell apart. So, too, did Scott's prospects for glory and self-actualization through rebellion.

Lunch: To the Press

It took until lunchtime to piece together the rumour that had so drawn my students' imaginations and ire. Stacy, a Grade 12 student enrolled in my Grade 11 English class, had been suspended for saying "Merry Christmas"; this sparked righteous anger, and some students began shouting the holiday greeting as an act of solidarity and resistance. Mr P, acting out of anti-Christian animus, then proceeded to suspend those students in turn for taking up the forbidden phrase.

From my vantage point, this account was utterly implausible, so I took my questions to the principal. He finally explained the growing furor. Stacy had reposted an incendiary Facebook meme. The meme declared that immigrants had no right to change Christmas traditions or prevent the singing of the national anthem, and that whoever disagreed should "go back to their own f-ing countries." In sharing the meme, Stacy had personally added the suggestion that people ought to dress up as Santa Claus and scream "Merry Christmas" at those who held anti-Christmas or anti-anthem views. Implicitly, this imagined anti-Christmas, anti-Canadian faction meant immigrants and visible minorities. A fellow student saw the post, determined that it was offensive or threatening, and reported Stacy to Mr P. He then summoned Stacy to his office on the Wednesday, the day before the events described here.

Under board policy, students could be suspended for behaviour that negatively impacted the school's "moral tone," whether in-school or online. Mr P suspended Stacy from classes for three days. The school was buzzing that Thursday because earlier that morning, Stacy had returned to dispute her suspension. Mr P informed her that she could not be on school property while suspended and sent her away. Hearing of this, likely from Stacy herself as she left the school in anger, a few students decided to run around screaming "Merry Christmas" at visible-minority students – especially those whom they took to be Arab, and presumed to be Muslim. Those who were caught were then promptly suspended by Mr P for harassment. Word of their suspensions got back to Stacy, and Stacy called the press. Within the hour, she appeared on the main page of a newspaper's website in a video with an accompanying article.

The video opens close up on Stacy's face. She stands in the parking lot of a local strip mall, and squints into the sun as she speaks. "I was suspended over something I believe. Over this 'Merry Christmas' thing ... about not being able to say 'Merry Christmas' and how it might offend some religious families," she says.

"Have they – have the students been told that they cannot say 'Merry Christmas' to each other?" the reporter asks. He is not in the frame; the camera stays fixed on Stacy for the duration of the interview.

Stacy hesitates for a split second and deflects: "Uhh ... not that I've heard, but a few of my friends have said yes, that's what they've been told."

He asks about her Facebook re-post and Stacy gives a halting paraphrase: "It said that ... it's sad that we can't say 'Merry Christmas' in our own country, and that our soldiers fought for – under our own Canadian anthem and our flag, and if other religious families do not like it, and they do not like our customs, then they're just gonna have to deal with it. We have to deal with theirs, so why not deal with ours?"

The reporter does not explain how the post is connected to her suspension, or revisit her claim about being prevented from wishing people "Merry Christmas." Instead, his next question is almost a prompt: "Now, I think one of the reasons they argue that we shouldn't be doing too much 'Merry Christmas' is because they want it to be all-inclusive and not everyone celebrates Christmas. Is that … a problem?"

It is unclear if he is taking her lead or going with what he or his editor recognizes as the more provocative angle. Taking the bait, Stacy subtly perks up. While her earlier responses are guarded and hesitant, she now speaks more quickly: "Well, I believe that if you don't celebrate Christmas, just ignore it. Let us be happy with what we celebrate, in our traditions. So, if you have – they have their traditions, we have ours. They celebrate theirs at a certain time, we celebrate ours."

The reporter wraps up with a half-hearted fact-check: "Now … you were told, uh, to stay away from school until Monday?"

Stacy explains that she had gone to school that day in an attempt to talk to the vice-principal after he had shooed her off the property the previous day. "He told me, 'Come back on Monday, get out of my school.' So I went there today and he … said that, if he has to, he'll … uh, give me a trespassing … warrant. That I'm not allowed back."

Having told the story of her exile, Stacy stops as though awaiting the next prompt. The video ends there.

Response

Public response was swift. The story, which the local newspaper published before fact-checking with the school, went viral and began drawing vitriolic comments. Its initial version conveyed, albeit with some room for ambiguity, that students had been suspended for wishing others a "Merry Christmas." Even after the newspaper published an updated version later in the day to clarify that this was not the case, and to include a reassuring statement from the school board, calls from outraged parents and members of the public quickly overwhelmed both Carson's administration and the school board office. Meanwhile, with some misinformed students continuing their belligerent verbal "defense" of Christmas, teachers had their hands full sending offenders to the vice-principal and keeping the lid on outbursts and threats of retaliation.

As the consequences continued to ripple outward, it occurred to me that with Windsor's powder keg of economic anxieties and prime conditions for nativist resentments, the backlash could be nasty. I was also painfully aware that many of my colleagues lacked the training, experience, or intercultural literacy to navigate a situation involving racism, anxiety, xenophobia, and misconceptions about ethno-religious groups. Still, while the stakes were high, so too was the potential for teachable moments. And so, despite reservations about my own presumption, I spent the remainder of my lunch break composing an email to the staff. In it I outlined the confusion in the morning classes, included a primer on key terms (covering, for example, the difference between "Muslim," "Arab," and "Arabic" – words I had heard staff and students alike using interchangeably), and suggested some possible approaches to discussing the situation with our students.

The efforts of Carson's staff and administration notwithstanding, the crisis continued unabated. That afternoon, hours after the video's release and after the initial wave of suspensions, elaborate rumours saturated the school. The only common thread was that students were allegedly being suspended for saying "Merry Christmas." In one especially puzzling version of the story, a student supposedly wished our principal a merry Christmas, and he promptly suspended her because the word "Christmas" contains "Christ" – and *that would be offensive to Catholics.* The next day, we also learned that police had been called to the school as a preventative measure: with ethnic tensions running high, there had been reports that a group of boys from a nearby Catholic school with a high Arab-Canadian population were coming to settle scores with the students who caused the initial fuss.

The school board was horrified by the turn of events and scrambled to put out a reassuring statement to the press – thereby proving the value of its in-house "Chief Diversity Officer," whose job was to manage precisely such a scenario. Carson's Parent Council was similarly horrified and wished to counter the negative publicity. The main thrust of these efforts was to deny that Christmas was under threat, to affirm Carson's Christmas credibility in the eyes of all the angry racists who had emerged to condemn the school, and to soothe ruffled feathers by affirming the board's inclusive and non-threatening diversity. In short, the message had two strands: first, we are all about Christmas, Canada, and patriotism! Second, our diversity is about all traditions, and all traditions are Canadian! Our principal also enlisted me to draft a letter to the local newspaper in an effort to untangle the misconceptions. I produced this letter over the weekend in collaboration with my English department colleagues, taking time out to supervise the Children's Christmas Party on the Saturday. The irony was not lost on me as I watched our enthusiastic student helpers – some of whom were Muslim girls sporting Christmas-coloured headscarves under reindeer antlers – shepherd underprivileged local children through a battery of festive activities. Reports of Christmas's demise at Carson were greatly exaggerated. As we discovered, however, once this sort of story got out, the truth was quite irrelevant to those who reacted most vehemently.

Aftermath: Personal and Political

In the public response to this fabricated crisis in a single Canadian school, it was evident that the "War on Christmas" narrative was powerful enough to override facts, local circumstances, and basic civility on the parts of students and adult onlookers alike. The newspaper ultimately published the Parent Council's letter instead of our staff letter, but corrective measures made little difference. The hate mail and angry calls took weeks to abate. The ongoing trickle of angry letters in the newspaper demonstrated that nothing quite dispelled the stubborn belief that Christmas needed defending from both immigrants (namely Muslims) and political correctness (which was supposedly also the fault of Muslims). The incident drew out xenophobes as far as Vancouver and Australia who seemed deeply invested in this narrative, and gladly used this incident to fuel their animus against immigrants. It had little to do with what had in fact transpired, and everything to do with emotion – specifically, a kind of outrage shading into anger.

After the 2016 US election, this story's motifs have been often echoed and compounded in more violent versions, making our Christmas crisis seem almost trite. But that December in 2011, the first Obama term had not yet drawn to a close, and few had reason to think that the combination of white working-class resentment, online misinformation, and the triumph of gut feelings over fact would fuel one of the biggest political spectacles of the era. In light of how neatly Carson's crisis telegraphed the major movements of the Trump campaign and presidency, it seems likely that for many years prior, in towns and social media spaces across America, similar local crises and storylines had been unfolding, quietly setting the stage for the drama to come.

Carson's Christmas crisis, short-lived as it was, was not exclusively confined to the board's publicity apparatus. The principal, who was white, and Mr P, the vice-principal who was of Arab descent, bore the brunt of the personal attacks. Some callers riffed on the principal's name, taunting him with a vaguely Middle Eastern–sounding nickname, as though that were inherently pejorative.[11] Many were openly racist toward Mr P. School staff members were generally taken aback, unsettled by how the norms of civility and lived multiculturalism they had daily taken for granted in their workplace could be so suddenly and vehemently disrupted. The ugly, muddied nature of the incident, its rapid escalation and unleashing of spiteful energies in the public at large, also left students by turn sobered, sheepish, and disgusted. Those who had no affinity for xenophobic provocations simply clucked in disapproval and continued with their lives.

Of the many who had believed the rumours, some seemed relieved to have no cause for grievance. The few active agitators went silent – whether they were truly mollified, I could not tell. By the following week, embarrassment won out as students and staff continued to be on the receiving end of misplaced outrage from their families, non-school acquaintances, and the public at large: Carson's students wanted to clear the school's name and leave the whole mess behind. With that, things took another turn. As if by consensus, students began vilifying Stacy, singling her out for besmirching Carson's reputation. Rather than reflecting on the surge of racism and ignorance, or on their own willingness to accept the rumours, the same people who had found her cause so believable began calling her a troublemaker. Contempt must have been an effective deflection, because I heard no expressions of remorse from these students. For all of the story's false starts, false premises, and unsatisfying conclusions, it did find its villain. It proved easier to blame one person than to exorcise the lingering sense of unease.

Christmas Crises: A Genre

The arc of Carson's Christmas crisis may feel familiar because similar stories are regularly reported in Western media.[12] In Canadian contexts, the dominant "War on Christmas" pattern is as follows. First, an institutional entity alters or removes a Christmas tradition. Whether the act is an earnest effort to make an environment more inclusive or simply to appear politically correct in a multicultural society – and whether these are even distinct motives – is subject to interpretation. Second, a public outcry follows wherein some groups or individuals blame non-Christians, non-whites, immigrants, or some combination thereof (Muslims have lately been a favoured target) for changing or destroying Canadian traditions. Less xenophobic objectors tend to focus blame on secularists, multiculturalists, liberals, urban elites, "PC Police," or some combination of the above for spoiling what they perceive as harmless seasonal fun. Still others spread the blame equally between these targets.[13] While specifics vary across settings, it is clear that real or perceived threats to Christmas have an extraordinary capacity to provoke a firestorm of unwanted publicity and outsized backlash.

David R. Berry, a retired American principal and professor of education, discusses his experience in an article entitled "A Not So Merry Christmas: Dilemmas for Elementary School Leaders."[14] Berry relates how once, following a parent complaint over Christmas celebrations in their Tennessee school, he wrote an email asking his staff to be mindful of their diversifying school population and of the separation of church and state ahead of the holiday season. Within days, someone distributed copies of his email in neighbourhood mailboxes. A local Concerned Christians group then placed an advertisement using his email text, asking supporters to defend "traditional Christian ways" from "outsiders."[15] Like mine, Berry's piece devotes a section to the aftermath, documenting staff's discomfort, the involvement of the school board chairman (who, Berry notes, was also a licensed lawyer), the media coverage, and the largely negative public response. Reflecting on the "unintended consequences" of such scenarios, Berry observes that "schools may become divided by emotional reactions to whatever policy is followed in connection with Christmas. Others may be silently discontented, fostering internal unrest."[16]

Deborah J. Levine also presents a Christmas-crisis anecdote in which she was personally embedded – not as a teacher, but as the leader of a community interfaith group called Network. In her Chicago suburb, a local principal moved the school's Christmas tree to a less prominent location in pre-emptive deference to increasing cultural diversity in the population. Outraged, students marched through the streets (all the while shouting racist slogans at onlookers) to the town's other high school, which had kept its prominent Christmas tree display. As with Carson, police involvement and heavy media coverage ensued. Levine explains that students "treated objections as threats to the school culture and ... to the religious heritage of the majority. [They] singled out classmates who advocated changes that would deprive them of on-going school traditions or new opportunities to augment the holiday season."[17] As with Carson, there was one prominent line of imagined ethno-religious distinction despite the presence of many minorities; in Levine's community, it fell between Christians and Jews, with other groups playing more marginal roles.

In our accounts, Levine and I are not only narrators, but also interveners. Noting the palpable "discomfort and confusion" of principals over the issue of religious diversity and seeing that too much rested on teachers with "little conflict management training, little education in multi-faith issues, limited religious training of their own beyond childhood, and little guidance from legal precedent," Levine stepped in to conduct religious and cultural diversity training for staff.[18] Levine's Network went on to hold many such seminars for educators, provide policy guidelines, and consult on similar issues both locally and nationally. Indeed, the language of threat and defense, loss and deprivation, and majorities vs. outsiders in all these cases hint that while Christmas crises may be political and symbolic battles, they are above all driven by emotions relating to identity.

As a traditional nexus for gatherings, stories, and a sanctified seasonal habitus in the dominant culture, Christmas is an optimal stage for pitching or perpetuating ideas. While brands, institutions, and politicians have long competed for the hearts and minds of their respective publics through seasonal self-promotion, I argue that informal and inchoate forces of identity politics do the same at Christmastime. In the most emotionally charged storylines, Christmas is a zero-sum battle of resisters, heroes, or martyrs who fight for cultural survival against the encroachments of deracinated elites, bureaucrats, and foreigners. While many scholars have attempted to "solve" the conflicts of multiculturalism through the development of theoretical models of ideal modes of engagement and the skillful application of policy, their approaches are rarely intended to address intimate, embodied, and affective negotiations of difference and disparity.[19] In the era of social-media echo chambers and hyper-partisan "dog-whistle" politics, there is an urgent need to examine the seemingly extreme or unreasonable responses that arise when personal and local grievances are projected onto a broader political-symbolic stage. Such examination would by no means justify white cultural entitlement or the abuse of minorities, but would instead illuminate how the grander narratives of identity politics have a way of overtaking local encounters with a predetermined repertoire of cultural scripts, roles, vernaculars, and interpretations.

As with all stories, one's identity and worldview determine the extent to which a given War-on-Christmas narrative seems plausible, representative, or compelling. Scholars of everyday multiculturalism remind us that worldviews are not developed around perfectly calibrated personas in a vacuum, but are mediated by place, proximity, material conditions, and genealogies of culture and identity reaching back to before one's birth. For poor white teenagers like Scott and Stacy, whose identities seemed disproportionately founded on a hazily defined combination of whiteness and Canadianness, the idea of losing their right to celebrate Christmas because their school was taking the side of immigrants seemed entirely possible – they eagerly took it as one more outrage in a perceived history of marginalization and displacements of people like themselves. Who, then, were these students identifying with? At Carson, students like Scott and Stacy often had defiant attitudes that masked their academic and socio-economic vulnerability. This vulnerability, rather than race, was arguably the defining characteristic of this subset. Its members were *more likely* to be white and very few were of Asian or Middle Eastern descent, but they did not socialize exclusively along racial lines. Prone to linger near the "Smokers' Pit" at the edge of school property, these students were the chronically disembedded: most lacked supportive home environments and reliable adult role models and were not plugged into Windsor's many robust ethno-cultural communities. They could claim few extracurricular activities and associations and little by way of academic or career goals. Perhaps the "War on Christmas" presented an irresistible opportunity to transform a vague sense of cultural inferiority and racial animus into heroic, countercultural resistance.

Resistance and Radicalization

Tracing the fraught relationship between multiculturalism and so-called "redneck" identity among working-class whites in Canada, Anne O'Connell argues that Canadian diversity and multiculturalism are strongly associated with urban settings, while rural regions are implicitly coded as white and culturally backward.[20] In her formulation, negative characterizations of rural whiteness constitute the negative space that defines and legitimates what she calls "hegemonic whiteness." Hegemonic whiteness is occupied largely by urban whites; unlike their less privileged counterparts who are confined to the space of a retrograde rural past, white elites enjoy cultural legitimacy and mobility in an urbanizing, globalizing world. O'Connell explains that this dialectic allows the establishment of a progressive Canadian multicultural brand while obscuring Canada's history of colonial crimes, ongoing racial violence or injustice in urban settings, and real issues of unemployment and crime in rural areas.

While O'Connell focuses on the urban-rural divide, I here foreground social class, which is less divided or racialized along urban-rural lines. Following the premise that hegemonic whiteness is imbricated within Canadian multiculturalism, it seems that cultural capital flows upward and disdain flows downward, despite racism not being limited to the lower end of the socio-economic ladder any more than racial acceptance is limited to the rich. O'Connell examines how those displaced by this hegemonic whiteness have lately reclaimed the "redneck" label: while it was once a term of contempt applied to poor whites who were presumably violent, lazy, or ignorant, it now recasts them as victims of post-industrial restructuring and counteragents of the current global order. Whether or not individuals actually embrace it consciously, the cultural phenomenon of redneck whiteness opens up a range of politicized narrative possibilities. By adopting the role and affect of an underdog minority "injured by economic suffering, isolation, exclusion, and more specifically marginality," conservative working-class whites are "well placed to challenge liberal multicultural values."[21] Though redneck pride in Canada may be less closely associated with white supremacist or right-wing politics than in the United States, O'Connell notes that it nonetheless positions rural whiteness as native to Canada and thus naturalizes an association between whiteness and Canadianness.[22] It is not hard to imagine how the events at Carson, or the War on Christmas more generally, are rooted in the spontaneous performance and anti-establishment appeal of redneck counterculture.

Could a seasonal display of nativist backlash, belligerence, and xenophobic solidarity be described as a catalyzing moment for cultural radicalization – or perhaps as a litmus test for radicalization that has already taken place? Does resisting the multicultural order by weaponizing "Merry Christmas" constitute radicalism? The Facebook post that Stacy shared was ostensibly addressed to anyone offended by Christmas celebrations or the singing of the anthem: "go back to your own f-ing country," it said.

Stacy herself framed the post with similarly hostile language. While it may seem far-fetched to apply the language of extremism and radicalization to this incident, it is worth considering the possible ramifications if another student – perhaps one identified as Muslim – had not posted a xenophobic rant about Christmas grievances but instead shared a xenophobic rant about grievances over Western military interventions in the Middle East. Rants like the one that Stacy posted are generated daily by a slew of racist, nativist, "alt-right," or white-supremacist sites and online communities. To what degree do they differ from similar rants generated by the social media fronts of international terror networks? Perhaps more importantly, would institutional and media responses have differed had the teenager in question not been white and female, and if the online rant had been of that other variety?

Porous Publics

Comparisons aside, it is important to ask what sort of public spheres Canadians – in particular young Canadians – inhabit, and how their online and offline communities shape their identity formation, affective allegiances, and disposition toward public institutions. Increasingly, the question of whether Canada's purported multicultural success and semblance of liberal consensus is sustainable depends on how young people experience or position themselves in relation to nationhood, belonging, and their fellow citizens. As the internet continues to fragment social life into webs of translocal affinities and interactions, can the wholesome multicultural branding and state education-and-outreach apparatus compete with innumerable countervailing ideologies and networks? An online meme communicates with incredible efficiency, needing no more than a single image paired with a line of text to generate feelings of outrage, solidarity, or indeed an entire cultural narrative. According to Michael Warner, a "public" is a space of reflexive circulation that comes into existence through an act of call-and-response: where one communicates and another chooses to pay attention, there you have a public.[23] A Facebook meme is a near-perfect indication of whether a given public exists: it is the mobile and shareable text *par excellence.* The fact that a pro-Christmas Facebook post not only drew Stacy's attention but also engendered a spontaneous solidarity in others – whether her supporters were fellow students, UKIP supporters, or local officials

– affirms the existence of a public that rallies around strident nativism and a disenchantment with the multiculturalist regime.

Given that the Christmas-crisis offenders and xenophobic commenters united around perceived disenfranchisement and anger against the multicultural establishment, however, "counterpublic"[24] may be the more accurate term. While participation in a self-organized public confers a sense of agency and empowerment, exclusion from a public – a common condition for the socially marginal – causes "political depressiveness, a blockage in activity and optimism."[25] Warner argues that this very condition of frustration and "friction against the dominant public forces" that produces a counterpublic also materializes as a space for strategic deliberation.[26] A counterpublic's discourse is necessarily incompatible with that of the dominant public, and at some level, it maintains an "awareness of its subordinate status."[27] On a political level, this embrace of anti-establishment cultural insurgency is precisely what both redneck whiteness and the white-supremacist "alt-right" are all about. Applied to a micro-sequence of Carson's crisis, Stacy's quickness to vent to her friends and call the media was an instinctual reach for a supportive counterpublic in response to a dominant force's crackdown. Because her "defense" of Christmas and Canadianness spoke to him, Scott's defiant but ultimately anticlimactic act of scrawling that blackboard message was his way of enlisting in the "War on Christmas" and signalling his belonging within that counterpublic.

For many students and community members, the Carson crisis was their first opportunity to mobilize on what had previously only been latent political affinities. This did not seem to impair their ability to merge local events into the transnational "War on Christmas," judging by the ease and fluency with which they did so. In fact, many online commenters responded to the cultural phenomenon while barely referencing the Carson case. Many invented details or accused school officials of actions beyond even what the erroneous initial report described. This suggests that details and accuracy are quite irrelevant once a broader discourse takes over. While Stacy's Facebook statement lacked polish and coherence (muddling race, ethnicity, nationality, and religious garb in a post about Santa, Christmas, *and* the national anthem), it still telegraphed a recognizable grievance tied to social difference. Semi, Colombo, Camozzi, and Frisina argue that the power to "create and use difference" is a primary means of shaping social reality for oneself and others, making it a potent resource and "tool for collective action."[28]

The "War on Christmas," with its implied ethno-religious fault lines and prominence in white working-class nativist circles, found great traction in Windsor's context of high immigration and equally high unemployment. Compared to neighbouring Detroit, however, whiteness in Windsor was an ambiguous category, rarely understood in opposition to blackness. While my students were aware of America's dominant racial binary, whiteness in their circles encompassed socio-economically and ethno-religiously dissimilar groups which had been in the region anywhere from two decades to two centuries. This did not stop its deployment as social shorthand, however. In that first day of the Christmas crisis, "whiteness" denoted a line of difference despite coding for meanings ranging from "white," "Christian," and "Canadian" to "not Muslim" and "not Arab." Students who believed the rumours about Mr P's alleged assault on Christmas seemed to share an intuitive sense of where the lines between themselves and Others were located, perhaps affirming the strength of Warner's counterpublic description. Meanwhile, Carson's less marginal students were more skeptical about the rumours and more critical of the scenario's projected social categories. I overheard one student scoffing at the logic behind treating all minorities as though they did not practise Christmas, given how many peers were walking, talking evidence to the contrary. A colleague described how another student said he "knew immediately" that the rumours could not be true.

Such is the strange reality of a contemporary multicultural public school: it is crowded with overlapping publics and counterpublics through which memes travel at lightspeed, and a crisis can spark fury in a hundred students while leaving their peers in the same cafeteria unmoved. Moreover, when publics form online, they are portable and porous; no sooner has a teenager staged a social-media performance than it slips beyond their control. As Stacy's moment in the spotlight demonstrates, what may appear to be semi-private, casual, and unoriginal acts of self-expression can have outsized consequences. Even when one seems to have found a community of the like-minded who will share one's grievances and worldview, even when a moment of solidarity and personal glory arrives and promises transformation and belonging to something greater than oneself, the plot can unravel. All it takes is for someone with a more compelling account, a more dominant public, or simply an irreconcilably different perspective to tell another story.

Notes

Helen Mo passed away in April 2017. She submitted her chapter in January 2017, and this version has been lightly edited by Pamela Klassen and Suzanne van Geuns. Helen's contributions to the study of religion are discussed in more detail in the notes on contributors and in the acknowledgments of this book.

1 The Official Languages Act of 1969 conferred official status to English and French, thus neatly marginalizing the cultural claims and language rights of Indigenous peoples.

2 Drohan, "Canada's Example."

3 See Kymlicka, *Multicultural Citizenship*; Fong, ed., *Inside the Mosaic*; Beaman and Beyer, eds., *Religion and Diversity*; Campolieti et al., "Immigrant Assimilation."

4 Mudde, "Putting Canada in a Comparative Context."

5 Wise and Velayutham, eds., *Everyday Multiculturalism*.

6 Semi et al., "Practices of Difference."

7 McLuhan, *Understanding Media*.

8 Levey, "Symbolic Recognition," 355, 368.

9 I will be using pseudonyms to protect the identities of this story's central figures and institution.

10 Li, *Ethnoburb*.

11 Just as Barack Obama's detractors pointedly refer to him as "Barack *Hussein* Obama" (emphasis theirs), particularly during his campaign and in the early years of his presidency.

12 Todd, "The War on Christmas."

13 See Rusk, "Toronto's Holiday Tree"; Selley, "Picking Sides"; Todd, "The War on Christmas."

14 Berry, "A Not So Merry Christmas."

15 Ibid., 38.

16 Ibid., 39.

17 Levine, "A Religious Diversity Tale," 214.

18 Ibid., 215.

19 Taylor, "The Politics of Recognition"; Kymlicka, *Multicultural Citizenship*; Levey, "Symbolic Recognition,"; Olsen and Morgan, "Happy Holidays"; Kinvall and Nesbitt-Larking, "Religion and Deep Multiculturalism."

20 O'Connell, "An Exploration of Redneck Whiteness."

21 Ibid., 547, 546.

22 Ibid.
23 Warner, *Publics and Counterpublics*.
24 Ibid.
25 Ibid., 56.
26 Ibid., 86.
27 Ibid.
28 Semi et al., "Practices of Difference," 68.

Bibliography

Beaman, Lori G., and Peter Beyer, eds. *Religion and Diversity in Canada*. Leiden, Netherlands: Brill, 2008.

Berry, David R. "A Not So Merry Christmas: Dilemma for Elementary School Leaders." *Kappa Delta Pi Record* 47, no. 1 (2010): 10–13.

Campolieti, Michele, Morley Gunderson, Olga Timofeeva, and Evguenia Tsiroulnitchenko. "Immigrant Assimilation, Canada 1971–2006: Has the Tide Turned?" *Journal of Labor Research* 34, no. 4 (2013): 455–75.

Chowdhury, Amit. "Windsor, Ontario High School … Student Suspended after Racist Facebook Tweet." *Pulse2*, 12 December 2011.

Drohan, Madelaine. "Canada's Example to the World: Liberty Moves North." *The Economist*, 27 October 2016. http://www.economist.com/news/leaders/21709305-it-uniquely-fortunate-many-waysbut-canada-still-holds-lessons-other-western.

Fong, Eric, ed. *Inside the Mosaic*. Toronto: University of Toronto Press, 2006.

Kymlicka, Will. *Multicultural Citizenship: A Liberal Theory of Minority Rights*. Oxford, UK: Clarendon, 1995.

Levey, Geoffrey Brahm. "Symbolic Recognition, Multicultural Citizens, and Acknowledgement: Negotiating the Christmas Wars." *Australian Journal of Political Science* 41, no. 3 (2006): 355–70.

Levine, Deborah J. "A Religious Diversity Tale: A Multi-Faith Case Study." *American Journal of Community Psychology* 37, no. 3–4 (1 June 2006): 203–10.

Li, Wei. *Ethnoburb: The New Ethnic Community in Urban America*. Honolulu: University of Hawai'i Press, 2008.

McLuhan, Marshall. *Understanding Media: The Extensions of Man*. Toronto: McGraw-Hill, 1964.

Mudde, Cas. "Putting Canada in a Comparative Context: Still the Multicultural Unicorn." *Nationalism and Ethnic Politics* 22, no. 3 (2016): 351–7.

O'Connell, Anne. "An Exploration of Redneck Whiteness in Multicultural Canada." *Social Politics* 17, no. 4 (2010): 536–63.

Rusk, James. "Toronto's Holiday Tree Returns to Christmas Roots." *The Globe and Mail*, 28 November 2002. http://www.theglobeandmail.com/news/national/torontos-holiday-tree-returns-to-christmas-roots/article1028439/.

Selley, Chris. "Picking Sides in the War on Christmas." *The National Post*, 4 December 2011. http://news.nationalpost.com/full-comment/chris-selley-picking-sides-in-the-war-on-christmas.

Semi, Giovanni, Enzo Colombo, Ilenya Camozzi, and Annalisa Frisina. "Practices of Difference: Analysing Multiculturalism in Everyday Life." In *Everyday Multiculturalism*, edited by Amanda Wise and Selvaraj Velayutham, 66–84. New York: Palgrave Macmillan, 2009.

Todd, Douglas. "The War on Christmas Smacks of 'Anti-Culturalism.'" *Vancouver Sun*, 7 December 2014. http://vancouversun.com/news/staff-blogs/the-war-on-christmas-smacks-of-anti-culturalism.

Warner, Michael. *Publics and Counterpublics*. New York: Zone Books, 2002.

Wise, Amanda, and Selvaraj Velayutham, eds. *Everyday Multiculturalism*. New York: Palgrave Macmillan, 2009.

10

Christmas on Orchard Road in Singapore: Celebrating the Gift of Jesus Christ between Gucci and Tiffany

Katja Rakow

Introduction

I board the Singapore Airlines aircraft at Frankfurt Airport, Germany, in December 2014, and enter a cabin decorated with Christmas bouquets featuring evergreens, red poinsettias, and golden bows. While "Joy to the World" softly plays from the cabin speakers, my fellow passengers on the flight to Singapore take their seats. A German couple entering the cabin regards the Christmas-themed surroundings with bewilderment: "Christmas decorations? But why? Aren't we flying to Asia?" the woman asks her companion. Her astonished question points to popular perceptions of Christmas as a holiday primarily associated with the northern regions of the Western Hemisphere and their Christian history; many are unaware that Christmas celebrations experienced a first wave of globalization in the wake of Christian missionary movements and a second wave in the wake of globalized consumer capitalism and event cultures.[1] Over recent decades, the tradition of German Christmas markets has been exported to various places around the world, including Singapore,[2] and China has become one of the main producers and exporters of Christmas decorations to the United States and Europe.[3] Today, the decorations that create much of the atmosphere of our Christmas are "Made in China," and the chances are good that the seasonal ornaments adorning the cabin walls of the Singapore Airlines aircraft stem from the same source. The notions of *Christmas* and *Asia* are not as oxymoronic as the German traveller's remarks suggest.

Maybe my fellow countryfolk are simply trying to escape the Christmas craze and the cold weather at home. In that case, the tropical city-state in Southeast Asia might not turn out to be the wisest choice of travel destination, because Singaporeans love Christmas. In 2011, Singapore's "Christmas on *A Great Street*" at Orchard Road, the city-state's premier shopping avenue, was ranked third on *Lonely Planet's* "Top 10 Christmas Markets of the World," the only Asian market on the list. Every year, "Christmas on *A Great Street*" attracts several million people.[4] In 2014, ten Christmas Markets offering shopping, food, and entertainment could be found around the island.[5] Throughout Singapore, Christmas is inescapable. Even the local supermarket at my usual living place in Tanah Merah on the eastern end of the island, far away from the buzzing downtown area and Singapore's tourist attractions, plays Christmas carols around the clock and features seasonal decorations starting early in November, suggesting that Christmas is not only enacted for the sake of the tourist business but rather is also entrenched in the Singaporean festive calendar.

Christmas celebrations came to Singapore with missionaries and colonial administrators.[6] In post-colonial times, Christians in Singapore celebrated Christmas mostly as part of their religious calendar, albeit not as a big public celebration. Christmas trees and decorations meant to attract Christmas shoppers were to be found in Singapore's big department stores and the little shops in Chinatown as early as the 1930s.[7] It was in the 1970s, however, that things in Singapore really began to change, as they did in other Asian countries in the post–World War II decades when Christmas was popularized by American TV and movie productions.[8] A Christmas wreath on the door indicated that the house's occupants celebrated Christmas, and contemporary pieces in Singapore's national newspaper advised readers on the latest decoration trends for Christmas wreaths and informed them about the meaning of the religious as well as the popular iconic elements of Christmas, such as the Christmas tree, Father Christmas, gingerbread, and reindeer.[9]

Since 1984, the annual Christmas Light-Up on Orchard Road in the middle of November has officially opened the festive end-of-year season with elaborate lights and decorations in the heart of Singapore's retail district. In its first two decades, the event was organized by the Singapore Tourism Board but has been taken over in recent years by the Orchard Road Business Association (ORBA). Both non-religious organizations emphasize the secular and commercial character of the Christmas Light-Up, viewing it as a means to promote the precinct and to create tourism and retail revenue rather than as a way of celebrating a religious holiday. The rising popularity of Christmas events in the 1980s coincided with a significant rise in the number of Evangelical Christians in Singapore's population.[10] The growth of Christianity was perceived as an effect of what many Singaporeans regarded as increasingly aggressive proselytization practices that threatened the social cohesion of Singapore's multi-ethnic and multi-religious population.[11] Such concerns also provoked discussions about the nature and role of Christmas in Singapore, in which fears were expressed that the import of Western traditions would happen at the expense of local traditions.[12] Early on, the national newspaper *The Straits Times* published several commentaries and opinion pieces. These pieces either argued that Christmas celebrations in Singapore should have a secular character or emphasized the religious nature of the holiday, situating it among the various religious holidays whose celebration expressed the multicultural and multi-religious nature of Singaporean society.[13] In 2004, a Christian organization called Celebrate Christmas in Singapore (CCIS) was granted permission to enrich the Orchard Road Christmas celebrations with Christian performances in order to reintroduce some of the religious meaning of Christmas into the commercial festivities.

Religious, secular, and economic aspirations intersect in popular public Christmas celebrations such as Orchard Road's "Christmas on *A Great Street*" and push the festivities back and forth along the axis laid out in the introduction to this volume. This chapter discusses Christmas and its related discourses and practices in the context of Singapore's multi-ethnic and multi-religious society. As in other places in the world, secular and religious discourses as well as consumer and religious practices intermingle in Singapore's Christmas celebrations; the Singaporean case provides an interesting example of the role of religion in a strictly regulated public sphere. First, I will address the multi-ethnic and multi-religious character of Singaporean society and its role in public discourse as well as the regulations concerning religion within the city-state. Second, I will sketch some of the history and success of Orchard Road's Christmas celebration in the context of Singapore's tourism business and retail sector. Third, I will discuss how the popularity of public Christmas celebrations allows Singaporean Christians to express their religious convictions within the public sphere, albeit in limited and highly regulated ways.

The Singaporean Context: The State's
Commitment to Multiculturalism

After World War II, Singapore became an increasingly self-governed colony of the United Kingdom. In 1963, Singapore entered the Federation of Malaya and thereby became independent from the UK. The merger failed due to the ethnic politics of the Federation and its preferential treatment of Muslim Malays over Singaporean Chinese, as well as economic inequalities between Singapore and Malaya. In 1965, Singapore was expelled from the Federation and became the Republic of Singapore. In contrast to the Muslim-led government of Malaysia with Islam as its official religion, Singapore deliberately employed a secular ideology to keep the political and religious spheres separated.[14]

Since gaining independence in 1965, Singapore has undergone rapid industrialization, modernization, and economic development. Today, it has reached the second highest per-capita income in Asia and has one of the highest population densities in the world.[15] The 2010 census documents the complex ethnic and religious composition of Singaporean society, where 76.1% of residents are Chinese, 15.0% are Malays, and 7.4% are Indians.[16] In Singapore, the practice of religion is closely bound to racial-cultural identities.[17] That the majority of Singapore's residents are Chinese accounts for the high percentage of people practising a religion associated with Chinese heritage, such as Buddhism (33.3%) or Daoism (10.9%). According to the 2010 census, Christians, at 18.3%, are the second-largest religious group, followed by Muslims (14.7%) and Hindus (5.1%).[18] The significant growth of Christianity from 10.6% in 1980 to 18.3% in 2010 is attributed mainly to the success of neo-Pentecostal and independent churches, closely followed by non-Pentecostal evangelical churches, among the urbanized, affluent, English-speaking, university-educated Chinese.[19] The religious heterogeneity of Singapore's citizenship is also visible in the various religious buildings found throughout the island and its diverse public celebrations, such as Vesak (Buddhist), Deepavali (Hindu), Hari Raya Puasa (Muslim), and Christmas (Christian).

Singapore is a secular society with no official state religion. The state grants religious freedom and freedom of worship. The official position towards religion is guided by the state's "commitment to multicultur-alism,"[20] which is expressed through the equal treatment of all cultural groups – and thereby all religious groups – regardless of their minority or majority status. The official state policy includes a general endorsement of religious values as the moral backbone of Singaporean society.[21]

At the same time, religious heterogeneity and multiculturalism are seen as possible sources of unrest and conflict and thereby as a threat to racial and religious harmony. According to a statement by First Deputy Prime Minister and Minister for Defence Goh Chok Tong in 1990, "harmony" makes up the very foundation of social cohesion and peace and is considered a necessary condition for Singapore to prosper as a nation: "I consider racial and religious harmony as the most important bedrock of our society. If there is no harmony there will be no peaceful prosperous Singapore. As simple as that. The Prime Minister and his colleagues have spent many years to build up this climate of harmony amongst Singaporeans and nurtured a climate of tolerance amongst people of different religions and I have every intention of ensuring that such a happy state of affairs remains."[22]

Aware that religious harmony cannot be taken for granted, the Singaporean government actively shapes policies to ensure that "moderation and social responsibility prevail in the practice of one's religious faith."[23] The state's policy towards religion in Singapore is characterized by "close scrutiny, interventionist surveillance, and ultra-sensitivity to perceived threats."[24] Therefore, legislation such as the *Internal Security Act (ISA)* (Cap. 143), the *Sedition Act (SA)* (Cap. 290), and the *Maintenance of Religious Harmony Act (MRHA)* (Cap. 167A) prescribes a strict separation of the political and religious spheres, punishes violations of the set boundaries, and attempts to forestall any religious extremism or interreligious tensions and conflicts.[25] Such legislation is used to regulate religious practices and the possibilities for religious expression by individuals and groups in private and in public. For example, the *MRHA* allows the minister to issue restraining orders against any religious spokesperson or member of a religious organization who may have caused or attempted to cause "feelings of enmity, ill-will or hostility between different religious groups."[26] In contrast to punitive instruments such as the *ISA* or *SA*, the *MRHA* has a preventive purpose; it is meant to de-escalate instances of religious disharmony before they can grow into public conflicts. The act does not define what actions count as transgressions under the *MRHA*, leaving it to the minister and the Presidential Council for Religious Harmony to decide which behaviours, actions, or statements are out of bounds.[27] Due to the looseness of the key terms, religious groups are compelled to be extra cautious in their relations with other religious organizations and their comments about any other religious group in order to avoid any possibility of "ill feelings" between them or attributed intentions of ill-will. The work of the Presidential Council and the actions of the minister regarding the application of the MRHA are not visible to the public. There are no public reports of the warnings issued by the minister, and the proceedings of the Council are secret.[28] This means that the regulation of religious harmony happens "behind closed doors";[29] the effects of the Act are "actively restrictive and explicitly policing and reinforcing the boundaries between the religions"[30] and ethnic groups.

In order to avoid ethnic-religious tensions and to enhance religious harmony, the state treats all religious groups equally. This equal treatment becomes quite visible in providing sites for religious worship. Due to the high population density and scarcity of space in Singapore, "the state takes a functional approach to religious places" in urban planning and land-use policies.[31] The government's planning standards for sites of religious practice and worship in newly developed town centres correspond to the percentage of Singaporeans belonging to the main religious traditions present in Singapore. For example, Singaporeans of Chinese background adhering to Buddhism or Daoism are the largest religious group, making up 44% of the population. Therefore, for every 9,000 dwelling units, a Chinese temple site will be set aside. Christians are the second-largest religious group, making up 18% of the population. Therefore, for every 12,000 dwelling units in new town centres, a site for a church will be designated.[32]

The general procedure followed to gain permission to use one of these allotted spaces is to tender for it, but religious organizations are only permitted to tender for spaces allocated to their particular religion (Buddhism, Christianity, Islam, etc.). As land is scarce and there are not enough allotted spaces to account for the denominational diversity of Christianity and its growing need for worship spaces, many churches convert existing "secular" spaces for religious purposes. This could include using flats and apartments in housing complexes or renting public, civic, or commercial spaces as temporary meeting grounds. Such spaces could include conference rooms in hotels, theatres, cinemas, or school halls.[33] But the conversion or utilization of existing buildings or secular spaces for religious purposes is also controlled and regulated by the government.[34] Flats in high-rise HDB[35] buildings are restricted to residential use only. Using such flats for religious purposes is strictly speaking a violation of regulations. As for commercial spaces, there exist possibilities to apply for permission to change the designated use of land or existing buildings. Whether a change in usage is approved by the authorities or not depends on several factors, such as the location of the building, the expected impact on traffic in the area, and the existence of adequate parking facilities. In the 1980s, some congregations obtained permission to convert old disused cinemas into churches.[36]

In July 2010, the ongoing practice of renting commercial spaces for religious purposes prompted the Urban Redevelopment Authority (URA) of Singapore to issue new mandatory guidelines for the limited and non-exclusive use of commercial spaces for religious activities. In general, religious activities are not allowed in commercial spaces, but the URA permits some exceptions in a very limited way as long as the religious use does "not exceed two days a week" or cause any "disturbances to the public," "such as noise, traffic or parking problems." Moreover, no display of religious signs, advertisements, or posters announcing religious use is allowed on the premises or the exterior of the building.[37] Similarly to the regulation of religious attitudes and expressions by the MRHA, the government's planning standards for buildings and policies concerning religious and non-religious spaces simultaneously "serve to segregate and balance the major religions"[38] in the secular state of Singapore.

The state's "doctrine of religious harmony"[39] is deeply intertwined with what in the Singaporean context is called "legislated multiculturalism" or "legislated multi-racialism."[40] Once it was inscribed into Singapore's constitution, multiculturalism (or multiracialism) could serve as an instrument of governance, legitimizing policies and administrative practices with regard to race and religious affiliation.[41] The policies are meant to ensure the equal treatment of all ethnic and religious groups in order to prevent disharmony, conflict, or racial riots. The state's policies include official language policies (there are four official languages: Malay, Mandarin, Tamil, and English) as well as housing quotas and designated team structures for candidates in elections, which are designed to ensure the equal distribution of ethnic groups in public housing and public office. Other instruments of governance such as Racial Harmony Day on 21 July or constitutional soft laws such as the *Declaration of Religious Harmony* are meant to encourage positive attitudes toward multiculturalism among Singapore's citizens and to counter the repressive nature of the state's policies in managing religion and race. The declaration, issued in 2003, reads: "We, the people in Singapore, declare that religious harmony is vital for peace, progress and prosperity in our multi-racial and multi-religious Nation. We resolve to strengthen religious harmony through mutual tolerance, confidence, respect, and understanding. We shall always recognise the secular nature of our State, promote cohesion within our society, respect each other's freedom of religion, grow our common space while respecting our diversity, foster inter-religious communications, and thereby ensure that religion will not be abused to create conflict and disharmony in Singapore."[42]

In balancing the different religions in Singapore through legislative measures, the state also manages and circumscribes possibilities for public festivities and religious celebrations. Instruments for the management of these possibilities include the official appointment of public holidays that correspond to religious festivals and the appointment of dates and spaces for religious activities in the public sphere.[43] The Christmas celebration on Orchard Road is an event that falls under this scheme of policing religious festivities in the public sphere.

Christmas on *A Great Street*:
The Orchard Road Light-Up

Since 1984, Orchard Road, Singapore's premier shopping locale, has been lavishly decorated and illuminated during the Christmas season. Stretching from Tanglin Mall to Plaza Singapura, the illuminated decorations feature a new design and colour scheme every year and extend along 2.88 kilometres of Orchard Road.

The first illuminations were organized by the Singapore Tourist Promotion Board[44] and are now hosted by Community Chest (a charity organization) and the Orchard Road Business Association (ORBA). Various large international sponsors such as Hitachi and Mastercard also finance the event.

Beginning three decades ago, the "Light-Up event" – the date in the middle of November when the Christmas lights are turned on – marks the beginning of the end-of-year celebrations in Singapore. According to the private and public stakeholders who organize the event, the Christmas Light-Up has turned Orchard Road into "a compelling destination with strong local character ... delighting locals and tourists of all ages."[45] The elaborate lights and lavish decorations on Orchard Road are accompanied by a range of performances, street art, music, dancers, and carollers to "entertain shoppers as they delight in their festive shopping and bond with their loved ones."

Figure 10.1   Orchard Road Light-Up, 2015.

In recent years, Christmas on Orchard Road has been the most photo-graphed event in Singapore. Illuminated themed landscapes in front of the ION Orchard mall invite passers-by to take selfies with reindeer, huge candy canes, and lollipops, while in the Ngee Ang City mall a giant Christmas tree featuring hundreds of little presents wrapped in Tiffany's iconic light blue packaging fills the high-ceilinged lobby. A little stage invites shoppers to have their picture taken in front of the Tiffany-themed Christmas tree. Navigating the strolling masses on Orchard Road, it becomes obvious that the selfie stick is a ubiquitous accessory, and many of the seasonal decor-ations cater directly to this popular picture-taking practice. Christmas on Orchard Road even has its own hashtag for use on social media: "Share your love for Christmas on Orchard Road by simply hash-tagging #orchardrdx-mas on your Facebook, Instagram or Twitter post. Celebrate with us and share your joy with loved ones!"[46] By spreading pictures of Orchard Road's Christmas decorations on social media, users are also by default providing advertising for the brands that make up the backdrop of the illuminations on Orchard Road. The chances are good that the trademark lettering of Gucci, Dior, or Tiffany's provides the background for numerous selfies and atmospheric pictures taken on Orchard Road, where all the stores, malls, and buildings compete with each other for the best Christmas decorations and thus for shoppers' attention and international recognition.

The Light-Up on Orchard Road has become known and is actively branded as "Christmas on *A Great Street*."[47] Over the years, the event has gained huge popularity and recognition outside of Singapore. In 2010, it attracted seven million people.[48] In the eyes of Singaporean business associations and the Tourism Board, this counts as a huge success and tallies with the nation's ambitions to be a global city as well as a tourism and financial services hub.[49]

In addition to economic ambitions, Christmas on Orchard Road has also been incorporated into the national multiculturalism discourse. The 2014 decorations featured large, multicoloured stars hanging like Christmas tree ornaments from the huge trees framing Orchard Road. The Singaporean newspaper *The Straits Times* reported, "Orchard Road Goes Colourful for Christmas to Celebrate Singapore's Diversity."[50] The chairman of the Orchard Road Business Association explained, "the many colors reflect Singapore's diversity as it celebrates 50 years of nationhood next year,"[51] whereby she invoked Singapore's ideal of a multicultural nation-state. The public work of Christmas in the context of the stakeholders of "Christmas on *A Great Street*" affirms a range of Singaporean self-understandings and aspirations, while pushing the seasonal festivities – to invoke the editors' idea of the "coordinates of Christmas"[52] – along the axis towards the end of commercial activities (i.e. materiality), and the state ideology of economic success and an affirmation of Singapore's multiculturalism (i.e. ideology and culture).

"The Reason for the Season": Spreading the Message of Christmas

While the Christmas decorations on Orchard Road might feature angels among other seasonal images, and Christmas carols celebrating the birth of Jesus Christ might be heard everywhere along the street to invoke the "seasonal habitus,"[53] the event is rather devoid of overtly religious content. The one big exception is the department store Tangs, which invokes the spirit of Christmas through prominently displayed, embellished, and illuminated quotations from the Bible.

Built in 1958, Tangs is one of the oldest stores on Orchard Road. It is easily recognizable with its sloped, green-tiled Chinese-style roofs, which provide a stark contrast to the postmodern metal and glass structures of the ION Orchard building. A Christian family of Chinese origin founded Tangs in 1932, and their prominent display of Bible quotations in the storefront during the Christmas season has a long history.[54] In 2013, the verse "Blessed are those who dwell in the house of the Lord" (Psalm 84:4) was framed by a large peacock and brightly glowing flowers. In 2014, a huge golden heart, surrounded by lights and little crosses and adorned with a stylized tree and exotic birds, displayed John 15:12, "Love each other as I have loved you." The chosen quote for the 2015 Christmas season was John 8:12, "The Lord is the light of the world," displayed with large luminescent letters and accompanied by star clusters in white, gold, and red.

Tangs's practice of illuminating Bible quotations as a part of their Christmas decorations is older than the aforementioned regulation introduced in 2010, which prohibits religious signs on non-religious buildings, such as department stores. It also seems that public displays of Bible verses are much more acceptable in the context of Christmas, which is officially recognized as a Christian holiday, although, as the following example shows, many voices lament the loss of its religious content in the process of commercialization.

Figure 10.2   Christmas decorations at Tangs department store, December 2015.

In 2004, a group of Christians joined forces to "bring the message of peace and joy of Christmas back into an otherwise commercial festive occasion" because they were concerned "that many may have lost the true meaning of Christmas."[55] They named their organization Celebrate Christmas in Singapore (ccis), and it is supported by various denominational bodies, churches, and para-church organizations in Singapore. According to information from ccis, the "annual event at Orchard Road became a hallmark of the Christian community in Singapore in reaching out and blessing the community with the message of love. Together with participants from other parts of the world, ccis is celebrated to commemorate the Gift of Jesus Christ during the first Christmas, through a multimedia celebration of performances, interactive activities, carols, floats, mass choirs, and much more!"[56]

A week before Christmas, there is a flurry of activity on Orchard Road as preparations for seasonal entertainment, including activity tents and performances by various Christian groups, Christian choirs, and dance troupes, are made. These performances and activities are meant to reach out and bless the community, share the meaning of Christmas through

Figure 10.3   Photo wall inviting passers-by to pose with characters from the Christmas story, December 2014.

creative storytelling, and thereby inform shoppers about the "the reason for the season."[57] Although the stated aim of CCIS is to inform shoppers and tourists on Orchard Road about the Christian story that underlies the history and meaning of Christmas celebrations, it is not regarded as an opportunity to evangelize among the public: "This is by no means an evangelical call. All around the world, people take part in the festivities in some way. We hope everyone in Singapore can learn why Christmas is celebrated."[58]

As the organizers are aware of the boundaries clearly marked by the state for public declarations of religious beliefs and Christians' difficult position when it comes to evangelizing in the public sphere, the program usually includes something called "creative storytelling." In 2014, volunteers from CCIS dressed as Romans and the Three Wise Men posed in front of photo walls telling the Christmas story and invited passers-by to enact the Nativity scene and to take pictures or selfies.

Both the consumer-oriented secular celebration on Orchard Road and the Christian event encourage the popular activity of taking pictures. In 2006, CCIS hosted the "Night Photo Contest" themed "Capture the Spirit

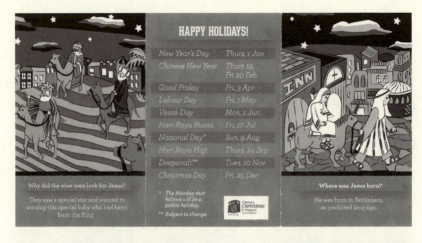

Figure 10.4   CCIS leaflet handed to passers-by, December 2014.

of Christmas in Singapore," which was supported by NIKON Singapore and jointly organized by The Photographic Society Singapore.[59]

Another activity in 2014 that invited pedestrians to briefly interrupt their stroll through the tropical shopping street was a large colouring tapestry with scenes from the Christmas story and the Nativity. Young Christians handed out coloured felt pens, inviting passers-by to colour the tapestry. While they were colouring, the volunteers explained the story of Jesus Christ and handed out small, credit card–sized flyers showing a miniature of the tapestry; the flyers briefly explained a version of the Christmas story in pictures and short sentences.

The back of the flyer presented a short list of all of the religious holidays in Singapore; this list is a small detail, but it clearly illustrates one of the many ways in which Singaporeans enact the official commitment to multiculturalism and diversity, even while displaying their religious particularities.

The main attractions during the days leading up to Christmas Eve are usually two stages for performances. In 2014, most of the performances were dance, choir, carol singing, or other musical performances, all of which mainly focused on interpreting popular Christmas carols. Neither the moderator who spoke in between performances nor the performers themselves framed the performances in overtly Christian terms. Performing the songs is regarded as a way to spread the message of Christmas, and no further comment on or explanation of the content of the carols seems to be needed. On the one hand, the absence of such elaborations can be interpreted as an effect of the strict regulation of religious propagation in public spaces, which leaves religious actors without clear ideas of what is appropriate and what already counts as a transgression. On the other hand, the program is clearly meant as entertainment for passers-by, who might not commit to staying for the full duration of a performance, much less for the whole evening program. A program that basically contains the singing of different songs and drum and dance performances set to Christmas carols invites passers-by to stop and experience a short moment of delightful diversion.

In addition to the performances during the days leading up to Christmas, ccis hosts the big celebration on Orchard Road on Christmas Day, when parts of the street are closed for traffic to allow visitors to enjoy the mass carolling concert and celebrate Christmas. The program includes not only performances and activities created by local Christian churches and organizations representing different denominations, but also Christian performers from Sri Lanka, Indonesia, the Philippines, the United States, and Brazil. Over the course of more than ten years, the annual Christmas event has become "a hallmark of the Christian community in Singapore," commemorating the "Gift of Jesus Christ"[60] in a public space mainly through the performance of Christmas carols without further elaboration on their content and its meaning. Reading materials occasionally offered to the interested audience are accompanied by warning signs declaring that the material contains the Christian message.

Figure 10.5   Christian reading material printed with the disclaimer that it contains the Christian message, December 2014.

In 2014, a musical dance-cum-storytelling performance by the group Singapore Youth for Christ (SYFC) provided a contrast to the brief windows of diversion and entertainment provided by the CCIS program. The SYFC performance lasted twenty minutes, contained a narrative arc, and demanded the investment of time by the audience. The story took the form of a Christian testimony performed on stage, which further heightened its contrast to the other performances.

Inviting pedestrians to stop and watch the upcoming performance, a young woman from Singapore Youth for Christ explained that they were "here to spread a little bit of Christmas cheer. If you are wondering what is the true love, joy, and peace of Christmas, we hope that our little performance will shed a little light on that."[61] The play told the story of a young family (a father, a mother, and their teenage daughter) caught up in their busy everyday lives: the father works in an office, the mother is a housewife who does the daily chores of cleaning, cooking, etc., and the daughter attends school and studies for her exams. All three miss the festive feeling Christmas promises and dream of escaping from their dreaded everyday lives in ways that are portrayed as rather superficial: the father dreams of holidays at the beach, the mother dreams of expensive shopping tours, and the daughter dreams of hanging out with her friends. While they are all sitting around the dinner table, a stranger knocks at their door. The stranger wants to spread the joy of Christmas by singing a song. They invite the girl into their apartment.

The guest introduces the song she is about to perform, which is titled "Christmas Isn't Christmas Anymore." Before she starts to sing, she explains that it is a song about the "true love, joy, and peace of Christmas," which she wants to sing because many people have the wrong idea when it comes to Christmas. They want to take a vacation; they want to find joy in mundane life; they want to share love through presents. She tells her audience – the family on stage as well as the larger audience of the performance standing in front of the stage – that the "true love, joy, and peace of Christmas" are "summed up in the person Jesus Christ – the *Christ* of *Christ*mas." She continues by saying that "through Jesus Christ, God offers love … because he gave his precious son to save us." Explaining that Jesus was "punished at the cross for our sins … to become our saviour," she connects her words to the famous carol "O Holy Night" and the line "It is the night of the dear Savior's birth!" She addresses the topic of peace next, referring to the popular Christmas phrase "Peace on earth and goodwill to men." Our peace, she explains, comes from Jesus's death on the cross and "our relationship to God through Jesus Christ." Finally, she addresses the third element – joy. Here, the message is that God raised Jesus from the dead, that Jesus is alive, which is a reason to rejoice and the reason why the famous Christmas carol goes "Joy to the world, the Lord is come! Let earth receive her King." This is the moment when the story takes the form of a testimony: "Our Saviour is in control. And knowing that allows me to live with true unchanging joy no matter what the circumstances of life." She finishes her explanations with the statement that "Christmas ain't Christmas if we don't realize that it is all about God's gift to us, Jesus Christ. And if you know him, everlasting love, joy, and peace can be yours this season and beyond." Then she performs the song, which delivers the message that Jesus Christ is "God's gift to you and me." After the performance, the group gave little presents to the audience that contained the lyrics of the song.

The Singapore Youth for Christ (SYFC) performance is remarkable in two ways. Not only was it a performance that presented a single cohesive narrative, it was also the most explicit in terms of its religious message. The deliverance of this message is in accordance with the mission statement of the organization of CCIS, which aims to educate visitors about the meaning of Christmas. But compared to the other performances, it was the only one making the Christian message as explicit as it could get, almost leaving the bounds of education and venturing into the realm of proselytism. The SYFC performance was not simply a story of Christmas featuring Mary and Joseph, the baby in the manger, and the three magi. It was a story that placed emphasis on the message of salvation that is contained in the Christmas story. Whereas popular statements refer to Christmas in broad and universal terms as "the season of joy and celebration" when everyone wishes for "peace on earth and goodwill to men," the narrative developed on stage clearly linked these well-meant wishes to a religious message, one that only unfolds its "true" meaning and transformative power when "God's gift to us" is acknowledged. The performance contains the unspoken message that the popular celebrations and festivities on Orchard Road and elsewhere are not "Christmas" in the strictest sense: "Christmas ain't Christmas anymore when the love of God isn't told." Thereby, it clearly posits Christmas at the other ends of the various axes that form the "coordinates of Christmas": emphasizing the Christian roots, the religious nature, and the "true meaning" of Christmas in the commercial and touristic context of Orchard Road, CCIS and more specifically SYFC are pushing the Christian holiday towards the "religious," "spiritual," and "authentic" ends of the axes.

Conclusion

In the Christmas celebrations on Orchard Road, consumption, entertainment, state policies, and religion intersect in many ways. Singapore's official commitment to multiculturalism and its regulation of religion clearly circumscribe public expressions of religious sentiments and convictions. Although there are possibilities for each of the major religions present in Singapore to celebrate their most important holidays with public events, these events do not include activities that could be read as active proselytizing or evangelizing. Many of the public religious celebrations are at once a celebration of a particular religious holiday

Figure 10.6   LED screen during the Youth for Singapore Performance, December 2014.

and a festive acknowledgment of Singapore as a multi-ethnic and multi-religious nation.[62] The Christmas celebrations on Orchard Road reference these discourses in various ways, for example by interpreting the choice of colours for the decorations as acknowledgment of Singapore's diversity and by printing a list of all religious holidays on the back of the little leaflet about the story of Christmas.

In Singapore, particular religious affiliations such as Buddhist/Daoist, Muslim, or Hindu are associated with ethnic groups (Chinese, Malay, and Indian, respectively). The only religion that runs across ethnic lines is Christianity, which, in addition, is not seen as a "proper" Asian religion, but as a Western import.[63] One way for Christians to conform to the discourse of multiculturalism is to perform what could be called *inherent multiculturalism* instead of representing one clearly distinguishable ethnic/cultural group that contributes to Singapore's multiracialism. The performance of inherent multiculturalism was mirrored in the cultural and ethnic diversity of the Christian artists on stage at the 2014 celebration, who came from Singapore, the Philippines, Sri Lanka, the United States, and many other places. Such portrayals of inherent diversity help to promote Christianity as a universal and thereby multi-ethnic religion that fits into a society that praises diversity – this despite the perception of Christianity as a foreign religion that has to recruit its members at the expense of local traditions and thereby endangers religious harmony. Due to this perception, Christians' activities in the public sphere are watched with scrutiny. The decision to allow Christian organizations to metaphorically and literally take centre stage on Orchard Road during the end-of-year celebrations is considerably influenced by the economic and touristic advantages that the season promises Singapore's retail and tourism sectors. The double-sided nature of Christmas as a secular, globalized, consumer-oriented holiday and a religious holiday with a distinctly religious message allows it to both create touristic and economic possibilities and offer legitimation for the presentation of a religious message in the public sphere. The ambivalent nature of Christmas creates a certain grey area where performances and creative storytelling might be able to open up spaces for evangelizing practices that do not require a warning sign that says "Contains Christian message." Therefore, it might not be a surprise that the little flyer telling the story of the birth of Jesus Christ that was handed to shoppers on Orchard Road made a concession to multiculturalism by listing all of the religious holidays celebrated in Singapore on the back.

The Christmas celebrations and decorations are in and of themselves a material witness to diversity and the malleability of this particular holiday, which accommodates secular as well as religious significations, stimulates modern consumer sentiments as well as religious feelings, and incorporates themes, symbols, and structures from various cultural backgrounds. Upon entering Changi Airport on 23 December 2014 to fly home, I am greeted by an almost-familiar scene. The German seasonal greeting "Frohe Festtage" (Happy Holidays) adorns the entrance to Changi Airport's own Christmas paradise featuring a large wooden pyramid (a typical German Christmas decoration traditionally produced in the Erzgebirge) and a small version of Neuschwanstein Castle. I have to think of my fellow German travellers from the beginning of the journey, and I wonder what they thought about Singapore's interpretation of German Christmas traditions.

Notes

1 Moore, *Christmas: The Sacred to Santa*, 167–88.

2 In 2014, the first "Christmas Wonderland" fair at Singapore's Gardens by the Bay featured a European-style Christmas Market with little wooden huts selling wine, sweets, and artisanal products, all surrounded by seasonal light sculptures and entertainment. The month-long event attracted more than 900,000 visitors in its first year and has since become an annual seasonal attraction for Singaporeans and tourists alike. See Kaur, "Gardens by the Bay's Christmas Wonderland to Charge for Admission This Year."

3 Sigley, "A Chinese Christmas Story," 101; Jackson, "Visuality," 52.

4 Singapore Tourism Board, "Placemaking."

5 Said, "Jolly Markets."

6 See for example the report of Christmas festivities at various churches and Christian institutions in 1909: "Christmastide. Seasonable Celebrations in Singapore. Festivities at Local Institutions."

7 "Colony Cavalcade," 2.

8 Moore, *Christmas: The Sacred to Santa*, 177–85.

9 "Eastern Touch for X'mas Wreaths," 23; "Dress Up Your Door for X'mas," 3; "A to Z of Christmas," 2.

10 Tong, *Rationalizing Religion*, 60.

11 Hill, "Conversion and Subversion," 11; Tey, "Excluding Religion," 122.

12 "PM Calls for Update," 1; "Don't Celebrate Xmas," 14; Villanueva, "Christmas Is Universal," 24.

13 Ooi, "Keeping the Spirit of Christmas," 24; "Make Orchard Road Light-Up Permanent," 14.

14 Sinha, "Theorising 'Talk'"; Chia, "Malaysia and Singapore," 82–7.

15 GDP per capita based on PPP (purchasing power parity) in 2016: #1 Qatar, #2 Luxembourg, #3 Macao SAR, #4 Singapore; see Knoema, "World GDP per Capita."

    Population density (people per sq. km. of land area) in 2015: #1 Macao SAR, 19,392.9; #2 Monaco 18,865.5; #3 Singapore 7,828.9; see Knoema, "Population Density."

16 Singapore Department of Statistics, "Population in Brief 2016," 18.

17 Goh, "Christian Identities in Singapore," 4; Tong, *Rationalizing Religion*, 61–5.

18 Singapore Department of Statistics, "Census of Population 2010," 11.
19 Tong, *Rationalizing Religion*, 60; Goh, "State and Social Christianity,"
    54–5.
20 Kong, "Negotiating Conceptions," 344.
21 Tan, "Keeping God in Place," 56.
22 Goh Chok Tong in a parliamentary debate; see Parliamentary Debate on
    the "Maintenance of Religious Harmony Act," col. 1150.
23 Tan, "Keeping God in Place," 58.
24 Ibid., 59.
25 Thio, "Constitutional 'Soft' Law"; Neo, "Seditious in Singapore!"; Tey,
    "Excluding Religion"; Winslow, "Legislation Comment and List."
26 The *Maintenance of Religious Harmony Act*, sec. 8 (1) (a).
27 Tey, "Excluding Religion," 133–5.
28 *The Maintenance of Religious Harmony Act*, sec. 7.
29 Tey, "Excluding Religion," 120.
30 Goh, "Christian Identities," 5.
31 Kong, "Negotiating Conceptions," 346; Kong, "Ideological Hegemony,"
    27.
32 Kong, "Ideological Hegemony," 28.
33 Kong, "In Search of Permanent Homes."
34 Goh, "Christian Identities," 6.
35 HDB is the acronym for public housing built and administrated by
    the Housing and Development Board (HDB), the statutory board of
    Singapore's Ministry of National Development.
36 Kong, "Ideological Hegemony," 28.
37 Urban Redevelopment Authority, "Limited & Non-Exclusive
    Religious Use."
38 Goh, "Christian Identities," 6.
39 Tey, "Excluding Religion," 121.
40 According to Chua Beng Huat, the term "multi-racialism" is more
    commonly used in Singapore than "multiculturalism." See Chua,
    "Multiculturalism in Singapore," 58. My quotation refers to the use of
    the term "legislated multiculturalism" in an advertisement for the book
    50 Things to Love about Singapore, printed in *The Straits Times*, December
    2014. See Long, ed., *50 Things to Love About Singapore*. In the actual
    chapter referring to this topic, the term "legislated multi-racialism" is
    used (Chang, "The State Will Help You Get Along"). Although not an

academic source, the advertisement as well as the chapter in the collection indicate how deeply entrenched the discourse on racial and religious harmony and its connected policies are in public discourse.

41 Chua, "Multiculturalism in Singapore"; Goh, "The Space of Race."

42 "Declaration of Religious Harmony."

43 Kong, "Religious Processions," 242; Chua, "Multiculturalism in Singapore," 60.

44 Now shortened to Singapore Tourism Board.

45 Quotations taken from one of the "Christmas on Orchard Road Exhibition" signs, placed at Shaw House Urban Plaza, November–December 2014.

46 Sign placed next to the illuminated "Christmas on *A Great Street*" sign on the sidewalk of Orchard Road in front of the ION Orchard, December 2014.

47 "Christmas on *A Great Street*."

48 Reed, "Singapore Becomes Christmas Island."

49 Goh, "Christian Identities," 10.

50 Lin, "Orchard Road Goes Colourful."

51 Ibid.

52 See the introduction to this volume.

53 See the contribution by Pamela Klassen in this volume.

54 "About Tangs." See Ooi, "Keeping the Spirit of Christmas," 24.

55 Celebrate Christmas in Singapore (CCIS), "About CCIS."

56 Ibid.

57 Celebrate Christmas in Singapore (CCIS), "CCIS Promo."

58 "Don't Rain on My Parade," 2.

59 "Capture the Spirit of Christmas in Singapore Contest," 62.

60 Celebrate Christmas in Singapore (CCIS), "About CCIS."

61 Performance by Singapore Youth for Christ on 20 December 2014 at Orchard Road, Celebrate Christmas in Singapore. All quotes are taken from my field notes.

62 During the celebrations of Vesak Day in Chinatown in 2014, a display informed onlookers about the religious holidays of all of the major religions present in Singapore.

63 Goh, "Rethinking Resurgent Christianity in Singapore," 105; Chia, "Malaysia and Singapore," 82–3; Goh, "Christian Identities," 9–10.

Bibliography

"A to Z of Christmas." *The Straits Times*, 23 December 1983.

"About Tangs." *Tangs*. Accessed 1 December 2016. https://www.tangs.com/Content/about/about-tangs.

"Capture the Spirit of Christmas in Singapore Contest." *Today*, 15 December 2006.

Celebrate Christmas in Singapore (CCIS). "CCIS Promo." *YouTube*, 2014. https://www.youtube.com/watch?v=-jXxbF419Go.

– "About CCIS." Accessed 1 December 2016. http://ccis.sg/about-celebrate-christmas-in-singapore-ccis/about-celebrate-christmas-in-singapore-ccis/.

Chang, Rachel. "The State Will Help You Get Along." In *50 Things to Love about Singapore*, edited by Susan Long, 39–42. Singapore: Straits Times Press, 2015.

Chia, Edmund Kee-Fook. "Malaysia and Singapore." In *Christianities in Asia*, edited by Peter C. Phan, 77–94. Oxford, UK: Wiley-Blackwell, 2011.

"Christmas on *A Great Street*." *Orchard Road*. Accessed 1 December 2016. http://www.orchardroad.org/christmas/.

"Christmastide. Seasonable Celebrations in Singapore. Festivities at Local Institutions." *The Straits Times*, 27 December 1909.

Chua, Beng Huat. "Multiculturalism in Singapore: An Instrument of Social Control." *Race & Class* 44, no. 3 (2003): 58–77.

"Colony Cavalcade. High Tide in the Singapore River. A Christmas Tree in Chinatown." *The Straits Times*, 22 December 1932.

"Declaration of Religious Harmony." Accessed 1 December 2016. http://iro.sg/about/declaration/.

"Don't Celebrate Xmas 'at Expense of Own Traditions.'" *The Straits Times*, 25 December 1989.

"Don't Rain on My Parade." *The Straits Times*, 22 December 2006.

"Dress Up Your Door for X'mas." *The Straits Times*, 23 December 1982.

"Eastern Touch for X'mas Wreaths." *The Straits Times*, 11 December 1975.

Goh, Daniel P.S. "Rethinking Resurgent Christianity in Singapore." *Southeast Asian Journal of Social Science* 27, no. 1 (1999): 89–112.

– "State and Social Christianity in Post-Colonial Singapore." *SOJOURN: Journal of Social Issues in Southeast Asia* 25, no. 1 (2010): 54–89.

Goh, Robbie B.H. "The Space of Race: Multicultural Policy and Resistant Discourses." In *Contours of Culture: Space and Difference in Singapore*, 111–42. Hong Kong: Hong Kong University Press, 2005.

– "Christian Identities in Singapore: Religion, Race and Culture between State

Controls and Transnational Flows." *Journal of Cultural Geography* 26, no. 1 (2009): 1–23.

Hill, Michael. "Conversion and Subversion: Religion and the Management of Moral Panics in Singapore." Asian Studies Institute Working Paper 8. Kelburn, NZ: Victoria University of Wellington, 1999. http://researcharchive.vuw.ac.nz/handle/10063/3189.

Jackson, Mark. "Visuality, 'China Commodity City,' and the Force of Things." In *Visuality/Materiality: Images, Objects and Practices*, edited by Gillian Rose and Divya P. Tolia-Kelly, 39–58. Farnham, UK: Routledge, 2012.

Kaur, Gurveen. "Gardens by the Bay's Christmas Wonderland to Charge for Admission This Year." *The Straits Times*, 29 October 2016. http://www. straitstimes.com/lifestyle/gardens-by-the-bays-christmas-wonderland-to-charge-for-admission-this-year.

Knoema. "Population Density." Data and Charts. *Knoema*. Accessed 1 December 2016. https://knoema.com/search?query=population%20density.

– "World GDP per Capita." Data and Charts. *Knoema*, 19 April 2017. https:// knoema.com/sijweyg/world-gdp-per-capita-ranking-2016-data-and-charts-forecast.

Kong, Lily. "Ideological Hegemony and the Political Symbolism of Religious Buildings in Singapore." *Environment and Planning D: Society and Space* 11, no. 1 (1993): 23–45.

– "Negotiating Conceptions of 'Sacred Space': A Case Study of Religious Buildings in Singapore." *Transactions of the Institute of British Geographers* 18, no. 3 (1993): 342–58.

– "In Search of Permanent Homes: Singapore's House Churches and the Politics of Space." *Urban Studies* 39, no. 9 (2002): 1573–86.

– "Religious Processions: Urban Politics and Poetics." *Temenos: Nordic Journal of Comparative Religion* 41, no. 2 (2005): 225–50.

Lin, Melissa. "Orchard Road Goes Colourful for Christmas to Celebrate Singapore's Diversity." *The Straits Times*, 13 November 2014.

Long, Susan, ed. *50 Things to Love About Singapore*. Singapore: Straits Times Press, 2015.

The Maintenance of Religious Harmony Act. Pub. L. No. Cap. 167A, The Statutes of the Republic of Singapore (2001). http://statutes.agc.gov.sg/aol/ download/0/0/pdf/binaryFile/pdfFile.pdf?CompId:2e0559d8-8eb6-4e82-80aa-a3fb434d7496.

"Make Orchard Road Light-Up Permanent." *The Straits Times*, 31 December 1986.

Moore, Tara. *Christmas: The Sacred to Santa*. London: Reaktion Books, 2014.

Neo, Jaclyn Ling-Chen. "Seditious in Singapore! Free Speech and the Offence of Promoting Ill-Will and Hostility between Different Racial Groups." *Singapore Journal of Legal Studies* (2011): 351–72.

Ooi, Suzanne. "Keeping the Spirit of Christmas." *The Straits Times*, 21 December 1986.

Parliamentary Debate on the "Maintenance of Religious Harmony Act." § Parliament of Singapore (1990). http://sprs.parl.gov.sg/search/report.jsp?currentPubID=00069609-ZZ.

"PM Calls for Update on Some Customs: Poser for Chinese Singaporeans: Seek Forms which Suit the Times." *The Straits Times*, 22 February 1988.

Reed, Chris. "Singapore Becomes Christmas Island." *Singapore Business Review*, 6 December 2012. http://sbr.com.sg/media-marketing/commentary/singapore-becomes-christmas-island.

Said, Nabilah. "Jolly Markets; Ring in the Festive Season with a Spot of Shopping and Good Eats at 10 Christmas Markets around the Island." *The Straits Times*, 12 December 2014.

Sigley, Gary. "A Chinese Christmas Story." In *Discourse as Cultural Struggle*, edited by Xu Shi, 91–104. Hong Kong: Hong Kong University Press, 2007.

Singapore Department of Statistics. "Census of Population 2010 Statistical Release 1: Demographic Characteristics, Education, Language and Religion." 2011. http://www.singstat.gov.sg/docs/default-source/default-document-library/publications/publications_and_papers/cop2010/census_2010_release1/cop2010sr1.pdf.

– "Population in Brief 2016." 2016. http://www.nptd.gov.sg/Portals/0/Homepage/Highlights/population-in-brief-2016.pdf.

Singapore Tourism Board. "Placemaking." 9 July 2015. https://www.stb.gov.sg/about-stb/what-we-do/Pages/Placemaking.aspx.

Sinha, Vineeta. "Theorising 'Talk' about 'Religious Pluralism' and 'Religious Harmony' in Singapore." *Journal of Contemporary Religion* 20, no. 1 (2005): 25–40.

Tan, Eugene K.B. "Keeping God in Place: The Management of Religion in Singapore." In *Religious Diversity in Singapore*, edited by Lai Ah Eng, 55–82. Singapore: Institute of Southeast Asian Studies, 2008.

Tey, Tsun Hang. "Excluding Religion from Politics and Enforcing Religious Harmony – Singapore Style." *Singapore Journal of Legal Studies* (2008): 118–42.

Thio, Li-ann. "Constitutional 'Soft' Law and the Management of Religious Liberty and Order: The 2003 Declaration on Religious Harmony." *Singapore Journal of Legal Studies* (2004): 414–43.

Tong, Chee Kiong. *Rationalizing Religion: Religious Conversion, Revivalism and Competition in Singapore Society.* Leiden, Netherlands: Brill, 2007.

Urban Redevelopment Authority. "Limited & Non-Exclusive Religious Use in Commercial Buildings." 2016. https://www.ura.gov.sg/uol/guidelines/development-control/change-use-premises/sections/guidelines-different-uses/others/others/Limited%20and%20Non-Exclusive%20Religious%20Use%20in%20Commercial%20Buildings.

Villanueva, Adrian. "Christmas Is Universal, Not Western." *The Straits Times,* 28 December 1989.

Winslow, V.S. "Legislation Comment and List: The Separation of Religion and Politics: The Maintenance of Religious Harmony Act 1990." *Malaya Law Review* (1990): 327–31.

11

A Cathedral Is Not Just for Christmas: Civic Christianity in the Multicultural City

Simon Coleman, Marion Bowman, and Tiina Sepp

Introduction: An Embarrassment of Riches

We begin with a telling moment in a master's thesis entitled "Christmas Is Not Just for Christmas."[1] Rachel Phillips focuses her research on the Christmas story as understood by people attending the Festival of Nine Lessons and Carols held at York Minster,[2] in the north of England. Assessing whether the seasonal narrative is a help or a hindrance in conveying the broader religious message of the Church, Phillips quotes Anglican theologian David Brown's anguished remark that this time of year reveals "the paradox of Christianity being apparently at its most appealing ... at a point where many a theologian and preacher finds the imaginative details at their most embarrassing."[3] How, Brown seems to ask, might the diminutive Christ Child be glimpsed behind the hulking figure of Santa? Or, if we are permitted an unfortunate pun, how does sanct-ification of the season relate to its seemingly inevitable Santa-ification?

This chapter addresses the question of how Christmas presents both an opportunity and a challenge for a particular kind of Christian institution. Our reflections emerge from an interdisciplinary study of four English cathedrals: Canterbury, Durham, and York (all Anglican), and Westminster (Roman Catholic).[4] We focus on the contemporary functioning of distinctive ecclesiastical spaces that house complex intersections of numerous agendas and expectations – not only religious but also civic, urban, commercial, and at times political. As huge buildings that frequently dominate the profiles of both cities and religious denominations, cathedrals combine the spiritual with the spectacular. Yet, in today's multicultural England, they are also fascinatingly ambiguous contexts whose roles may shift only with some unease between the religious and the civic, the liturgical and the historical. They are possessors of prestigious "high" cultural capital and yet democratically open to all comers[5] – elite institutions that simultaneously constitute a public good. They represent a religion, Christianity, that is still considered important enough to merit representation in the House of Lords, and yet is increasingly challenged by falling engagement in parish life, non-institutionalized forms of spirituality, growing activism of non-Christian migrant faiths in the public sphere, and overt secularism.

Under such circumstances, Christmas helps to shine a public spotlight onto cathedrals and what they represent in theory, even as it poses an awkward question as to what exactly it is that they *do* represent. Christmas raises issues that go beyond a focus on cathedrals alone toward a wider examination of diffuse and often problematic articulations between Christianity, urban publics,[6] and the semiotics of mediation between the two. By "semiotics of mediation" we refer here to the challenges that Christmas can pose in requiring liturgical action to be related not only to overt religiosity but also to the civic realm and even to secular expectations – tracking between what Scheer in this volume has called the "religionization" or "culturalization" of Christmas. While this question of mediation is clearly a question that is relevant for cathedrals throughout the year as a whole, it is posed most acutely at Christmas, when public attention is focused most intently on cathedral spaces.[7] A sense of what is at stake was provided to us by an informant, Daniel, a middle-aged man who works as a verger at York Minster, and who like Phillips described the Festival of Nine Lessons and Carols at York.[8] He called the latter "very much a gift to the city" and "a great spectacle." Expanding on the Festival's effect on the diverse groups of people who fill the Minster at this time of year, he added: "It puts them in the mood for Christmas," which "is great and that's not a problem." So Daniel sounded largely positive. But we note the hint of an interlocutor contained in his phrase "not a problem": in effect, he is implying that in other people's eyes that is precisely what it *is*.

Beyond Re-invention

Admittedly, theological embarrassment is hardly an unusual emotion among Christians at this time of year. Christmas as catalyst for pious unease has a long history, ranging from Puritan attempts to ban celebration of the season in the seventeenth and eighteenth centuries on account of its problematically "pagan" aspects, to endless contemporary diatribes against commercialism that track between moral censure and mere cliché.[9] Scholarly and popular literatures regularly reproduce the tired trope of Christmas as (re-)invented Victorian tradition, as if a tradition's ability to renew itself must render it inherently inauthentic.[10] We point instead to two dimensions of Phillips's work that deserve more attention in an analysis of Christmas as a multicultural, urban, public, and ambiguously religious occasion.

First, there is the issue of Christianity's civic appeal at this time of year. Christmas possesses the capacity to capture the attention of an otherwise largely apathetic English congregational culture. A 2002 survey actually put the UK fourth from the bottom in European countries in terms of rates of regular, public worship, and the pulling-power of churches and denominations that have historically been the most powerful has been most precipitous in its decline in the postwar years.[11] Yet, while in October 2013 approximately a million people participated in an Anglican service each week, in the same year nearly two and a half million attended on Christmas Day or Christmas Eve.[12] The Church even caters to anticipated seasonal demand by deploying special "festival churches" – buildings that are only opened for special occasions such as Christmas and Easter.

Intriguingly, we see here an interaction as well as a possible tension between what the sociologist and Anglican priest Martyn Percy calls "episodic" and "dispositional" faith, in other words between faith that comes occasionally into view and that which is both everyday and seemingly organic.[13] Percy's diagnosis of this division expresses an ecclesiastical dilemma facing cathedrals at Christmas, for he sees the episodic character of such practice as indicating the marginalization of religion in public life. Interestingly, in the case of cathedrals we visited, such marginalization occurs precisely within the most visible, most "central" spaces of the Church.[14] Speaking in his dual role as clergyman and social scientist, Percy notes further:

The current boom in cathedral worship is one example of episodic belief on the rise: well-attended high quality religious services by increasing numbers, but with little evidence that this leads to an overall rise in actual Church of England membership. Indeed, what seems to flourish in modern European mainline denominational Christianity is pilgrimage, memorialisation and celebration, all of which are episodic in character, rather than intrinsically dispositional.[15]

Percy's reference to the boom in cathedral worship resonates with a 2012 report (Theos and The Grubb Institute) significantly called "Spiritual Capital," which dangles a tempting sociological morsel in front of those who would see cathedrals as centres of Anglican revival, suggesting that "their impact on and significance for English life extends far beyond their role as tourist destinations."[16] Again, Christmas appears to be an interestingly problematic occasion here. It clearly does not occur at the height of tourist season, when cathedral guides may be rushed off their feet in accommodating the tours demanded by international as well as national visitors; and yet it involves the engagement of the cathedral with very large numbers of incomers and "users." Many of the latter may or may not be religious, but they are frequently local, so that visiting the cathedral becomes part of their attachment to place. As one staff member of York Minster[17] put it to us, "You can't work in a cathedral and *not* have to do with Christmas," expressing the slightly harried sense of responding to public demands as well as the attempt to take advantage of the opportunity to engage more intensely with parts of the local community such as schools, businesses, and charities. Thus while we accept Percy's comment over the non-increase in conventional membership, we find his opposing of the episodic and the "intrinsically dispositional" less convincing in relation to Christmas: the crowds who come to cathedrals at this time may only come once a year, and many do not see themselves as Christian, but such visits might still be highly "dispositional," drawing on an annually kindled habitus of participation tied to the season, and indeed to regular familial, regional, or work-related obligations (we might compare this point with what Klassen in this volume calls a seasonal habitus). According to a guide and learning officer at the Minster, Joseph,[18] "It's almost like somebody kind of pushes a button in the people of York and goes – it's Christmas, we'd better go to the Minster."

The relative filling of cathedrals at Christmas also raises questions with regard to another sociological characterization of the ambiguities of religious practice in Britain as a whole: that it features populations who "believe" in some kind of spiritualized cosmology and yet choose not to "belong" to religious institutions.[19] In fact, Christmas might be said temporarily to reverse the values of this binary. Those who attend services at Christmas do not necessarily see themselves as convinced by the narratives contained in the Christmas story, but they appear to express a certain kind of belonging by their public occupation of cathedral space, if only for a short while.[20] As we shall see, such "occupation" is carried out by private individuals but also by more corporate bodies, eager to locate their seasonal festivities within a cathedral frame. On the one hand, such eagerness might be interpreted as indicating the very weakness of cathedrals as religious spaces, since so little appears to be at stake for a well-known business such as John Lewis[21] to locate its Carol Service in Westminster Cathedral, very close to its corporate headquarters. On the other hand, a cathedral offers more than just a capacious building for people to gather in: it offers access, and exposes them, to an elaborate religious and historical symbology.

To these questions about the periodic *appeal* of cathedrals to wider publics we add a second, perhaps less obvious dimension of Christmas: that of *reflexivity* – this time largely on the part of representatives of the Church. Phillips's thesis research was carried out with the strong support of York Minster, and it is one of a number of studies carried out by and for English Anglicans that draw attention to the special character of Christmas in the Church year. We thus see members of the ecclesiastical establishment trying to understand – and perchance to extend – a place in the limelight before all is lost in the secular freeze of the New Year. For instance, Holmes and Kautzer note how Anglican Church statistics give "pause for thought" in relation to attendance at Christmas and Easter.[22] While attendance figures for Easter 2012 were 54,700, the highest amount for a decade, those for services during Advent (leading up to but not including Christmas Eve and Day) were 745,900, a situation which is said to illustrate "the desire of an increasing number of people within the wider community as well as the regular cathedral worshippers to celebrate the great Christian festivals at a cathedral service."[23] What is especially notable about Holmes and Kautzer's analysis is that they contrast such apparently healthy figures with the much smaller number of *communicants* at such services – perhaps around 50 percent of total attendance – a situation that for them raises the pressing question of the extent to which sacramental life is becoming a peripheral activity in these events (although we would add that such non-participation may also be related to simple lack of awareness of what to do among people who come from a non-churched background). In a slightly later report published by the Church of England, concerned directly with the issue of congregational growth, the reference to Christmas is also telling. It is expressed through the words of a six-year-old boy, who lists what he likes about the Church: "Everything. Children's Church and everyone is friendly. Christingle, Christmas, Harvest Festival. I was christened here and it was amazing."[24] In the context of the report, worried as it is about the aging demographic of the people who inhabit the Church, Christmas becomes associated through the child's observations with generational as well as theological rebirth: here is a new voice expressing a commitment to Christianity, albeit through listing its more "fun" occasions.

Later in this chapter, we will reflect more theoretically on how cathedrals respond to these challenges and opportunities provided by Christmas, and thus to the question of how the semiotic mediations evident during this season can be thought of as emblematic of how Christianity relates to and articulates with ambiguously defined publics. However, we first wish to explore Christmas in the cathedral in more empirical terms. We shall do so in two ways, both of which highlight some of the dilemmas and challenges associated with reconciling "sanct-ification" with "Santa-ification." The first deals with the troubled relationship between Christmas and Advent, and indeed with another great event in the Church year, Easter, thus moving us toward questions of explicitly Christian temporality. The second deals in detailed ways with how cathedrals prepare materially and performatively for Christmas – through the paraphernalia of the crib, the tree, the star, but above all the Carol Service – and how such objects and actions can themselves form subtle bridges between semiotic and ontological worlds. We shall show that while Advent broadly expresses separation from the (secular) civic realm, occasions such as a Carol Concert express more of a reconciliation with its assumptions and expectations, and yet retain the sense that a subtle Christianization of the civic realm might still be possible.

Christmas "versus" Advent

One of the unanticipated responses to Christmas that emerged from our work with cathedral clergy and other staff was the expression of a sense of ambiguity, even ambivalence, over Christmas as opposed to the wider commemoration of Advent. One dimension of such unease involved the distinction between the relatively more secular and/or civic temporalities of the season and those of the Anglican and Roman Catholic Churches. Thus, as Ella, an education officer at York, put it to us:

> Christmas for the minster begins mid-October with Advent, and is not a full-blown celebration at that time, but a preparation; then when the rest of the world goes back to work, the Minster is in liturgical mode. [We] must recognize that for others, Christmas is over. For the Minster it goes on till Candlemas [2 February]. We are asked why we don't put lights up earlier and why the nativity is still there "after."

Ella points not only to the lack of "fit" between religious and wider conceptions of the scope of the season, but also the forms of misrecognition entailed in such encounters. The "liturgical mode" of the Minster is out of step with the demands of post-Christmas labour, while the questions asked about the "before" and "after" of Christmas reveal a public ignorance of the season as laid out in the Church calendar. Indeed, it is no accident that some of the richest data we have gathered so far on the relationship between Advent and Christmas have come from vergers and sacristans – precisely those figures in cathedrals who manage the spatio-temporal shifts in behavioural framing between various constituencies as they organize the material and liturgical moves between different activities. When we asked David, a verger[25] at Canterbury, to tell us about Christmas, he noted:

> Define Christmas, is my first question. For us, Christmas begins on Christmas Eve. Well, actually no, on the 23rd as it happens, for we are having an extra Carols … So on the 23rd we're having the first of the Cathedral Carol services, that's when Christmas begins here as a season and lasts until Candlemas, the second of February. That's Christmas. What most people mean is the Carol Service season which for us is the season of Advent, so there's an

immediate dichotomy because you've got the church keeping the penitential season.

In fact, this paragraph is merely the beginning of a detailed and lengthy response from David that illustrated both the overlaps and the distinctions between the penitential and the celebratory. But what is at issue here is not a straight distinction between, say, "purely" liturgical and "purely" secular, commercialized senses of the season, but two spatio-temporal framings that are in tension and yet mutually dependent. In the following, David provides another dimension to the sense of "confusion" and multiple framing that the season creates:

> The season of Advent is a real hotchpotch because we could do a jolly Carol Service in the afternoon and then at Evensong we're back into Advent mode, and then there's another Carol Service for another group.

This "Advent mode" parallels Ella's "liturgical mode" in its pointing to a degree of seriousness and penance in contrast to the jollity of a Carol Service, but it also indicates what, from the cathedral's point of view, appears to be a somewhat schizophrenic existence, shifting rapidly and somewhat jerkily from one behavioural frame to the other. It is therefore notable that David ultimately concludes that "I'm much happier with Lent, Holy Week and Easter because there's no secular pressure to do other stuff at that point," and in fact nearly all cathedral staff members we have talked to have said they preferred Easter to Christmas. The former may attract fewer people and be more inward-looking, but its participants are far more clearly oriented toward, and encased within, the spatial and temporal assumptions of the Church.[26]

Material Mediations

If the "liturgical" and "Advent" modes are about preserving the spiritual identity of the Church within the context of an open, iconic, public building, workers within cathedrals may also play a more mediating role, seeking actively to find bridges between sanct-ification and Santa-ification, and possibly also pulling the public toward the former and away from the latter. Under such circumstances, the seasonal "props" of a cathedral (and of courses churches more generally) have the potential not only to declare the special character of the season, but also to prompt forms of spiritual (re-)orientation, both playing on and channelling symbols recognized by a wider public, while drawing on both verbal and non-verbal resources. For instance, when we asked Stella,[27] a tour guide and chaplain at York Minster, about how her guiding might change in relation to Christmas, she noted:

> Well, just as the very space of the Minster is different, so I point out the Advent wreath, and the last several weeks, of course, leading a tour on Monday morning, there's somebody moving chairs around, we're rearranging for Carol Service or something that has gone on or is going on, so it gives us the opportunity to talk about the activity and different events that go on in the Minster, invite people to come to some of those events. And now that the Nativity set is up, so to point that out. We want to be a welcoming church to all people, no doubt about that, but we are a Christian Cathedral, and so to reiterate that story and point out the pieces that are going on there.

Stella, who has both a religious and secular function in the Minster, is sensitive here to how a wreath can refer back to Advent (and thus not merely to Christmas), just as the rearranging of the space provides the chance to embark on a narrative that goes beyond the purely historical. Her mention of the idea of a "welcoming church" touches on a point of considerable debate and indeed strategizing in cathedrals, whose clergy spend much time considering how their self-conscious openness to the public at large can also be funnelled into a more religious trajectory and yet avoid the stridency of some evangelical discourse.[28] Stella adds:

> Because as people are visiting the city and visiting the St Nicholas market and going shopping and eating, they want to be in the Christmas spirit of the lights and the carols, and so, again I think it's one of those things that we're not sure where to meet people but it allows us to be inviting rather than being rigorous to the fact that we are not in the Christmas season, we are in the Advent season.

Thus seasonal "performances" are contexts of opportunity and unease, balancing welcome with rigour, involving the potential for translation as well as risking embarrassment. The Advent/Christmas axis provides the chance to make theological points through a language of material semiosis that plays on what is assumed to be known and unknown among the public. The verger Daniel, for instance, describes how York speaks its Christmas message through a symbol that both links to and subtly alters expectations:

> The week preceding Christmas we will have put the crib up in the North Transept, but the crib will be empty. And people again, come in, see the crib, are puzzled as to why there's nothing in it, and then we have to explain that actually we're not at that point yet in the year where we actually have the figures in the crib … the Christ Child doesn't go into the crib until Christmas Eve.

Once again, we see battles over temporality as well as materiality evident at Christmas here, with "liturgical" and secular "lay" expectations being significantly out of kilter. The reference to puzzlement has an interesting parallel with Susan Harding's depiction of evangelical discourse surrounding the American preacher Jerry Falwell as constituting a kind of semiotic snare, as the gaps and aporias around a charismatic symbol invite the narrative victim in, seeking to find an answer to what seems to be not quite right or incomplete in the story being told to them.[29] As with the disordered chairs described by Stella, the material culture of the cathedral may act as a prompt toward explanation for the unexpected. The "puzzle" of the empty crib also takes us back to Phillips's discussion of the Christmas Story, and the Festival of Nine Lessons and Carols, for she notes how York Minster developed a practice, towards the end of its Service, of having a carol choir looking not to the Crib but to the Cross: a kind of embodied, proleptic, theological leap intended ultimately to mutually articulate, even to conjoin, the lay and the liturgical gaze – even as it perhaps provided a form of in-house signalling to cathedral staff in suggesting the presence of an esoteric and value-added meaning to their action, and thus one not evident to outsiders.[30]

The crib, as a central point in the Christmas narrative as well as a spatial centre of attention, takes on considerable symbolic weight in all of our cathedrals, even though it is deployed in different ways. In Canterbury, unlike York, the Christ Child goes into the crib as soon as the Nativity scene is set up. In this case, therefore, no attempt is made to intrigue the viewer by confounding their expectations, but the crib still expresses a "bridging" spiritual strategy. As one of the canons of the cathedral remarked, "In reality we have Jesus in the crib because so many visitors see their visit as an early celebration of Christmas and the baby in the manger illustrates the truth that Jesus was born and died and rose again and is always with us."[31] Temporality is again invoked, but here it appears to collapse birth and death, crucifixion and resurrection, even as it suggests that the Christian story is "always" salient, and not just for one season. ·

In Durham, meanwhile, Jesus is customarily placed in the crib early on, but is covered by hay until Christmas Eve, when he is removed and then placed back during the Midnight Mass.[32] Volunteers are informed that he must be hidden until the appropriate point of the service – his constant presence but final revelation a mixture of the York and Canterbury models. In December 2016 one of us, Tiina Sepp, spotted the child uncovered well before Christmas Eve and mentioned this fact to a steward, inducing a minor panic and a swift restoration of the layer of hay above the statue. The steward's interpretation of the prematurely exposed baby was that some parents had wanted to show their children the Baby Jesus and therefore removed the hay from him – indicating, in a small yet significant and materialized way, the differing expectations of visitors and cathedral staff.[33]

Although we focus on the experiences of cathedral staff in this article, we should also note that not all "non-liturgically-oriented" visitors to cathedrals at Christmas are there for celebratory purposes. Christmas is a notoriously hard time for the lonely and bereaved, and for instance at York Minster the Midnight Mass on Christmas Eve is attended by many people who are on their own. Graham, an elderly chaplain of Durham Cathedral, noted: "An awful lot of people come in, men particularly, just before Christmas … If you walk in here fortnight, 10 days before Christmas, you will always find those pews full of men who have lost their wives, either this previous year or maybe years gone by. And they cannot face Christmas on their own and they come in here and they unburden. You don't have to talk to them, but they are there. And the Lord does his thing with them, I don't know."[34]

Even the festive figure of the Christmas tree can be used to invoke attention but also redirect consciousness along more liturgical, reflective, and indeed penitential lines. At York Minster, for instance, the tree may be used as a "memorial" symbol where people are invited to hang notes with their messages. The Lullaby Carols Service, given by York Minster and the Lullaby Trust,[35] is dedicated to the memory of babies who have died suddenly and unexpectedly. Congregants are given a star, on which they can write a message in memory of a baby or other loved one. After the service the star can be placed on the Christmas tree.

As hinted at above, a key activity in bringing people into the cathedral, and thus one of the main occasions when seasonal "props" will be viewed by the largest numbers of people, is the Christmas Carol Concert. It is the organization of these occasions that takes up so much of vergers' time, even as they attempt to choreograph them in ways that permit proper recognition of Advent to occur. In the context of considering semiotic mediation and ritual action, the Christmas Carol is itself an intriguing form. Adam Kuper describes how Dickens's book of that name was produced in the 1840s very much at the cusp of the creation of the modern Christmas in England, with its associations of nostalgia and beneficence.[36] He also notes, however, that it was evangelicals who were particularly instrumental in reviving the singing of carols with the publication in 1871 of *Christmas Carols Old and New*, indicating perhaps the assumed power of such singing to drag congregants back on to theological message, ultimately shifting attention from carol to creed.[37] Nowadays, the singing of carols seems to provide a prime catalyst and qualification for entry into cathedral space, although the conditions of such entry display significant distinctions. A Carol *Service* should not be confused with a Carol *Concert*, for instance. This distinction may seem trivial, but it plays on one of the key points of ambiguity and debate amongst administrators of cathedrals throughout the year: should one charge for entry into a cathedral, and if so for which activities, given that the same space may seem ontologically different for the believer as opposed to the tourist, even as no definite sign or visible criterion distinguishes the former from the latter?[38]

These issues become highlighted at a place such as York Minster, which normally charges entry to tourists, although attendance at religious services is free.[39] The Minster also has free entry throughout Christmas Eve and Christmas Day, though the exact motivation for and enactment of such liberality did not emerge clearly from our discussions with staff.[40] One guide said that the Minster would in fact be closed for visitors on these days and that there would only be "services" on offer (thus justifying the lack of charging by implying that only Church business was going on). However, a Minster host refuted this point and said the building would indeed be open for all comers, including for "visitors who come to the services."

What we might characterize more generally as "carol performances" seem significant in their capacity to crystallize both ambiguity and overlap in relation to different framings of cathedrals as public spaces, even amongst staff themselves. During her visit to York Minster in December 2015, Tiina Sepp chatted to Susan, a tour guide for the Minster, and recorded the following in her field notes:

> I tell Susan that I'm going to the Carol Concert on Friday. She says, "Lucky you!" I ask if she has ever been to one, and she says, much to my surprise: "No, never. I'm an atheist."

Tiina's own comment on this incident is as follows:

> The Christmas Carol concert is a very interesting "genre" and as such the best example of a cathedral as a confused and confusing place. For example, why wouldn't a Minster volunteer guide [like] Susan go to the Carol Concert, even though she is an atheist? Because of the couple of prayers that are thrown in at the beginning and end of the concert?

In our terms, it is this very sense of confusion expressed by Tiina as she voices Susan that indicates the complex ontology but also potentiality of the cathedral as public arena, depending on the particular liturgical and/ or ideological frame that it adopts at any given time. But whatever Susan's sensibilities might be, carol performances are interesting precisely because of the accessibility and sense of temporary ownership they grant within the space-time of the cathedral at Christmas, not least as numerous groups seek representation. A further sense of the profusion as well as confusion of such events is provided by David, the verger at Canterbury:

> Because we anticipate Christmas over four weeks with endless Carol Services, and we're not complaining about that because that's part of what we're here for ... There's one commercial group that we do, which is a steam train that arrives in Canterbury for a day out, and they have a Carol Service in the Crypt ... But otherwise ... all the Carol Services that we do are either Canterbury or Kent-based organizations with whom we have a link. So obviously the King's School, St Edmund's School ... the two universities, the local

regiment ... and the Mothers' Union, the W[omen's] I[nstitute]. All the local groups, we don't live apart from the world in which we're set, we live within this huge wall which encloses us.

Perhaps David's "not complaining" sounds a little like Daniel's "no problem" earlier, but in fact we see the Carol Service becoming a point of quasi-liturgical contact and articulation between civic institutions and cathedral in this account, as the latter metaphorically breaks down its enclosing wall. Such contact not only indicates the links between the cathedral and certain corporate bodies (we can assume that not all would be appropriate), but also starts to break down the division between sanct-ification and Santa-ification. We are not proposing a functionalist account of Christmas here – not least because the contradictions and ambiguities we have highlighted are too evident for such deterministic social reasoning to apply. However, we do argue that the Carol Service, if kept within certain behavioural limits, can become liturgically productive through its engagement of publics that are allowed to develop a dispositional connection with the cathedral. Thus, while we previously learned of Holmes and Kautzer's worries over the loss of sacramentality as evidenced by the relative lack of communicants at such services, we see here if not a sacramental then at least a potential immanent link being established between life "outside" and "inside" the wall metaphorically and materially enclosing the cathedral.[41]

Broader Reflections: Christmas in Public

In common with much recent work on what is often called "the material turn" in studies of religion, Birgit Meyer claims that media and mediation must be seen as intrinsic to religious practice.[42] Her argument is directed partly against more Protestant views that have influenced scholarly analysis, traceable to such figures as Max Weber and William James, according to which personal and direct experience of the divine is privileged above church structures, outward behaviours, and deployment of images in the understanding of genuine religious experience.[43] Meyer thus coins the phrase "sensational forms" to grasp the ways in which form and content must in fact be considered together, and she defines such constructs as "relatively fixed modes for invoking and organizing access to the transcendental, offering structures of repetition to create and sustain links between believers in the context of particular religious regimes."[44] While our discussion of the signs, symbols, and rituals of the Christmas period generally chimes with this materializing thrust in the study of how religion is actually lived, we are also demonstrating the need for considerable flexibility and nuance in understanding what might be perceived as the mediating practices of religion. In the spaces we have examined in this chapter, Advent services provide relatively conventional embodiments of religious regimes, whereas the celebration of Christmas indicates the porosity, ambiguity, and fragility of ways in which ritual forms might organize "access to the transcendental." Indeed, attendees at Christmas concerts or services may not be conventional believers and thus have little interest in the transcendental as such, and their dispositional orientations toward "structures of repetition" will vary considerably.

Thus one of the interesting characteristics of Christmas is its location between material regimes of social commitment, between shifting and not always coherent civic and religious "representational economies."[45] The semiotic mediations provided by a crib, a Christmas tree, or a Carol Service, especially in a public space such as a cathedral, may not work at all in forming links between ecclesiastical and secular orientations; or at times they may do their bridging work in subterfuge, expressing a Christian message in ways designed not to cause offence or even be consciously noticed by the public. Thus the crib that remains empty until a given time in Advent, or the Christmas tree that retains both a reflective and a mourning function, are "sensational forms" that both draw on and subtly subvert the expectations of the religiously apathetic or ignorant, and yet they do their work by accommodating secular expectations as well as religious aspirations.

Our emphasis on semiotic mediation also has resonances with the work of an anthropologist who has recently been concerned with examining the interactions between English Christianity, publics, and forms of publicity in complex urban spheres: Matthew Engelke.[46] The British and Foreign Bible Society Engelke studies, like the cathedral staffs we have been describing, is constantly engaged in reflexive deployment of semiotic and aesthetic registers that bridge "cultural" and "Church-based" repertoires.[47] In both cases, a sense of what Engelke calls the "ambience" of mainstream religion plays precisely on what is already known or assumed about Christianity by complex and multicultural publics, thus also perhaps bridging the chasm that Martyn Percy sees as existing between episodic and dispositional ways of interacting with Anglican practice. But our real point is that while the Bible Society must go out on the street, seeking to publicize symbols and activities that can form a pathway for members of the public to shift consciousness from the secular to the sacred, the Christian cathedral at Christmas actually has a sizable portion of the public beating down its ancient doors to seek entry. As Martyn Percy suggests, only the most optimistic believer would see such occasions as sufficiently effervescent in themselves to revive the entire Church: their long-lasting social effects are not always obvious. What is revealed, however, is the cathedral's shape-shifting ability to mediate between the civic and the sacred, asking afresh what it means to constitute a public in a space that is set up to both accommodate and subtly subvert civic and secular orientations. Clearly we cannot go too far in our claim, since our focus has been on the strategies and assumptions of cathedral staff rather than their visitors and attendees. Nevertheless, we hope to have indicated the potentiality of Christmas to be used to engage its varied constituents in sometimes subtle, sometimes powerful ways. Such engagement works not primarily through theologically explicit versions of the seasonal narrative as described by Rachel Phillips at the beginning of this chapter, but through materialized means that risk theological and cultural "embarrassment" and yet simultaneously retain their mediating force precisely through embracing some of the iconography of popular culture.

We do not claim that the kinds of predicaments we have been describing are exclusive to cathedrals, or to Western Christians, alone. Certainly, many other religious institutions – synagogues, temples, mosques – must face similar strategic questions in determining how to retain the interest or engagement of those whose presence is episodic, linked to major feast days and festivals. Such similarities do not weaken our argument but give it more applicability. Where we think that the cathedrals we have been studying do display some particular characteristics, however, is in their considerable scale within, and centrality to, the religious and civic landscapes that they inhabit. Christmas is striking by its ubiquity even across multi-religious Britain, (pre)occupying domestic, commercial, educational, and religious spaces and soundscapes. But Christmas in a cathedral gives access to a civic and seemingly gently spiritual realm of "belonging" that can conflate the historical, the regional, and the ecclesiastical in ways that are deeply dispositional even if they are also highly diffused.

Notes

1 Phillips, "Christmas Is Not Just for Christmas."
2 The word "minster" is an honorific title given to some church buildings, including the cathedral at York. It is derived from the Latin "monasterium," or monastery.
3 Brown, *Tradition and Imagination*, 2.
4 See "Pilgrimage and England's Cathedrals: Project Overview." This chapter concentrates on the Anglican cathedrals we have studied, though some comparisons are made with Catholic Westminster Cathedral (not to be confused with Westminster Abbey).
5 Though some cathedrals, when they function as heritage sites, may also charge for entrance. Our sample contains two "free" (Durham and Westminster) and two "charging" (Canterbury and York) cathedrals. See note 39.
6 Of course not all cathedrals are especially urban, but the majority are, and until the nineteenth century in England and Wales the designation of "city" was dependent on the presence of a cathedral.
7 With the exception of one-off events, such as royal weddings and state funerals.
8 Interviewed 29 July 2015. All informants' names used in this chapter are pseudonyms.
9 For the former, see e.g. Schmidt, *Consumer Rites*, 177.
10 See e.g. Bingham, "How Britain Invented Christmas."
11 Woodhead, "Introduction," 6.
12 "Statistics for Mission 2013." The Anglican Cathedral Statistic report for 2015 notes: Christmas attendance was 125,200 in 2015, the highest figure since 2011. There were 33,100 communicants at Christmas in 2015. Services during Advent, the period leading up to Christmas, attracted an attendance of 824,300 in 2015, the highest figure for the past decade. All events and services from the beginning of Advent to 23 December are captured in the Advent total. See Research and Statistics, "Cathedral Statistics 2015."
13 Percy, *Anglicanism*, 70.
14 Ibid., 69.
15 Ibid., 125.
16 Theos and The Grubb Institute, "Spiritual Capital," 10. One census has revealed a 21 percent rise in attendance at Anglican cathedral services between 2000 and 2004. Brierley, *Pulling Out of the Nosedive*, 198.

A frankly astonishing 27 percent of the adult population of England visited an Anglican cathedral at least once in the year before the Theos Report came out. Theos and The Grubb Institute, "Spiritual Capital," 15. This number adds up to around 11 million adults, covers the entire demographic spectrum, and includes Christians, non-Christians, and non-believers.

17   Ella, Education Officer, interviewed 12 February 2015.

18   Interviewed 15 July 2015.

19   Davie, *Religion in Britain since 1945*.

20   See also Day, *Believing in Belonging*.

21   The John Lewis Partnership is an employee-owned UK company which operates John Lewis department stores in the UK, selling household goods and clothes. It regularly holds a Christmas Carol Concert in the Cathedral in December.

22   Holmes and Kautzer, "Report on Strand 3a," 57.

23   Ibid.

24   "From Anecdote to Evidence," 27.

25   Interviewed 12 August 2015. At Canterbury, the role conventionally termed "verger" is actually spelled "virger." A verger works as the "caretaker" of an Anglican cathedral, and may also play a minor role in services. The broad equivalent at Westminster Cathedral is the sacristan.

26   It is notable that Easter was not mentioned as one of the "fun" parts of the Church by the six-year-old boy, quoted above from the 2014 Church of England report.

27   Interviewed 16 December 2015.

28   The current statement of Anglican strategy called "Renewal and Reform" resulted, among other things, in the idea of "a Christian presence in every community," illustrating an immanent sense of a Church that is "local" rather than "gathered." The phrase is now incorporated in the banner of the Anglican Church website, visible in every section. See "Renewal and Reform."

29   Harding, *The Book of Jerry Falwell*.

30   Phillips, "Christmas Is Not Just for Christmas," 215.

31   In Durham, meanwhile, presents placed under the tree are then given away by the Salvation Army to the poor. This quote is taken from Canon Yvonne's address in the Christmas 2016 issue of Canterbury Cathedral Visit Department's newsletter *Through the South West Door*. This newsletter is only distributed among the staff and volunteers of Canterbury Cathedral.

32 The Durham Nativity set also contains interesting allusions to the local mining industry – a key dimension of the area's identity and economic development since the industrial revolution. The donkey in the set is in fact a pit pony, and the crib is a "choppie box" in which the ponies were given their feed underground. The innkeeper is dressed as a miner and the dog in the set is a whippet (akin to a small greyhound, and a popular local pet and working dog in the past). The figures were carved by Michael Doyle, a retired pitman, during 1975 and 1976.

33 At Westminster Cathedral, the crib is likely to be placed on show around mid-December, but the Baby Jesus will not be placed into the crib until 24 December. Nowadays, the Infant is screwed into his crib, after an attempted theft.

34 Interviewed 28 May 2015.

35 A UK-based charity dedicated to helping people affected by sudden infant death.

36 Kuper, "The English Christmas and the Family," 159–61.

37 Ibid., 161. It should be noted that there exists in England a strongly regional carolling tradition outside ecclesiastical settings: "groups of people maintain local traditions of Christmas carolling, which are quite distinct in style, performance practice, and repertoire from the popular national conception that has its roots in the Victorian era. The origins of these 'village carols' predate those of the popular repertoire by at least a century." Russell, "Working with Tradition," 17. See also Addley, "God Rest Ye Merry Gentlemen."

38 What is deemed appropriate in the cathedral context, for both services and concerts, is a matter for negotiation, and in some cases veto; the secular clustering of Christmas songs (which include popular carols, vernacular markers of Christmas such as "Jingle Bells," and popular hits) becomes carefully differentiated in this space.

39 As opposed to Durham and Westminster, but the Minster has this in common with Canterbury. The question of whether/when to charge for entrance is a matter of considerable concern for all cathedrals, which are generally regarded as a public good and yet must be financially self-sufficient. Durham's ability not to charge for entry is dependent in part on the income it derives from property holdings, but it does require payment for its more heritage-oriented exhibition "Open Treasure." Although York and Canterbury levy a visitors' fee that is directed at tourists, access to attend a service or to come explicitly as a pilgrim is offered gratis. More

generally, the Christmas season may provide a useful source of income. Thus businesses such as John Lewis pay a "donation fee" to Westminster Cathedral for the use of its space, and the Cathedral's choir may also be hired. According to an interview carried out with Westminster Cathedral staff on 12 December 2016, a Carol Concert held by one firm that year was a fundraiser for the Cardinal Hume Centre, which caters to homeless young people in London. Cathedral shops also stock goods oriented toward Christmas.

40 Conversations held on 23–24 December 2015.

41 In the context of a space such as Canterbury; the very ambiguities and affordances of the wall that surrounds the cathedral are highly significant, offering security and exclusivity but also a form of architectural aloofness and physical barrier of which staff are very aware.

42 Meyer, "Mediation and Immediacy," 23.

43 Ibid., 28.

44 Ibid., 29.

45 Keane, "Semiotics." Keane notes that the term "representational economy" draws "attention to the dynamic interconnections among different modes of signification at play within a particular historical and social formation." See Meyer, "Mediation and Immediacy," 410. Thus how people understand and handle material goods and how they use words may be mutually implicated.

46 Engelke, *God's Agents*.

47 We might think here also of the words of the cultural theorist Stuart Hall ("The Question of Cultural Identity," 310): "Everywhere, cultural identities are emerging which are not fixed, but poised, in *transition*, between different positions; which draw on different cultural traditions at the same time; and which are the product of those complicated cross-overs and cultural mixes which are increasingly common in a globalized world." In our account, religious identities might easily be substituted for cultural identities in this quotation.

Bibliography

Addley, Esther. "God Rest Ye Merry Gentlemen: The Thriving Culture of Pub Christmas Carols." *The Guardian*, 14 December 2014. https://www.theguardian.com/lifeandstyle/2014/dec/14/god-rest-ye-merry-gentlemen-thriving-tradition-pub-christmas-carols.

Bingham, Harry. "How Britain Invented Christmas." *The Telegraph*, 15 December 2007. http://www.telegraph.co.uk/news/uknews/1572625/ How-Britain-invented-Christmas.html.

Brierley, Peter. *Pulling Out of the Nosedive: What the 2005 English Church Census Reveals*. London: Christian Research, 2006.

Brown, David. *Tradition and Imagination: Revelation and Change*. Oxford, UK: Oxford University Press, 1999.

Church of England. "Renewal and Reform." N.d. https://www. churchofengland.org/renewal reform.aspx.

– "Statistics for Mission 2013." London: Archbishops' Council, 2013.

– "From Anecdote to Evidence – Findings from the Church Growth Research Programme 2011–2013." Church Growth Research Programme, 2014. http://www.churchgrowthresearch.org.uk/UserFiles/File/Reports/ FromAnecdoteToEvidence1.0.pdf.

– "Research and Statistics." *Cathedral Statistics 2015*. London: Statistics Unit, 2016.

Davie, Grace. *Religion in Britain since 1945: Believing without Belonging*. Hoboken, NJ: Wiley-Blackwell, 1994.

Day, Abby. *Believing in Belonging: Belief and Social Identity in the Modern World*. Oxford, UK: Oxford University Press, 2011.

Engelke, Matthew. *God's Agents; Biblical Publicity in Contemporary England*. Oakland, CA: University of California Press, 2013.

Hall, Stuart. "The Question of Cultural Identity." In *Modernity and Its Futures: Understanding Modern Societies*, edited by Stuart Hall, David Held, and Tony McGrew, 273–327. Cambridge: Polity Press, 1992.

Harding, Susan Friend. *The Book of Jerry Falwell: Fundamentalist Language and Politics*. Princeton, NJ: Princeton University Press, 2000.

Holmes, John, and Ben Kautzer. "Report on Strand 3a: Cathedrals, Greater Churches and the Growth of the Church." Durham, UK: Church Growth Research Programme, n.d.

Keane, Webb. "Semiotics and the Social Analysis of Material Things." *Language & Communication* 23, no. 3–4 (2003): 409–25.

Kuper, Adam. "The English Christmas and the Family: Time Out and Alternative Realities." In *Unwrapping Christmas*, edited by Daniel Miller, 157–75. Oxford, UK: Clarendon Press, 1993.

Meyer, Birgit. "Mediation and Immediacy: Sensational Forms, Semiotic Ideologies and the Question of the Medium." *Social Anthropology* 19, no. 1 (2011): 23–39.

Percy, Martyn. *Anglicanism: Confidence, Commitment, and Communion.* Farnham, UK: Ashgate, 2013.

Phillips, Rachel. "Christmas Is Not Just for Christmas: An Exploration of the Christmas Story and Its Meaning." MA thesis. Nottingham, UK: University of Nottingham, 2011.

"Pilgrimage and England's Cathedrals: Project Overview." Christianity and Culture. *University of York*, n.d. http://www.christianityandculture.org.uk/research/pilgrimage-and-englands-cathedrals.

Russell, Ian. "Working with Tradition: Towards a Partnership Model of Fieldwork." *Folklore* 117, no. 1 (2006): 15–32.

Schmidt, Leigh Eric. *Consumer Rites: The Buying and Selling of American Holidays.* Princeton, NJ: Princeton University Press, 1995.

Theos and The Grubb Institute. "Spiritual Capital: The Present and Future of English Cathedrals. A Research Report Commissioned by the Foundation for Church Leadership and the Association of English Cathedrals." London: Author, 2012.

Woodhead, Linda. "Introduction." In *Religion and Change in Modern Britain*, edited by Linda Woodhead and Rebecca Catto, 1–33. London: Routledge, 2012.

12

Epilogue: Containing the World in the Christmas Mood

Hermann Bausinger

Introduction

The following sketch is intended to serve as an epilogue, as a sort of summary and closing, not by engaging with all the rich empirical detail that has been presented and interpreted in the contributions in this volume, but by attempting to describe in general terms the area of tension in which the concrete studies move. Tensions are already alluded to in the title of the book: Christmas as the recurring venue for debates over difference and belonging.

Underlying this confrontation, however, is another enduring opposition which influences the intercultural handling of Christmas as well as determining the *intra*cultural problematization of the holiday: the understanding of Christmas as a decidedly religious holiday versus the practical reality of it being a holiday season shaped by worldly concerns. During the course of the nineteenth century, an ever-larger section of society was able to materially equip and augment the holiday, giving more and more people a stake in Christmas. The critique of this ever-widening Christmas appeal emerges at the same time, though earlier in the United States than in Europe. But here, too, the critical voices have grown louder, so that gradually the critique has become the central topic in public discourse during the pre-Christmas season and, in part, even still during the holidays. Whereas the non-news-related parts of the daily newspapers in this season used to be dominated by contemplative texts with at least a light religious accent, in recent decades the worldly reshaping of the significance of this time of year has moved to the fore, whether as a realistic description of the plethora of celebration possibilities or as a criticism of the loss of its presumably "actual" meaning. The worry and the worldliness go hand in hand: detailed tips on luxurious seasonal arrangements – be they exuberant decorations with strings of light in front yards or plans for vacation journeys – lead to the call not to forget the inner core of the holiday, namely the Christian message, in the face of all the surface decorations and demonstrations.

Critical commentary on the "Christmas Rush" is quite popular. Such criticism also claims its place as a topic of day-to-day conversation. One's own complicity in it is not always ignored, but rather bemoaned or downplayed, while the excessive involvement of others is more easily highlighted. Discourse surrounding Christmas often concentrates on the questionably excessive range of goods available and the decorative commercialization of Christmas, on the arbitrary focus of the festival and the fickleness of consumers, oftentimes completely without reference to the religious context of Christmas. This context is nevertheless ever-present, and any serious discussion of the topic leads de facto to a contrasting juxtaposition between the religious and the secular natures of the season. This is not incorrect, but upon closer inspection, it is questionable just how clear this distinction can be.

The Worldly and the Local

The fact that this juxtaposition is generally accepted as an explanatory model points to the notion that, in broad sections of modern society, religious beliefs have been withdrawn into an ethereal realm. In actuality, religious faith draws much of its power and authority from the fact that it is *welthaltig*: worldly, or containing the world. This concept plays an important role in the study of fairy tales: one of their main characteristics is that they transcend reality while remaining connected to and thematizing the most important issues of life in the world, for which the Swiss folklorist Max Lüthi coined the term *Welthaltigkeit*.[1] In this way, the fundamental conditions of the human experience are mirrored in the tales. This power of worldliness can in turn be utilized to explain traditional religious matters and forms of modern religious practices. The Christmas tradition offers a perfect example in this regard.

Nowadays (and in fact for more than a century), Christmas is considered by large portions of society to be the most prominent and important Christian holiday. Various factors have contributed to the fact that Easter has been ousted from this position. Emphasis has often been put on the changing of the year as a literal turning point, on the need for homely comfort within middle-class family units and the beautification and softening of the austere winter season with gift-giving – and rightly so. However, elements of the perception and portrayal of the events of Christmas are likely to be more important. Where the mythical images of the Easter resurrection deviate from tangible experience, central parts of the Christmas story remain close to livable and indeed lived reality. Mary and Joseph's cumbersome journey, prompted by the census, and the meager shelter where they found accommodation are, in times of mass refugee movements and their worldwide coverage, a familiar theme.

The pious re-narration and presentation of these traditional events has, moreover, enriched the story with touches of reality which are usually scarcely historically justified, let alone reflective of the time in which the story came about. In dramatizations, the events of Christmas are often set in the respective present – be it authentic, satirical, or rather naive. For example, the eighteenth-century Baroque comedies of the German Premonstratensian preacher Sebastian Sailer relocate the bible story of Christmas in his own temporal and regional setting. In his Three Wise Men scene, the pope and the conflict between the Russians and the Turks are discussed. The three recognize their own image in the door gables of the houses they pass, and they use common Christian salutations.

Other authors of religious plays also rely on the humorous effect of such alienation techniques. I myself experienced this in Steiermark, Austria, at an informal play where the Magi searched for Jesus's address in the telephone book. The enhancement of the decoration of Nativity scenes with elements of actual, contemporary, everyday life provides a particularly obvious example, such as in church figurine arrangements, and smaller crèches in private homes have certainly experienced colourful makeovers as well. Connections to Christian tradition can certainly be made plausible. Such a large convergence of people descended on Bethlehem that it seemsed obvious to depict flourishing markets, artisanal activities, and agricultural labour within Nativity scenes. But the visual reconstruction of the circumstances at the time of Christ was supplemented and soon replaced by the endeavour to bring the Christmas scene into the local present and to situate it in the diversity of modern life.

Recent observations in the Catholic diocesan town of Rottenburg near Tübingen confirm this local temporalization of Christmas. The backdrop of the Nativity scene set up in the cathedral depicts the local houses in Rottenburg town and a nearby chapel; at the entrance to the city the official "Rottenburg" sign is visible; a shepherd is poring over the local newspaper, whose headline reads "Today Christ Is Born in Rottenburg," thus providing the religious reference. In many ways, the visual depiction of the Christmas story in the crèche has found a continuation in the stylistically similar model train sets, which for decades have been a popular Christmas decoration in many homes.

Religious Solemnity and the Festive

The Italian literary figure Luciano Crescenzo divided humanity, rather tongue-in-cheek, into *crèche-lovers* and *Christmas-tree-lovers*; among the former he suspected more love and poeticism, among the latter, desire for power and liberty.[2] One could venture a loose (and perhaps risky) correlation with denominational distinctions, since the Christmas tree initially became popular in Protestant homes whereas the Nativity scene was, for a long time, a Catholic institution. Heide Inhetveen used the terms "spectacle" (*Spektakel*) and "unobtrusiveness" (*Dezenz*) to describe the difference between Catholic and Protestant practices.[3] Though the assumption seems to be that the Catholic propensity for visual demonstrations of faith permeates and confirms the worldly forms of the holiday, it could just as well forbid and constrain the secular Christmas spectacle.

However, confessional distinctions have faded to a large extent, just as day-to-day doings and one's lifestyle in general are much less influenced by religion than they were in times gone by, to the best of our knowledge. The contours of belief have blurred; what has remained is the feeling and the notion of a transcendental sense of reality and virtue. Thomas Luckmann characterized this move as a step from "religion" to the "religious."[4] It is a move towards stronger privatization; the influence of the religious community and the church as an institution are less significant; in place of binding, dogmatic orientation there is much more room for individual exploration.

From a traditional stance of religious conviction and piety, this attitude is in danger of being branded dubious or phony. Hermann Hesse commented on the topic of Christmas in 1917, during the First World War. He not only asserted that it was a "tool of advertising, a base for fraudulent corporations, a feeding ground for kitsch" but he also made a sweeping attack on sentimentality, on "luxuriating in those feelings, which, in reality, one does not take seriously enough to make a sacrifice for, to ever turn them into any sort of action."[5] Though these sardonic observations are not plucked out of thin air, they do appear to be somewhat too drastic. A cursory glance at the increase in charitable donations during the Christmas period, which rise just as steeply as people's inclination to shop, is the most obvious refutation of this attack. There is no wall between sentimentality and feelings, and feelings are not simply vague affectivity, but rather contain a cognitive stake. Feelings are, therefore, coupled with an effort of understanding and the possibility of active implementation.

Religiosity – as a feeling not clearly defined nor definable – is not far from solemnity. Generally, one sees in it a feeling of a higher sphere and special experience underpinned by objective supports (such as various stagings). The label "solemn" (*feierlich*) is often used to characterize religious settings, but it can also be used in connection with festive events relating to purely secular occasions. This fluid crossover from the (more specifically religious) "solemnity" to the (more or merely secular) "festive" provokes criticism from within conservative church circles, but is nevertheless an opening and an invitation for people who have already taken leave of stricter orthodox religious forms.

In Germany, both an appreciation and a critique of solemnity-as-festivity could be observed in the years following the end of the Second World War. Many parishes had to take on large numbers of refugees fleeing from eastern German regions and neighbouring countries who then sought to find their feet in their new homes. Empirical research at the time looked into the religious attitudes of these new citizens. A novelty religious practice at the time was Christmas Eve Midnight Mass, which took place in many churches, including Protestant ones. This was accepted by the newcomers as a *so nicely festive* tradition, whereas others – including pious locals – criticized the event precisely because of its all-too-festive character. It was thought that the pomp and ceremony in music and song led to the loss of the cognitive meanings of the liturgy, implying that music is more emotionally moving than text. Even when lyrics are sung, they do not fully assert their message when embedded in the musical form.

Never Quite Secular

The valorization of festiveness indicates, on the one hand, a certain loss of importance of religion, but on the other hand, has provided a breeding ground for "religiousness," which can still remain present when the enactment of the festivity is rather more secular or worldly. The array of Christian symbols, as, for example, so often presented in museums, allows – even demands – other avenues of access besides the pious and faithful ones. Aesthetic ideals can barely break fully away from their religious associations. The tendency to aestheticize religious experience contributes on one side to the conservation of Christian symbols, while on the other, it can push them into a less dogmatically fixed context, which, of course, brings with it secular inclinations.

Philosopher Friedrich Theodor Vischer developed a symbol theory in the mid-nineteenth century which was later taken up and developed further by Aby Warburg. Vischer starts with the premise of a state in which interaction with symbols was "*dark and unfree*," and therefore a distance between the set meaning of the symbol was impossible.[6] Warburg speaks of a magical-concatenating (*magisch-verknüpfend*) stance, which precedes a logical-exclusive (*logisch-sondernd*) one.[7] Vischer inserts a concept between the aforementioned two, one he borrowed from his son's doctoral thesis: namely, sympathetic understanding (*Einfühlung*) of symbolic meaning. He explains this using the example of religious images of the Madonna, which among rational-thinking non-believers doesn't have the associations of virginity, but rather those of pure femininity. This is very much an idea of its time, but the notion of a transitional form between religious and rational is not obsolete.

It implies that even worldly understandings of festiveness and festivities can have their roots in religion. In the pre-Christmas period, shoppers with children can scarcely pass the chocolate and candy on offer, in shiny, enticing Santa-themed packaging. More often than not, the child is more interested in the contents than the wrapper. At the same time it should not be presumed that the religious context is completely unknown to the child in the act of opening the festive treat, even when he or she is not exactly versed in hagiography. This is a banal example quite parallel to Vischer's. To take it one step further, and following up on the reflections about festiveness, one can ask if the whole flamboyant enactment of Christmas in the shopping streets and department stores unavoidably brings an element of the religious with it – even in situations where the direct connecting factors are not present.

Since greeting cards have existed, they are sent in their greatest numbers – except perhaps for vacation postcards from more or less exotic locations – during the Christmas period. It is possible to establish that in the past they largely depicted religious symbols, whereas in more recent times, romantic winter landscapes are much more popular. Evidence of secularization? Perhaps. It is, however, also possible to think of this trend from the other perspective and to say that snowy forests and icy winter lanes contain a quiet Christian symbolism. These are formations of nature, which are part of the Saint Nicholas tradition, including his wintry home and animal helpers and sometimes – although far from meteorologically correct – the biblical Magi. The religious latency behind an image of a little angel peeping over snow-capped fir trees is not overtly revealed, but it is connected to the winter atmosphere.

The "Religious" and Difference

The above manifestations of the "religious" and the problems associated with it do not presuppose a coexistence or conflict of different religions, but this could and should be discussed. For a long time in Germany and in some other European countries, the most prevalent view onto this issue was rather restricted to the contrasts between different forms of Christianity. The much-sought overcoming or reconciliation of such differences was subsumed in the all-encompassing concept of ecumenism. To some extent, ecumenism resonated with the universal Christian missionary mandate at the same time that non-Christian world religions lay beyond the experience and consciousness of those invoking the ecumenic idea.

In many places in Germany and in some other European countries, relatively homogenous denominational affiliations were prevalent well into the twentieth century. Customs and rituals were observed accordingly. *Christkind, Martin,* and *Nikolaus* were the respective gift-givers in particular regions and were regarded as the legitimate representatives of a particular denomination or political unit – Catholic Saint Nicholas and Austrian *Christkind.* Crossovers or hybrids between these Christmas figures were extremely rare; the classifications were stable. By contrast, Father Christmas or Santa Claus, belonging to no particular denomination, having very secular connotations, and being highly commercially contaminated, overcame the existing antagonisms to such an extent that his secret ecumenical merit is undeniable nowadays. A certain weakening of religious interpretations can therefore redress differing attributions and so better facilitate the mixing of populations. The Advent wreath should also be mentioned in this context. It is in fact a Protestant invention, which, thanks to its unmistakable visual announcement of the coming Christmas festival, also found its way not only into Catholic homes but also into secular ones as a neutral form of festive decoration. It's no coincidence that year after year, new trends for Advent wreath colours, ribbons, and decorations are advertised. This insight into the diversity of Christian symbols and into the possibility of their coexistence is a bridge to the consideration of current multicultural circumstances.

Briefly I wish to discuss the question of which role Christmas plays in a mixed-religious society. The statistics provide numbers illustrating the distribution of religious creed in a particular country or region. It goes without saying that a balanced dispersion of many religious groups makes mutual tolerance and recognition of other faiths more probable, and therefore also encourages a widespread active interest in Christmassy things and events (Singapore!). But the focus must be narrowed: are we speaking of a major or minor city or a rural area? What residential district comes into question? How does the neighbourhood interact internally – are communal activities common or at least possible? What about particular family situations? There is a considerable number of "mixed" families creating religious patchworks.

But even beyond these direct fields of contact there are encounters and sources of friction. In areas where one religion dominates, the children of another faith or denomination come unavoidably into contact with the facts and festivals of the other religion through schools and educational institutions. Children and, in particular, young adults are strongly led by their peer group. How this works from case to case must be investigated to find out whether the "religious" has a place in these interactions. For young adults, but partially also for adults, there are possibilities of encounter in clubs and societies such as choirs, sports clubs, and hiking groups and it should be asked how much these opportunities are being exploited. All of these are areas which should not be speculated upon or generally judged, but which would benefit from the ethnographic observation and precise descriptions that would emerge from such research. These findings would also draw political attention. In the heated debate surrounding the integration of migrant populations, there are often calls for pat solutions which would be acceptable to everyone. This is, of course, an understandable desire in view of the tough decisions needing to be made by officials and administrators. But it should be made clear that such general provisions often do not meet the real requirements and needs of those affected.

Conclusion

Back to Christmas. The multifaceted collection of studies in this volume presents how different people, in different places and at different times, deal with a perhaps initially alien and unfamiliar festive season. Attention should be paid to the diversity of these responses, which points toward the heterogeneity of what is often perceived as a unified group of 'non-Christians.' For even when trying to escape from the colonial perspective by arguing that other religious persuasions be granted their own right, one often implicitly assumes the superiority of one's own religion.

The secular transformation of the "religious" sphere should not be presumed to be a trajectory of sheer decline. On that note, I would like to close by venturing a call for a detailed and individualized consideration of our Christmas problem on the basis of a generalized hypothesis, perhaps rather in contradiction to my previous arguments against generalizations. Analogous to the step from "religion" to the "religious," maybe it is possible that Christmas is less in demand than what might be called "the Christmassy." I titled this piece "In the Christmas Mood" to place this idea in the centre of our discussion, in an attempt to underline the ambivalence of the development. Our largely playful dealings with Christmas and its commercial wares are part of secularization, which accompanies modernity, and might be understood as a late and trivial form of demythologization; but the Christmas holiday nevertheless continues to carry with it its original religious substance.

The solid contours of a religion of revelation and mission prompt absolutization, which hampers tolerance of other faiths; a softer understanding allows even alien religious traditions to have their place. Their faithful may not be converted, but the festive mood evokes feelings which are familiar to them from their own use of religious forms and which, hopefully, can open the way to their neighbours. The religious, even in its more festive form – to incorporate this concept once more – is namely individualized and accordingly manifold, but it is, as a rule, more open to foreign worlds than religion itself.

Notes

This chapter was translated from German by Margaret Haverty.

1 Lüthi, *The European Folktale.*
2 Crescenzo, *Also sprach Bellavista.*
3 Inhetveen, "Dezenz und Spektakel: Traditionelle Frauenfrömmigkeit in der dörflichen Lebenswelt."
4 Luckmann, *Die unsichtbare Religion.*
5 Hesse, *Weihnachtszeiten.*
6 Vischer, *Das Symbol.*
7 Wind, "Warburgs Begriff der Kulturwissenschaft und Seine Bedeutung für die Ästhetik," 170–2.

Bibliography

Crescenzo, Luciano. *Also sprach Bellavista: Neapel, Liebe und Freiheit.* Stuttgart, Germany: Deutscher Bücherbund, 1988.

Hesse, Hermann. *Weihnachtszeiten: Erinnerungen, Betrachtungen, Gedichte.* Edited by Volker Michels. Frankfurt am Main, Germany: Insel Verlag, 2001.

Inhetveen, Heide. "Dezenz und Spektakel: Traditionelle Frauenfrömmigkeit in der dörflichen Lebenswelt." *Zeitschrift für Volkskunde* 82, no. 1 (1986): 72–94.

Luckmann, Thomas. *Die unsichtbare Religion.* Frankfurt am Main, Germany: Suhrkamp Verlag, 1991.

Lüthi, Max. *The European Folktale: Form and Nature.* Bloomington, IN: Indiana University Press, 1986.

Vischer, Friedrick Theodor von. *Das Symbol.* Leipzig, Germany, 1887.

Wind, Edgar. "Warburgs Begriff der Kulturwissenschaft und seine Bedeutung für die Ästhetik." *Zeitschrift Für Ästhetik Und Allgemeine Kunstwissenschaft* 25 (1931): 163–79.

Contributors

HERMANN BAUSINGER is professor emeritus of Empirische Kulturwissenschaft at the University of Tübingen, where he served as the department chair from 1960 to 1992. His habilitation thesis *Volkskultur in der technischen Welt* (1961), published as *Folk Culture in a World of Technology* (Bloomington, IN: Indiana University Press, 1990), is widely regarded as having helped initiate a fundamental paradigm shift in German *Volkskunde*. One of the leading figures in German folklore studies and European ethnology, he has published articles in many areas of German popular culture with a focus on folk narrative, social linguistics, and dialect studies, as well as the social and cultural history of everyday life. He co-edited the *Enzyklopädie des Märchens* (15 vols., Berlin: De Gruyter, 1975–2015) and his most recent book is a history of southwest German literature (18th–21st centuries) titled *Eine Schwäbische Literaturgeschichte* (Tübingen, Germany: Klopfer & Meyer, 2016).

MARION BOWMAN is senior lecturer in religious studies, The Open University, and is currently (2016–18) a visiting professor in the Department of Culture Studies and Oriental Languages at the University of Oslo. She is vice-president of the European Association for the Study of Religions. Her recent publications include *Vernacular Religion in Everyday Life: Expressions of Belief* (London: Routledge, 2012), edited with Ulo Valk. She was a co-investigator on the AHRC-funded project "Pilgrimage and England's Cathedrals, Past and Present" (http://www.pilgrimageandcathedrals. ac.uk/about).

JULIANE BRAUER is a research fellow at the Center for the History of Emotions at the Max Planck Institute for Human Development in Berlin. Having studied modern history and musicology at the Humboldt University of Berlin and the University of Bielefeld, she acquired her PhD from the Free University of Berlin in 2007 with a dissertation published as *Musik im Konzentrationslager Sachsenhausen* (Berlin: Metropol Verlag, 2009). She has just completed a manuscript for a book titled *Youth, Music and the Cultivation of Feelings in a Divided Germany*. Her research interests also include the history of education and the role of emotions in practices of remembrance.

SIMON COLEMAN is Chancellor Jackman Professor, Department for the Study of Religion, University of Toronto, and currently president of the Society for the Anthropology of Religion, American Anthropological Association. He co-edits the journal *Religion and Society: Advances in Research*. Recent publications include *Pilgrimage and Political Economy: Translating the Sacred* (New York: Berghahn, 2018). He was a co-investigator on the AHRC-funded project "Pilgrimage and England's Cathedrals, Past and Present."

YANIV FELLER is Jeremy Zwelling Assistant Professor of Jewish Studies and an assistant professor of religion at Wesleyan University. In 2015–17, he worked as an exhibition curator for the new permanent exhibition at the Jewish Museum Berlin. He is currently completing his first book manuscript, which is dedicated to the work of the rabbi and philosopher Leo Baeck.

PAMELA KLASSEN is professor in the Department for the Study of Religion at the University of Toronto. Her most recent publications are *The Story of Radio Mind: A Missionary's Journey on Indigenous Land* (Chicago, IL: University of Chicago Press, 2018) and *Ekklesia: Three Inquiries in Church and State* (Chicago, IL: University of Chicago Press, 2018), co-authored with Paul Christopher Johnson and Winnifred Fallers Sullivan. Together with a team of students and consultants from Kay-Nah-Chi-Wah-Nung Historical Centre of the Rainy River First Nations, she recently launched *Kiinawin Kawindomowin Story Nations* at http://storynations.utoronto. ca. She currently holds the Anneliese Maier Research Award from the

Humboldt Foundation in support of a five-year collaborative project entitled *Religion and Public Memory in Multicultural Societies*, undertaken together with Prof. Dr Monique Scheer of the University of Tübingen.

CHRISTIAN MARCHETTI studied Empirische Kulturwissenschaft and political science in Tübingen and Seville and attained his PhD in 2010 with a dissertation on Austrian *Volkskunde* during World War I. His current research project deals with German-speaking *Volkskunden* in southeastern Europe in the interwar period. His research interests include the history of ethnographic knowledge production, public and private festive culture, and popular forms of knowledge transfer.

HELEN MO was a PhD candidate in the Department for the Study of Religion at the University of Toronto. A brilliant scholar at the heart of several intellectual communities, Helen passed away in 2017, at the age of thirty-three. Helen had a promising career ahead of her as a scholar of religion in the public sphere in multicultural North America. She had completed the fieldwork for her dissertation, entitled "Evangelicals in the Ethnoburbs: Chinese Christian Imaginaries and the Landscape of the Canadian Dream," but had yet to write what was sure to be a critical and lyrical contribution to scholarship. A founder and editorial board member of several online publications, including *The Ethnic Aisle*, *The Elements Experiment*, and *The Sunday Morning Salon*, Helen conveyed her eloquence and insights to broad public audiences.

KATJA RAKOW is assistant professor of religious studies at Utrecht University. She received her PhD in religious studies from Heidelberg University, Germany, in 2010 with a dissertation on transformations of Tibetan Buddhism in the West. Her postdoctoral projects looked at contemporary forms of Evangelicalism and Pentecostalism in the United States and Singapore. Recent publications include "The Bible in the Digital Age: Negotiating the Limits of 'Bibleness' of Different Bible Media," in *Christianity and the Limits of Materiality*, edited by Minna Opas and Anna Haapalainen (London: Bloomsbury, 2017), and (with Esther Berg) "Religious Studies and Transcultural Studies: Revealing a Cosmos Not Known Before?" in *Transcultural Studies* (2016).

SOPHIE REIMERS received her PhD in social and cultural anthropology at the Viadrina University in Frankfurt/Oder in 2017, with a dissertation on the educational paths of three generations of German-Turkish families. In 2018, this research was published as *Migration, Bildung und Familie: Ethnografische Annäherung an den Alltag dreier Generationen zwischen türkischem Dorf und Neuköllner Kiez* (Bielefeld, Germany: Transcript Verlag).

MONIQUE SCHEER is professor of historical and cultural anthropology at the University of Tübingen, where she also serves as vice-president for International Affairs. Most recently, she co-authored *Emotional Lexicons: Continuity and Change in the Vocabulary of Feeling* (Oxford, UK: Oxford University Press, 2014), co-edited with Birgitte Schepelern Johansen and Nadia Fadil a volume titled *Secular Bodies, Affects and Emotions: European Configurations* (London: Bloomsbury, 2019), and is currently completing a monograph on the cultural practice of enthusiasm in modern Germany.

TIINA SEPP is a research fellow at the Department of Estonian and Comparative Folklore, University of Tartu. She was a postdoctoral research assistant on the AHRC-funded project "Pilgrimage and England's Cathedrals, Past and Present," and her role was to research contemporary models of pilgrimage. Her other research interests include belief narratives, fieldwork methodology, and vernacular religion.

ISAAC WEINER is associate professor of religious studies in the Department of Comparative Studies at Ohio State University. He is the author of *Religion Out Loud: Religious Sound, Public Space, and American Pluralism* (New York: NYU Press, 2014). He is also the co-editor, with Joshua Dubler, of *Religion, Law, USA* (forthcoming, NYU Press), and co-director, with Amy DeRogatis, of the Religious Sounds Project (http://religioussounds.osu.edu).

Index